IAAI–2001

Proceedings of the Thirteenth
Innovative Applications of
Artificial Intelligence Conference

Edited by
Haym Hirsh and Steve Chien

AAAI Press

Menlo Park • California • USA

Contents

Deployed Applications

Emerging Applications

AAAI Organization

Officers

President
Bruce G. Buchanan, University of Pittsburgh

President-Elect
Tom M. Mitchell, Carnegie Mellon University

Past President
David L. Waltz, NEC Research Institute, Inc.

Secretary-Treasurer
Norman R. Nielsen, AtomicTangerine

Councilors

(through 2001):

Henry Kautz, University of Washington
David McAllester, AT&T Labs — Research
Johanna Moore, The University of Edinburgh
Michael P. Wellman, University of Michigan

(through 2002):

Deborah McGuinness, Stanford University
Bart Selman, Cornell University
Reid Simmons, Carnegie Mellon University
Manuela Veloso, Carnegie Mellon University

(through 2003):

Craig Boutilier, University of Toronto
Rina Dechter, University of California, Irvine
Richard Doyle, Jet Propulsion Laboratory, California Institute of Technology
David Poole, University of British Columbia

Standing Committees
Conference Chair
Paul Rosenbloom, University of Southern California

Fellows/Nominating Chair
David L. Waltz, NEC Research Institute, Inc.

Finance Chair
Norman R. Nielsen, AtomicTangerine

Publications Chair
Kenneth Ford, UWF/Institute for Human & Machine Cognition

Grants Chair
Manuela Veloso, Carnegie Mellon University

Membership Chair
Reid Simmons, Carnegie Mellon University

Symposium Chair
Ian Horswill, Northwestern University

Symposium Cochair
Daniel Clancy, NASA Ames Research Center

Symposium Associate Chair
David Poole, University of British Columbia

AI Magazine
Editor
David Leake, Indiana University

IAAI-01 Program Committee

Conference Chair
Haym Hirsh, Rutgers University

Program Cochair
Steve Chien, Jet Propulsion Laboratory

IAAI-01 Program Committee
Bruce Buchanan, University of Pittsburgh
Robert S. Engelmore, Stanford University
Usama Fayyad, digiMine
Ronen Feldman, Clearforest Corporation
Randall Hill, USC/Institute for Creative Technologies
Neil Jacobstein, Teknowledge Corporation
Craig Knoblock, USC/Information Sciences Institute
Alain Rappaport, Carnegie Mellon University
John Riedl, University of Minnesota
Charles Rosenberg, Carnegie Mellon University
Ted Senator, DARPA/ISO
Howard Shrobe, Massachusetts Institute of Technology
Reid Smith, Schlumberger Limited
Shirley Tessler, Aldo Ventures, Inc.
Ramasamy Uthurusamy, General Motors Corporation
Marilyn Walker, AT&T Labs-Research

Invited Talks

Mass Market Intelligent Robots

Rodney A. Brooks, Director, MIT Artificial Intelligence Laboratory, Fujitsu Professor of Computer Science, and Chairman & Chief Technical Officer, iRobot Corporation

At iRobot Corporation we have been pushing intelligent robots into the mass market. The AI component differentiates them from the rest of the field but there are other equally difficult issues: costs, market creation, market penetration, and distribution.

Decoupling Art and Affluence

Harold Cohen, Professor Emeritus, University of California, San Diego, and Senior Research Professor, Center for Research in Computing and the Arts, University of California, San Diego

Preface

The Thirteenth Annual Conference on Innovative Applications of Artificial Intelligence (IAAI-2001) continues the IAAI tradition of serving as one of the premier venues for current work on artificial intelligence applications. As always, this year's conference features an outstanding selection of papers on deployed applications that use AI techniques, as well as papers on emerging technologies relevant to the design and development of AI applications.

The twelve papers presented at the conference and included in these proceedings were selected from thirty-seven papers submitted by authors from more than twelve countries. Five of these papers describe deployed applications, providing case studies on the design, management, and deployment of real-world systems incorporating AI technologies. The problems addressed range from a dialogue system for online sales to load planning for ships to a management advisor for grasshopper infestations, with a range of AI technologies including stochastic search, case-based reasoning, and natural language understanding. The remaining seven papers discuss emerging technologies, work whose goal is the development of technologies relevant to the design and development of systems using AI technology. Problems addressed by these papers include protein crystallography, spelling correction, and aircraft collision avoidance, with technologies ranging from machine learning to constraint satisfaction to case-based reasoning and image analysis.

This year's conference was collocated with the International Joint Conference on Artificial Intelligence (IJCAI-01), with coordinated programs and a single registration fee so that attendees could move freely between the two conferences. In addition to the above papers, IAAI-2001 also provided conference attendees with two invited talks — by Rod Brooks on consumer robotics, and by Harold Cohen on his work on AI and Art — as well as a panel on personalization organized by John Riedl.

Artificial intelligence continues to be an exciting and profitable area of investigation for people interested in building software systems that operate in realistic environments incorporating a range of uncertainties and complexities. We are eager to see what future innovations may further follow from the work presented at this year's conference.

– Haym Hirsh and Steve Chien

Deployed Applications

CARMA: A Case-Based Range Management Advisor

Karl Branting
LiveWire Logic, Inc.
5500 McNeeley Drive
Suite 102
Raleigh, NC 27562
branting@livewirelogic.com

John Hastings
Dept. of Computer Science and
Information Systems
University of Nebraska at Kearney
Kearney, NE 68849
hastingsj@unk.edu

Jeffrey Lockwood
Entomology Section
Dept. of Renewable Resources
University of Wyoming
Laramie, WY 82071-3354
lockwood@uwyo.edu

Abstract: CARMA is an advisory system for rangeland grasshopper infestations that demonstrates how AI technology can deliver expert advice to compensate for cutbacks in public services. CARMA uses two knowledge sources for the key task of predicting forage consumption by grasshoppers: cases obtained by asking a group of experts to solve representative hypothetical problems; and a numerical model of rangeland ecosystems. These knowledge sources are integrated through the technique of *model-based adaptation*, in which CBR is used to find an approximate solution and the model is used to adapt this approximate solution into a more precise solution. CARMA has been used in Wyoming counties since 1996. The combination of a simple interface, flexible control strategy, and integration of multiple knowledge sources makes CARMA accessible to inexperienced users and capable of producing advice comparable to that produced by human experts. Moreover, because CARMA embodies diverse forms of expertise, it has been used in ways that its developers did not anticipate, including pest management research, development of industry strategies, and in state and federal pest management policy decisions.

Introduction

Grasshopper outbreaks cause significant economic damage to livestock producers worldwide. Grasshoppers annually consume 21–23% of rangeland forage in the western United States, causing an estimated loss of $400 million (Hewitt and Onsager, 1983). Estimates of the value of forage lost to grasshoppers in the 17 western states in 1998 range from $408 million (assuming replacement by leasing land) to $1.02 billion (assuming replacement by hay) (Nelson, 1999). Similar losses were sustained in 1999. Various chemical and biological pesticides are available for treatment of grasshopper infestations, but the cost of using these agents often outweighs the value of the forage saved by their application.

Before 1996, the USDA paid the entire cost of treatment on federal land, one-half the cost on state land, and one-third of the cost on private land. In addition, the USDA provided intensive surveys and pest-management advice to

ranchers about treatment selection. Subsequently, however, the USDA stopped providing these subsidies (except for infestations on federal rangelands that represent an immediate threat to adjacent crops) and the level of survey and logistical support was substantially decreased. CARMA was developed to help compensate for the decreased availability of federal assistance to ranchers.

Task Description

CARMA's task is to help ranchers determine the most cost-effective responses to rangeland grasshopper infestations within user-defined environmental constraints. CARMA's performance objective is to emulate as closely as possible the performance of pest management experts. The shortage of human experts makes it important for CARMA to be sufficiently intuitive that it can be easily used and understood by ranchers, range managers (who often lack pest management expertise), and pest managers (who may lack experience with rangeland grasshoppers). Determining the most cost-effective response to a grasshopper infestation requires, at a minimum, estimating (1) the value of the forage that is likely to be consumed by grasshoppers if no action is taken, (2) the value of the portion of this forage that would be saved in current and future years under each treatment option, and (3) the cost of each option.

To explicate the process whereby experts make these estimations, we performed a protocol analysis of "solve-aloud" problem solving by several experts in rangeland grasshopper management at the University of Wyoming (Hastings et al., 1996). The protocol analysis suggested that experts predict the proportion of available forage that will be consumed by grasshoppers by comparing the current situation to prototypical cases.

An example of a prototypical case is a moderate density of emerging grasshoppers in a cool, wet spring. In this situation, only a low proportion of forage is typically consumed, because wet conditions both increase forage growth and promote growth of fungal pathogens that decrease grasshopper populations, and cool conditions tend to prolong the early developmental phases during which grasshoppers are most susceptible to pathogens and other mortality factors. In predicting forage consumption by comparing new cases to prototypical cases, such as the cool, wet spring prototype, experts appear to be using a form of case-based reasoning

(CBR) (Aamodt and Plaza, 1994).

If a particular new case differs in some ways from the most similar prototypical case, the expert can perform causal reasoning to adapt the prediction associated with the case to account for the differences. For example, if the population density of emerging grasshoppers in a cool, wet spring is high (rather than moderate), an expert might predict moderately low (rather than low) forage consumption because higher density generally means more consumption.

Experts seem to reason about prototypical cases in terms of abstract features that are relevant to the expert's model of rangeland ecosystems, such as grasshopper species, developmental phases, and population density. In contrast, a rancher's description is almost always in terms of directly observable features, such as the color, size, and behavior of grasshoppers, temperatures, and precipitation. As a result, determining the most similar prototypical case requires inferring the relevant abstract features from a set of observations provided by the rancher. Experts exhibit great flexibility in inferring these features. For example, if a rancher is unable to provide the information that discriminates most reliably among grasshopper species (e.g., whether the grasshoppers have slanted faces or a spur on their "throats"), the expert is able to ask questions that are less reliable but easier to answer (e.g., "Are the grasshoppers brown or green?").

If it appears that grasshoppers will consume forage needed by livestock, the expert determines which interventions are compatible with local conditions, using knowledge such as that wet conditions preclude the use of malathion and that chemical treatments are precluded by environmental sensitivity. Finally, the expert estimates the relative value of the forage saved in this and future seasons and the cost of each control measure based on market price. The expert then advises the rancher to take the most economical action, either applying the most cost-effective control measure or doing nothing. Experts can justify their advice by appealing to an underlying causal model, but seem to use this model only in explaining and adapting the predictions associated with prototypes and not in performing any sort of simulation.

The protocol analysis identified four important characteristics of human expert problem solving in this field:

- **Graceful degradation.** Human experts can use, but do not require, highly precise information of the type required for accurate model-based reasoning. Less accurate information may degrade the quality of advice an expert can give, but doesn't preclude useful advice. In the worst case, human experts can provide plausible advice based merely on the location of the rangeland and the date.

- **Speed.** Human experts can provide useful advice very quickly. This suggests that human experts can use highly compiled knowledge.

- **Explanations in terms of a causal model.** Although the speed and graceful degradation of human expert performance suggest that experts can use compiled knowledge, they can also readily provide causal explanations for their conclusions. Moreover, entomologists can generate causal predictions of the effects of incremental variations on case facts.

- **Opportunism.** Human experts can use a variety of different strategies to solve a single given problem depending on the available information. Human experts don't address the subgoals that arise in decision-making in an invariant order, but adapt their problem-solving behavior to the particular facts of a given case.

In summary, the protocol analysis indicated that experts in rangeland pest management use an eclectic approach that includes case-based reasoning for consumption-prediction, rules for inferring case features and acceptable control measures, and causal reasoning for adaptation and explanation. Moreover, expert problem solving is fast and tolerant of inaccuracies in data.

CARMA is designed to model the problem solving behavior of experts in managing grasshopper infestations as described in the previous section. CARMA emulates expert human advice by providing treatment recommendations supported by explanation in terms of causal, economic, and pragmatic factors, including a numerical estimate of the proportion of forage consumed and a cost-benefit analysis of the various treatment options.

Application Description

Overview

CARMA's consultation process, summarized in Figure 1, consists of the following steps:

1. Determine the relevant facts of the infestation case from information provided by the user by means of heuristic rules.

2. Estimate the proportion of available forage that will be consumed by each distinct grasshopper population (i.e., subcase) by matching and adapting the prototypical infestation cases that best match the facts of the current case.

3. Compare total grasshopper consumption with the proportion of available forage needed by livestock.

4. If the predicted forage consumption will lead to economic loss, determine what possible treatment options are excluded by the case conditions.

5. Provide an economic analysis for each viable treatment option by estimating both the first-year and long-term savings.

Determining Relevant Case Features

CARMA begins a consultation by eliciting observations from the user through a window-based interface. These observations are used to infer the relevant features of a new case, such as the species, population density, and developmental phases of the grasshoppers. CARMA uses multiple levels of rules for inferring each case feature, ordered by a qualitative estimate of each rule's accuracy or reliability. The rules are applied in succession until either the user can provide the necessary information or a default rule is reached.

Figure 1: The main steps in CARMA's consultation process.

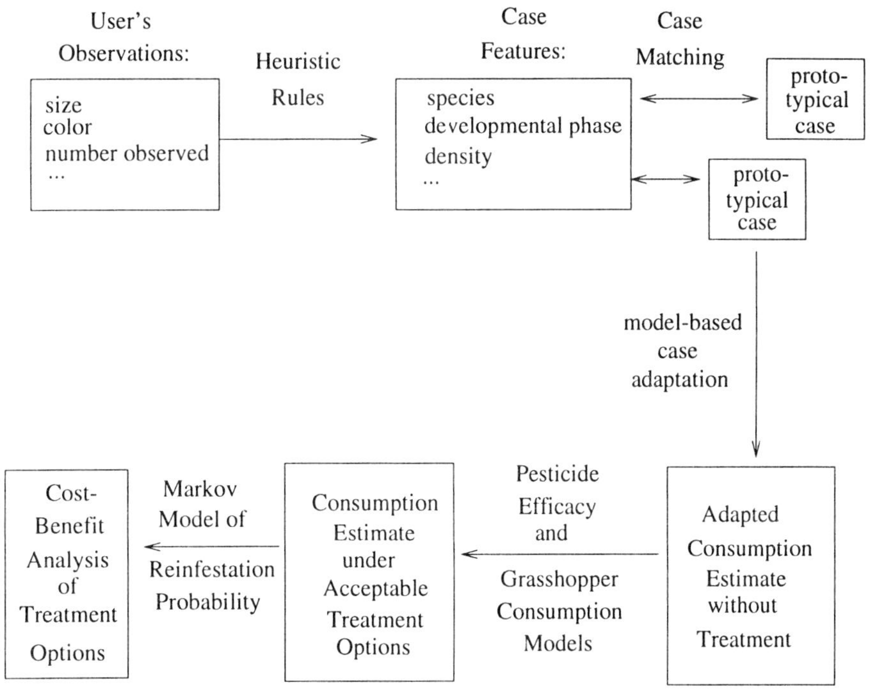

For example, if the value of the case feature "total number of grasshoppers per square yard" is unknown to the user, CARMA instructs the user to estimate the number of grasshoppers that would be present in 18 square-foot circles (2 square yards). If the user can't provide this information, the system attempts to infer this feature using the heuristic that grasshopper density is equal to 1.5 times the number of grasshoppers seen hopping away from the user with each step taken in the field. Otherwise, the value defaults to the historic average for the area. By applying rules in the order of their accuracy or reliability, CARMA reasons with the best information available.

A typical interface window for determining the observed grasshopper type distribution appears in Figure 2. It includes the options "Why" for describing why this information is important to the consultation, "Help" for advising the user about the various window features and their operations, "How To" to explain the proper procedure for gathering the required information, "Not sure" to trigger the selection of an alternative rule for inferring the feature, "Back" to move to the previous screen in the consultation, and "OK" to indicate that the user has chosen an answer. "Display planthopper" shows a small insect that the user should distinguish from a recently hatched grasshopper nymph.

Because a complete case specification is not always required for useful advice, CARMA fills in the facts of a new case opportunistically, asking the user for information only when the corresponding case feature is required for the reasoning process to continue. At the earliest point at which a decision can be made, the case-feature inference process

halts, advice is given, and the consultation is ended. For example, if the date and location of an infestation indicate that it is too early to assess the severity of a grasshopper infestation, CARMA advises the user to rerun the consultation at a later time without prompting for further information.

Case Matching

The protocol analysis indicated that pest managers estimate forage consumption by comparing new cases to prototypical cases. A tract of rangeland almost invariably contains multiple grasshopper species, which may differ widely in consumption characteristics. In particular, grasshoppers that spend the winter as nymphs consume far less during the growing season than grasshoppers overwintering as eggs. CARMA therefore partitions the overall population of a new case into subcases according to overwintering type. Prototypical cases each represent a single grasshopper population.

To predict the forage loss of a subcase, CARMA first retrieves all prototypical cases whose overwintering type matches that of the subcase. The weighted sum of feature differences between each prototypical case and the new subcase is calculated to determine the most similar prototypical case. Match weights are determined from the mutual information gain between case features and qualitative consumption categories in a given set of training cases. The forage-loss prediction associated with the given case is then adapted to compensate for differences between the current case and the most similar prototypical case using *model-based adaptation*, discussed in the next section.

Figure 2: Elicitation of grasshopper type information in CARMA.

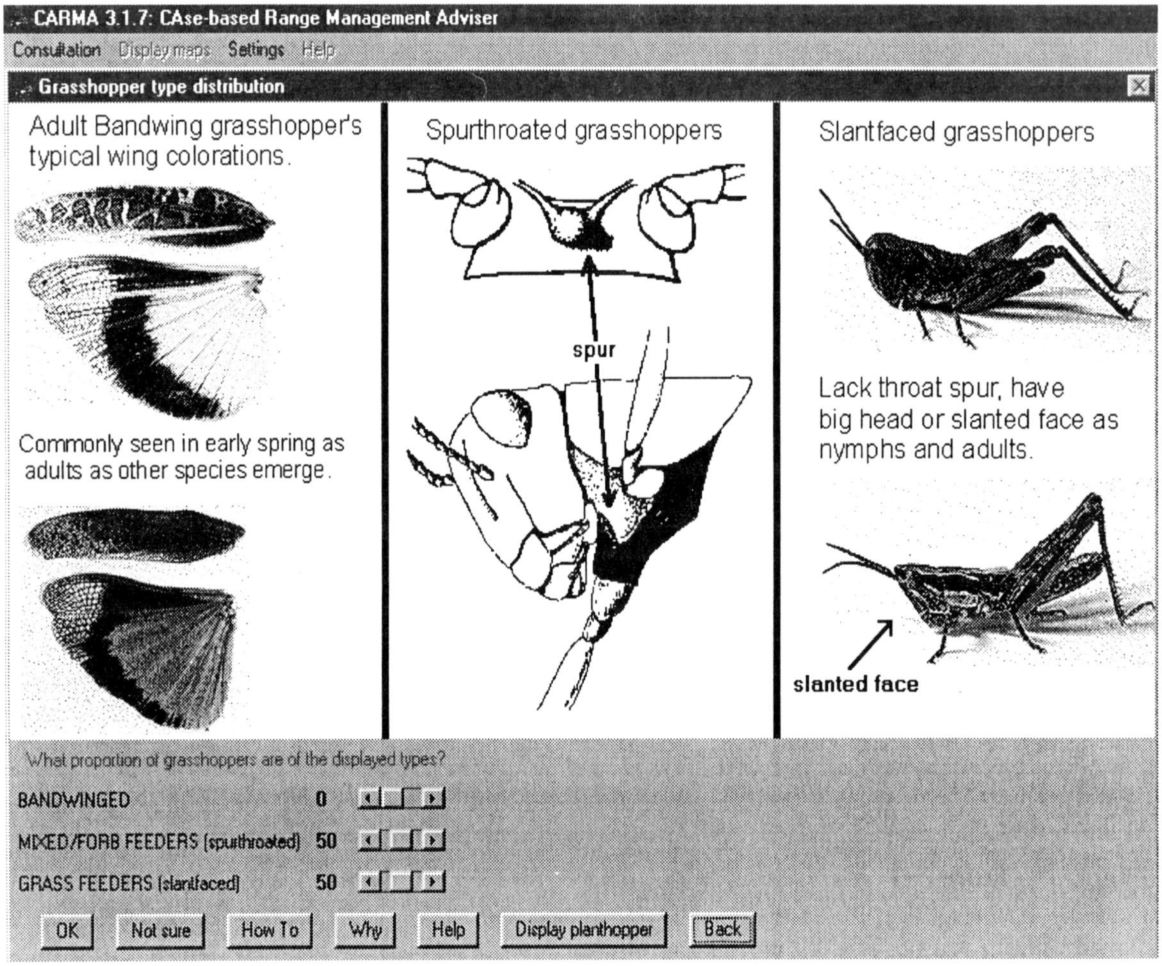

Forage Loss Estimation

After adaptation, the consumption predictions for each sub-case are summed to produce an overall consumption estimate. If the proportion of available forage that will be lost to grasshoppers and the proportion needed for livestock (and wildlife) exceeds 100% of the forage available, CARMA concludes that grasshoppers will cause economic losses.

Determining Treatment Options

If grasshoppers will cause economic losses, CARMA applies a set of rules to determine the treatment options that are excluded by the conditions of the case. Some of the information necessary for determining exclusion is already known from the case features (e.g., the presence of grasshoppers in the first nymphal instar indicates an ongoing hatch, which precludes malathion and carbaryl bait from consideration). Other conditions must be determined from further user input (e.g., "Will it be hot at the time of treatment?" If so, exclude malathion).

Treatment Recommendation

For each acceptable treatment option, CARMA provides estimates of the reduced probability of future reinfestation and current-year and long-term savings. From the estimated savings, CARMA recommends the treatment or treatments that are most economical. Explanation text in this and other CARMA windows is produced using conventional schema-based techniques (Moore, 1995).

CARMA calculates the total reduced probability of future reinfestation for each treatment type using a Markov model of infestation probability for each location derived from historical data collected by the USDA and synthesized by the University of Wyoming Entomology Section (Lockwood and Kemp, 1987). CARMA computes the current-year savings as the difference between the value of forage saved and the treatment cost. CARMA calculates the savings for future years for each treatment type via multiplying the reduced probabilities of reinfestation by the estimated forage loss for each subsequent year.

A typical treatment recommendation window including estimates of future reinfestation and economic savings ap-

Figure 3: CARMA's treatment recommendation screen.

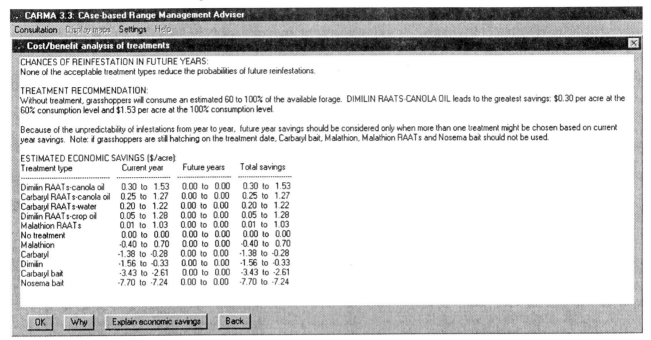

pears in Figure 3. CARMA lists both worst- and best-case scenarios for most calculations. Note that this analysis includes "no treatment" as an option and that negative savings indicate a loss.

CARMA recommends the treatment that is estimated to save the most under a worst-case scenario and the treatment that is estimated to save the most under a best-case scenario. Usually, the worst- and best-case scenarios produce the same recommended treatment. Following the treatment recommendation, the consultation is complete.

Uses of AI Technology

CARMA uses AI technology in two distinct ways. First, as described above, CARMA's control strategy emulates human experts' speed, opportunism, explanation capability, flexibility in eliciting relevant case features through a variety of alternative heuristic rules, and ability to integrate multiple knowledge sources. Second, CARMA uses model-based adaptation for the key reasoning step of predicting the amount of forage that will be consumed by grasshoppers.

Model-based adaptation consists of using CBR to find an approximate solution and model-based reasoning to adapt this approximate solution into a more precise solution. Model-based adaptation is useful in domains in which both cases and models are available, but neither is individually sufficient for accurate prediction. Such domains are typified by chemical or biological systems with well-developed, but imperfect, models. Model-based adaptation has been applied for bioprocess recipe planning in Sophist (Aarts and Rousu, 1996; Rousu and Aarts, 1996), for selecting colorants for plastic coloring in FormTool (Cheetham and Graf, 1997), and in design reuse (Goel, 1991).

Model-based adaptation is appropriate for CARMA's advisory task because both empirical knowledge, in the form of cases, and a grassland ecology model are available, but neither is individually sufficient for accurate prediction of forage consumption, given the information that ranchers can typically provide.

Case-Based Reasoning in CARMA The initial impetus for using CBR for forage consumption prediction was cognitive verisimilitude. The protocol analysis suggested that human experts in this domain reason using prototypes. This is consistent with various cognitive studies that have demonstrated that examples or prototypes often play a central role in human concept structure (Klein and Calderwood, 1988; Smith and Medin, 1981).

During the development of CARMA, however, CBR's ability to facilitate knowledge acquisition grew in importance. Few precise records of rangeland grassland infestations are available. However, there are a number of expert pest advisors with many years of experience with rangeland grasshopper infestations.

To capture human expertise, we sent questionnaires describing hypothetical Wyoming infestation cases to entomologists recognized for their work in the area of grasshopper management and ecology. Each expert received 10 cases randomly drawn from a total of 20 representative cases. The descriptions of the 20 cases contained at least as much information as a rancher ordinarily provides to an entomologist. The questionnaire asked the expert to estimate the probable forage loss[1]. Eight sets of responses were received from

---
[1]The questionnaire also asked the expert to identify the most appropriate course of action. This information was used in the val-

Figure 4: Projection of a prototypical case PC to PC' to align its developmental phase with new case NC.

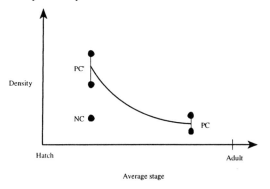

Wyoming experts, who had a mean of 18.0 years experience[2]. CARMA's case library consists of the 20 hypothetical cases. The consumption prediction associated with each case is the mean of the experts' predictions for that case.

Adaptation CARMA uses three techniques for adaptation: temporal projection; feature adaptation; and critical period adaptation. Two of those techniques—temporal projection and critical period adaptation—make use of the rangeland ecosystem model. Temporal projection is needed because the feature values of each prototypical case are represented at a specific point in the life history of the grasshopper population. To determine the match between the grasshopper population densities of each prototypical case and a new subcase, the life history of the prototypical case must be projected forward or backward to align its average developmental phase with that of the new subcase. This requires using a model to simulate grasshopper attrition, which depends on developmental phase, precipitation, and developmental rate (which in turn depends on temperature) throughout the interval of the projection.

Figure 4 illustrates how the population in prototypical case PC must be projected backward in time to PC' to match the average developmental stage of new subcase NC. Projection backward in time increases grasshopper density by removing the effect of attrition over the interval of the projection, whereas projection forward in time decreases grasshopper density by adding attrition during this interval. The vertical bar corresponding to PC and PC' indicates the confidence range for grasshopper density, which always increases (indicating greater uncertainty) as a function of the interval projected.

In feature adaptation, the forage loss predicted by the

best matching prototypical case is modified to account for any feature differences (other than average developmental phase) between it and the subcase. The modification is a linear function of the feature differences. The coefficients of the linear function are determined by a form of *introspective learning* (Leake et al., 1995; Hanney and Keane, 1997), consisting of hill climbing through parameter space to optimize leave-one-out predictive accuracy on the case library.

Critical-period adaptation is needed because grasshopper consumption is most damaging if it occurs during the portion of the growing season during which forage losses cannot be fully replaced by forage growth, termed the *critical period*. The forage loss predicted by a prototypical case must be adapted if the proportion of the lifespan of the grasshoppers overlapping the critical period in the new case differs from that in the prototypical case. This requires determining, for both the new case and the prototypical case, the proportion of the grasshopper population's lifetime consumption occurring in the critical period. For a more complete description of model-based adaptation in CARMA, see Branting et al. 1997.

Experimental Evaluation of Model-Based Adaptation

The design of CARMA's forage consumption component was based on the hypothesis that an integration of model-based and case-based reasoning can lead to more accurate forage consumption predictions than the use of either technique individually. This hypothesis was based on the observation that neither the causal model nor the empirical data available for rangelands are individually sufficient for accurate prediction. To test this hypothesis, an ablation study was performed in which CARMA's empirical and model-based knowledge components were each tested in isolation and compared the results to the performance of the full CARMA prediction system.

Each predictive method was tested using a series of leave-one-out tests in which a set of cases (S) from a single expert was split into one test case (C) and one training set (S − C). The methods were trained on the forage-loss predictions of the training set and tested on the test case. This method was repeated for each case within the set (S).

CARMA's empirical component was evaluated by performing leave-one-out tests for CARMA's forage consumption module with all model-based adaptation disabled. CARMA's forage consumption module with model-based adaptation disabled is termed *factored nearest-neighbor prediction* (factored-NN), because under this approach prediction is based simply on the sum of nearest neighbor predictions for each subcase. Two other empirical methods were evaluated as well: decision-tree induction using ID3 [3] (Quinlan, 1986) and linear regression using QR factorization (Hager, 1988) to find a least-squares fit to the feature values

idation of CARMA's advice, but did not become part of CARMA's knowledge base.

[2]The mean standard deviation of forage loss predictions for all the hypothetical cases was 12.4%, a variation sufficiently high to call into question the reliability of experts for this task. However, the issue of the validity of human expertise in this field is beyond the scope of this project. Instead, our goal was to emulate the judgments of human experts under the assumption that these judgments are valid.

[3]ID3 classified cases into 10 qualitative consumption categories representing the midpoints (5, 10, 15, ... , 95) of 10 equally sized qualitative ranges. ID3's error was measured by the difference between the midpoint of each predicted qualitative category and the expected quantitative consumption value.

and associated predictions of the training cases.

The predictive ability of CARMA's model-based component in isolation was evaluated by developing a numerical simulation based on CARMA's model of rangeland ecology. This simulation required explicit representation of two forms of knowledge implicit in CARMA's cases: the forage per acre based on the range value of the location, and the forage typically eaten per day per grasshopper for each distinct grasshopper overwintering type and developmental phase.

The accuracy of each approach was evaluated using leave-one-out testing for the responses from each of the eight Wyoming experts and for a data set consisting of the median of the predictions of the Wyoming experts on each case. The full CARMA prediction system was tested using both global adaptation weights (CARMA-global) and case-specific adaptation weights (CARMA-specific).

The root-mean-squared error for each of the methods are set forth in Table 1. These provide initial confirmation for the hypothesis that integrating model-based and case-based reasoning through model-based adaptation leads to more accurate forage consumption predictions than the use of either technique individually. The smallest root-mean-squared error rate was obtained by CARMA-specific. On the Wyoming Expert Sets, the root-mean-squared error rate was 13.3% for CARMA-specific and 14.2% for CARMA-global. The root-mean-squared error rate was higher both for the empirical approaches—21.1% for factored-NN, 34.9% for ID3, and 25.6% for linear regression—and for the purely model-based approach—29.6%. CARMA-specific and CARMA-global were also more accurate than the alternative methods on the Wyoming median set, although linear regression was only slightly less accurate.

The initial confirmation of the hypothesis that integrating model-based and case-based reasoning through model-based adaptation leads to more accurate forage consumption predictions than the use of either technique individually is tentative because the relatively low level of agreement among experts and the absence of any external standard give rise to uncertainty about what constitutes a correct prediction. A detailed description of the empirical evaluation of CARMA is set forth in (Branting et al., 1997).

Application Use and Payoff

In June, 1996, CARMA 2.0 was distributed to University of Wyoming Cooperative Extension Offices and Weed and Pest District Offices in each of Wyoming's 23 counties and was made available to be downloaded from a University of Wyoming website. CARMA 2.0 was used by Wyoming ranchers and pest managers every summer from 1996 to 2000. CARMA has been endorsed and advocated for use by pest managers by the United States National Grasshopper Management Board (NGMB, 2001). Perhaps the greatest interest in the system has been expressed by the county-level Weed and Pest District supervisors, who—with the withdrawal of USDA support—have become the "front line" agency in grasshopper pest management. Workshops to train these individuals in the optimal use of CARMA were developed and delivered at the request of the agency.

Although CARMA was designed as an advisory system for ranchers, CARMA's ability to robustly integrate a variety of knowledge sources led it to be applied in several ways that were not imagined when the program was developed. First, CARMA's economic analysis has been used to justify pest management policy decisions. In 1998, CARMA's economic analysis was used to generate a declaration of grasshopper disaster areas by Wyoming County Commissions, leading to low interest, federal loans by the Farm Service Administration. CARMA's economic analysis played a role in the National Grasshopper Management Board's recommendation of a new treatment approach, Reduced Agent Area Treatments (RAATs) (Nelson, 1999), a strategy now adopted in six states.

Second, CARMA's analysis was incorporated into industry strategies. Uniroyal (CK Witco) developed recommendations for the use of Dimilin, a new chemical pesticide, using CARMA's analysis. Similarly, RhônePoulenc (Aventis) developed recommendations for the use of Fipronil based on CARMA's analysis.

Finally, CARMA-based economic analysis was incorporated into pest management research in (Lockwood et al., 1999) and (Lockwood and Schell, 1997).

Development, Deployment, and Maintenance

CARMA was developed as a dissertation project (Hastings, 1996). The out-of-pocket development costs were small, consisting of several years of graduate research assistant support and the license fees for Franz Allegro Common Lisp, the language in which CARMA was developed. However, the path to the development of CARMA was quite circuitous, with a variety of different approaches to grasshopper advising having been developed, tested, and rejected. Thus, the development costs would have been much higher outside of an academic environment.

In the years since the distribution of CARMA 2.0, there have been a number of changes in pest-treatment practices. In 2000, CARMA 2.0 was updated to CARMA 3.0 to reflect these changes and to include a spreadsheet for calculating per acre treatment costs under various alternative economic conditions. CARMA's declarative knowledge representation made revising the program straightforward. These changes were funded by a grant from a producer of a pesticide introduced after the distribution of CARMA 2.0 and therefore not included as a treatment option in the earlier version. The pesticide maker's interest in being incorporated into the CARMA revision demonstrates the perception that this advisory system is an important tool in pest management.

Conclusion

CARMA demonstrates how AI technology can be used to deliver expert advise to compensate for cutbacks in public services. CBR proved to be an appropriate AI technique for the forage-prediction component both because experts in this domain appear to reason with cases and because asking experts to solve example cases was an effective knowledge-acquisition technique. Model-based adaptation provided a mechanism for incorporating rangeland ecosystem models

Table 1: Root-mean-squared error rate (in %) for leave-one-out test results.

	CARMA		Empirical Only			Model-Based Only
	Specific weights	Global weights	Factored-NN	ID3	Linear regr.	Numerical simulation
Wyoming expert sets	13.3	14.2	21.1	34.9	25.6	29.6
Wyoming median set	9.7	10.0	22.8	35.2	11.9	28.8

into the system without the slow performance, sensitivity to noise, and diminished explanation capability that would have resulted from a purely simulation-based approach.

A key factor in CARMA's acceptance among users is its simple interface and speed, which make using CARMA very straightforward. The combination of a a simple interface, flexible control strategy, and integration of multiple knowledge sources makes CARMA accessible to inexperienced users and capable of producing advice comparable to that produced by human experts.

Acknowledgements

This research was supported by a grant from the University of Wyoming College of Agriculture, a Faculty Grant-in-Aid from the University of Wyoming Office of Research, NSF Career Grant IRI-9502152, and a grant by Uniroyal (CK Witco).

References

Aamodt, A. and Plaza, E. (1994). Case-based reasoning: Foundational issues, methodological variations, and system approaches. *AI Communications*, 7(1):39–59.

Aarts, R. and Rousu, J. (1996). Toward CBR for bioprocess planning. In *Proceedings of the Third European Workshop on Case-Based Reasoning (EWCR-96)*, pages 16–27, Lausanne, Switzerland.

Branting, K., Hastings, J., and Lockwood, J. (1997). Integrating cases and models for prediction in biological systems. *AI Applications*, 11(1):29–48.

Cheetham, W. and Graf, J. (1997). Case-based reasoning in color matching. In *Proceedings of the Second International Conference on Case-Based Reasoning*, pages 1–12, Providence, Rhode Island. Springer.

Goel, A. (1991). A model-based approach to case adaptation. In *Thirteenth Annual Conference of the Cognitive Science Society*, pages 143–148.

Hager, W. (1988). *Applied Numerical Linear Algebra*. Prentice Hall, Englewood Cliffs, New Jersey.

Hanney, K. and Keane, M. (1997). The adaptation knowledge bottleneck: How to ease it by learning from cases. In *Proceedings of the Second International Conference on Case-Based Reasoning*, pages 359–370, Providence, Rhode Island. Springer.

Hastings, J. (1996). *A Mixed-Paradigm Reasoning Approach to Problem Solving in Incomplete Causal Theory Domains*. PhD thesis, University of Wyoming.

Hastings, J., Branting, K., and Lockwood, J. (1996). A multi-paradigm reasoning system for rangeland management. *Computers and Electronics in Agriculture*, 16(1):47–67.

Hewitt, G. and Onsager, J. (1983). Control of grasshoppers on rangeland in the United States: a perspective. *Journal of Range Management*, 36:202–207.

Klein, G. A. and Calderwood, R. (1988). How do people use analogues to make decisions? In *Proceedings of the DARPA Workshop on Case-based Reasoning*, pages 209–218, Clearwater, Florida. Morgan Kaufmann.

Leake, D., Kinley, A., and Wilson, D. (1995). Learning to improve case adaptation by introspective reasoning and CBR. In *Lecture Notes in Artificial Intelligence 1010*, pages 229–240, Sesimbra, Portugal. Springer.

Lockwood, J. and Kemp, W. (1987). Probabilities of rangeland grasshopper outbreaks in Wyoming counties. *Wyoming Agr. Exper. Sta. Bull.*, B(896). externally reviewed.

Lockwood, J. and Schell, S. (1997). Decreasing economic and environmental costs through reduced area and agent insecticide treatments (RAATs) for the control of rangeland grasshoppers: Empirical results and their implications for pest management. *Journal of Orthoptera Research*, 6:19–32.

Lockwood, J., Schell, S., Foster, R., Reuter, C., and Rachadi, T. (1999). Reduced agent-area treatments (RAATs) for management of rangeland grasshoppers: efficacy and economics under operational conditions. *International Journal of Pest Management*, 46:29–42.

Moore, J. (1995). *Participating in Explanatory Dialogues*. MIT Press.

Nelson, D., editor (1999). *Proceedings of the National Grasshopper Management Board meeting*, Colorado. National Grasshopper Management Board.

NGMB (2001). National grasshopper management board position statement. In *Proceedings of the National Grasshopper Management Board meeting*, Denver, Colorado.

Quinlan, J. R. (1986). Induction of decision trees. *Machine Learning*, 1:81–106.

Rousu, J. and Aarts, R. (1996). Adaptation cost as a criterion for solution evaluation. In *Proceedings of the Third European Workshop on Case-Based Reasoning (EWCR-96)*, pages 354–361, Lausanne, Switzerland.

Smith, E. E. and Medin, D. L. (1981). *Categories and Concepts*. Harvard University Press.

TALPS
The T-AVB Automated Load Planning System

Paul S. Cerkez
DCS Corporation
46641 Corporate Drive
Lexington Park MD 20653
(301)-862-2390 ext 317
FAX: (301) 863-0324
pcerkez@dcscorp.com
pcerkez@acm.org
Affiliations:
AAAI, ACM: (SIGART and SIGRAPH), IEEE Computer Society

Abstract

Due to military drawdowns and the need for additional transportation lift requirements, the US MARINE CORPS developed a concept wherein they had modified a commercial container ship to support deployed aviation units. However, a problem soon emerged in that there were too few people who were expert enough to do the unique type of planning required for this ship. Additionally, once someone did develop some expertise, it was time for him or her to move on, retire or leave the active duty forces. There needed to be a way to capture this knowledge. This condition was the impetus for the TALPS effort. TALPS is now a fielded, certified application for Marine Corps Aviation.

T-AVB Background Information

Background:
Historically, one of the most difficult problems facing Marine Aviation Logistics planners was finding an affordable, flexible, and rapid means of providing intermediate maintenance capability for forward-deployed aircraft. To overcome these challenges, in the mid 1980's, the Department of the Navy purchased the T-AVBs and the Marine Corps introduced the Marine Aviation Logistics Support Program (MALSP).

MALSP incorporates a flexible "building-block concept," known as Contingency Support Packages (CSPs) that follows a pre-arranged deployment and employment scenario for assembling the right mix of Marines, support equipment, Mobile Facilities (MF), and spare parts within a Marine Aviation Logistics Squadron (MALS) to support deployed aircraft. The key word is "flexible." Contingency Support Packages can be rapidly configured to support the contingency aircraft mix and marshaled for movement. CSPs are comprised of either the fixed-wing or rotary-wing common support, and/or the peculiar IMA and Supply support for the various deploying aircraft. Initial support packages (30 days of

spare parts) are flown in to the operational theater as part of the Fly-In Echelon (FIE); the balance of the Marine Air Ground Task Force (MAGTF) commander's tailored aviation logistics support arrives in theater aboard the T-AVB. Without the T-AVB, it would require more than 140 C-141 cargo aircraft flights to deploy a MALS with an IMA level capability to a crisis area.

The T-AVB ships were acquired as a result of a Marine Corps "Feasibility Study of the Aviation Logistics Support Ship" (USMC 1983). Two ships have been modified for use by USMC I-Level aviation maintenance and supply organizations. The Department of Transportation Maritime Administration (MARAD) maintains the ships in a 5 day reduced readiness status using a civilian, commercial U.S. Merchant Marine retention crew stationed aboard each ship to monitor equipment conditions and conduct vessel maintenance and repair.

The Mobile Facility (MFs) work centers used by the Marine Corps conform to the standard commercial International Standardization Organization (ISO) container dimensions, which are 8'x 8'x 20'. Figure 1

Figure 1: MF being prepared for loading

shows a typical work center MF being prepared for loading. Figure 2 shows a special doublewide arrangement. Access modules are used to access 2nd and 3rd tier MFs that are 'complex'd' for IMA Level repair capability. Figure 3 shows a typical access module.

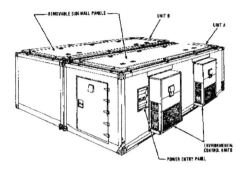

Figure 2: MF Double wide configuration

The modifications to the ships to support an MF setup allows a MALS to operate fully functional work centers on board a ship or in an expeditionary mode ashore, or both. Two basic load out configurations exist for each ship: TRANSPORT mode and OPERATIONAL mode.

In the TRANSPORT configuration, the ship is loaded for maximum capacity. In this mode, MFs are not accessible nor can the equipment contained therein be operated. In this configuration, more than 650 Twenty-foot Equivalent Unit (TEU) containers can be loaded. In this mode, the ship is a standard container ship and

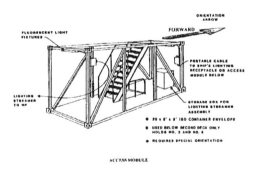

Figure 3: Access Module

supports re-supply operations and missions. The function of re-supply is the secondary mission of the T-AVB.

In the OPERATIONAL configuration, the ship is loaded such that MFs can be placed in a functional, operating condition. What you have in effect is a tailorable, floating, aviation repair facility. Officially, in this configuration, 300 MFs and 42 Access Modules can be loaded, or 342 TEUs. This configuration allows the embarked work centers to process and repair defective or

broken aircraft components while en route to an operational theater, or should the concept of operations in theater dictate, continue operating until finally moved ashore (referred to as operating "in stream"). This describes the primary mission of the T-AVB and the most difficult area of load planning.

Load Planning Overview:

The embarking Marines responsible for a particular ship must develop the load plan for that ship. The civilians manning and loading the T-AVB will load the ship any way the Marines tell them, as long as it does not put the ship in an unsafe condition. Unsafe is defined as any condition that would 'hazard' the vessel. For example, if the ship were loaded so that is was top heavy or too heavy on one side, it would put the ship at risk of capsizing. (La Dage and Van Germert 1990)

T-AVB load planning is a time consuming, inflexible process made more so by the high tempo of operations and pressure to execute operational orders in the time allotted in a time of war. The manual system of load planning is not responsive (in a timely manner) to modifications in the force structure, concept of employment or both. There is no formal training, and On-The-Job Training (OJT) opportunities for implementing and exercising load planning considerations are scarce. The lack of this experience and training was abundantly evident when the T-AVBs had to be loaded for Desert Shield/Storm. At that time, the T-AVB concept was still new and there were no experts. It took 5 full 24-hour days to load one of the ships for the desert. With all of the changes, the actual manifest and inventory had to be manually validated after the ship set sail. Changes were being made right up until the very end.

The following facts exist:
- Load planning is complex and tedious.
- No formal training is available.
- Attrition of experienced personnel occurs regularly, (orders, retirement, force reductions, etc.).
- If the load plan is found unstable or modified after being presented to the ship's First Mate/Master, it must be redone.
- For a variety of reasons, T-AVB will not be exercised often enough to maintain a knowledge base readily available to plan loads and deploy.

To develop a load plan, the planner must have a listing of all MFs and cargo to be loaded. MFs embarked include not only maintenance work centers, but also supply department MFs, bulk cargo and rolling stock. That list must identify:
- MF/container power requirements
- MFs needing air and/or water hookups
- MFs/containers needing access
- MF interconnection requirements (shop integrity)
- Ownership of the MFs (Rotary Wing, Fixed Wing, Work Center, etc.).
- Type of MF.

- Projected off-load priority.
- The availability and locations of facility assets on the ship (air, power, etc.).
- Special limitations on locations or MFs.
- Types of additional cargo, (rotor blades, nose cones, rolling stock (MMGs (Mobile Motor Generators), mobilizers, etc.), POLs (Petroleum, Oils, Lubricants), etc.).
- Pier side facilities at both departure and destination ports.
- Status of the Ship's cargo handling equipment, MF support systems, and ship access points (hatches, ramps and doors).

Once the load planner has all the requisite data in hand, he must compare what is needed against the ship's facilities and develop a proposed load plan. After the load plan is completed it must be presented to the ship's First Mate/Master for approval. If the load plan is found to be unsafe, (i.e., "…the ship floats upside down"), the load plan must be redone. Any modifications to an approved plan require resubmission.

Taking into account the above listed conditions, if it takes the load planner only 1 minute per item of cargo to identify where to place it in the ship, with over 350 MFs and access modules, it will take over 5 hours to develop a load plan. Now, add to that rolling stock and other bulk stores/cargos that may take two minutes per item due to irregular shapes, sizes and ability to stack (or lack of). Assuming NO CHANGES in what is to be loaded, an experienced, seasoned load planner can develop a load plan to present to the ship's First Mate/Master in about 8 to 10 hours. In reality, it takes anywhere from 1.5 to 2.5 days to develop the initial load plan.

Prior to TALPS, T-AVB load planning had always been done manually, (the "stubby pencil" method). The particular problems presented by this unique situation made it an ideal candidate for automation.

Solution

Automation Of the Load Planning Process
The purpose of the T-AVB Automated Load Planning System (TALPS) is to automate the T-AVB load planning process. The TALPS program uses artificial intelligence (AI) to follow the same logical steps that an expert uses in completing complex tasks associated with load planning.

The ability to develop load plans with a prolog-based expert system was proven in the early 1980's when SRI International developed the Automated Airload Planning System (AALPS) for the military (U.S. Air Force) using Quintus Prolog. AALPS was constraint based, but like a number of other load planning programs, it requires the user to place the item of cargo. The aircraft cargo loading system then validated the load against all constraints. Stanley & Associates developed a ship loading program called CAEMS (Computer Aided Embarkation Management System) using a Paradox Database driving an AutoCad user interface, interfaced using the C Language, for the United States Marine Corps in the late 1980's.

CAEMS was used to help load the ships coming back from Desert Storm and a much improved, updated version is still in use by the Marine Corps embarkation community today. "AutoShip" (Autoship Systems Corporation) is another software tool available to commercial shipping companies that supports loading containerized cargo. AutoShip, is a ship type/class specific tool and is configured at purchase time for the vessel(s) it will support. The US Army Military Traffic Management Command had an application called CODES that is in the process of being upgraded, modernized and renamed to ICODES (Integrated Computerized Deployment System). ICODES is being developed by the CAD Research Center, California Polytechnic Institute in San Luis Obispo and has seen limited fielding.

CAEMS, ICODES, and AutoShip operate primarily the same way for ships that AALPS does for aircraft loads; the user loads the cargo and the system validates the load against constraints. These programs are designed to be extremely flexible in that they never know what kind of ship or load they may have to develop. All three are 'template' based. CAEMS does have an AI module that does 'auto-pro-ration' (a term used to describe how the module computes the flow of cargo into a location) while ICODES is an AI 'Agent' based application (originally built using CLIPS and now being developed in C++) that will automatically place cargo items in a template developed by the user. These routines analyze the cargo to ensure it can get to it's designated cargo storage location, (i.e., can it fit through the hatch, make the turn onto a vehicle ramp, etc) and assigns specific cargo items to the template locations. The templates act as 'greedy attractors' (locations trying to pull certain types of cargo to them) to specific cargo types and individual serialized items are then stowed. For example, if the template shows a position for a M1A1 tank for Unit A, any one of Unit A's tanks could end up there unless the user designates a specific one. Developing these templates is the most time consuming operation of load planning, it is in effect, manual load planning.

While TALPS will support this manual cargo placement method of operation also, the significant difference with TALPS is that it can also place the cargo automatically. With most of the other systems, a domain expert is doing the template and load plan development. Due to the unique mission of the T-AVB, all of the 'template' knowledge for any type of load the ship is capable of carrying is in the TALPS fact and rule bases. Because of the unique functionality provided by the ship, there are extremely few people with T-AVB load planning expertise. The problem is that there are domain experts for the ship, there are domain experts for the cargo, and there are experts in ship loading, but there are extremely few experts in all three domain areas. TALPS combines the expertise from all three domains for this application. The prolog development environment for this expert system is "PDC Visual Prolog".

The Advantages of TALPS

One important feature of TALPS is it automatically considers the ship's load and stabilization requirements. As such, the ship's First Mate/Master will not reject a load plan as being unsafe. CAEMS and ICODES must export the load to another application for Trim, Stress and Stability (TSS) verification. This represents the single most significant benefit of TALPS: TIME SAVINGS. With a manual load planning time of 8 to 10 hours per session (that could be rejected as unsafe, thus restarting the 10 hour clock), the time to develop a load plan can be significant. In actual planning exercises, the time to complete a load plan with TALPS from start to finish, has been under 1 hour.

Additionally, TALPS provides cargo preparation schedules, load team assignments, and cargo flow schedules. These additional items are by-products of the load planning process within TALPS that normally would have to be prepared manually after the plan is approved. Each of these products would normally take hours by themselves to produce. All of these products increase the efficiency of the loading evolution. CAEMS and ICODES do not provide these additional capabilities.

The Evolution of TALPS

The TALPS efforts began in 1992 with a proposal from the Naval Aviation Maintenance Office to Headquarters Marine Corps, Department of Aviation. From 1992 through 1997, the TALPS development team participated in every T-AVB training exercise as observers, interviewed all load planners involved with each exercise and extracted knowledge from the few load planning manuals that existed for the ships. From that effort, a T-AVB load-planning manual was written and the TALPS software was produced.

During the initial development efforts, the load plan generation routines went through a couple of revisions. The most notable being the attempt to use a Genetic Algorithm (GA) (Goldberg 1989) to generate a load plan and then have it evaluated against the fact bases for fitness. This effort was attempted however the GA would never advance beyond 50% fitness. After 6 months, the effort was abandoned due to product delivery requirements and budgetary limitations. The lessons learned from developing the fitness function for the GA were then applied to the rule and fact bases.

In May 1997, TALPS, version 1.03c, was certified by American Bureau of Shipping (ABS) as a Safe Loading Instrument and the software was distributed to Marine Corps Aviation Logistics Squadrons (MALS). In 1999, DCS Corporation was contracted to update the software,

update the user interface, and update the rules and fact bases to account for additional modifications made to the ships after the initial release of TALPS. TALPS will be reviewed after the annual T-AVB exercise and updated or modified as required. TALPS version 2.1 was fielded in Nov 2000 and is currently being used to plan the 2001 T-AVB exercise. What follows is a discussion of the underlying methodologies of how TALPS works.

The Technology of TALPS

TALPS is primarily a constraint based, expert scheduling system. TALPS is configured to recursively process all cargo items and assigns them to cargo locations. After each complete iteration of cargo assignments, the ship's TSS characteristics are evaluated. If any safety parameters are exceeded, the plan is rejected, the system backtracks (via the internal prolog backtracking mechanism) and the system recalculates the load. By incorporating domain knowledge into the rules that process the cargo data, many of the conditions that would cause a plan to fail are avoided. By avoiding the known unsafe conditions, safe load plans are almost always generated correctly the first time.

As a result of the interviews during the initial TALPS development efforts, certain patterns emerged that later became 'iron clad'. Certain MFs will always be combined and co-located with particular other MFs and these 'blocks' will almost always go into a select few ship locations. A 'block' is normally made up of 2, 3 or 4 MFs. As a result, rules and facts were incorporated to take advantage of these heuristics. By building up a fact base of these 'standardized' blocks, their possible locations, and adding rules to process them, 'blocks' of MFs can be assigned in seconds, leaving only the unattached MFs to be dealt with by the system. One of the biggest challenges was to represent the knowledge and data so the prolog engines could process it. In TALPS, the block's data is represented as facts, each containing a single paired list that represents a block.

An example of the data representation of a single predefined block and three of the legal cell block sets is shown below.

The top level clause (autoLoad) controls the sequence of events and cargos are assigned in an order that prunes the search space rapidly. Access Modules are almost always placed in 42 specific locations on the ship. The autoLoad clause calls the sub-clauses that handle access modules very early in the process. This removes 42 cargo items from the search space. Dry stores and crew Reefers (refrigeration containers) are handled the

```
mf_blocks(["MV01B","2F32","MV02A","2F34","MV03","2A34","NA01","2A32"])
mf_blocks(["MV01B","2F33","MV02A","2F35","MV03","2A35","NA01","2A33"])
mf_blocks(["MV01B","3F32","MV02A","3F34","MV03","3A34","NA01","3A32"])
```

```
cargo_item(1,"NONE","DRY006","TAVB","000","TAVB00","Z","0","DRY006","000",ds,"AC","NA","TA
VB only")
cargo_params("DRY006",w(2500,2500,2500,2500,5000,5000,10000,"LBS"),d(240,"INCHES1",96,"INC
HES2",98,"INCHES",1306.67,37),b(120,58.8,48))
cargo_info("DRY006","Embark1","Debark1",0,0,0,0,0)
```

same way removing another 10. Next come deep stow cargos. They require no access and are always put into the same 54 cargo locations thus reducing the count. The system then searches for predefined blocks, potentially removing another 50 to 60 MFs from the search space. The previous steps are an application of the heuristics learned during the initial TALPS development efforts; the load planners always got these items out of the way first. By the time the system has to place individual cargo items, the search space has been reduced typically from 350 items to about 180, or about one half the search space.

Another example of the heuristics involved is predefined blocks. The system reads in a predefined block, determines if all of the necessary MFs are available and awaiting location assignment (i.e., not already assigned), and verifies that the cargo locations are available. If both are true, the block is then loaded and system stored parameters are updated to reflect the loaded cargo. If not, the system checks the next available set of preferred cargo locations. Once all of the locations are exhausted, the current block is rejected, the system backtracks and retrieves the next predefined block starting the process all over.

Structuring of the rules and data in this format allows the system to adapt for exceptions to the rules should there ever be a MF block in excess of 4 MFs. The exception is then handled in data without having to change any code.

Once all of the predefined types are assigned, the system then starts assigning cargo items individually based on the parameters listed earlier. If any cargo item is placed that has a 'user designated' partner, they are then treated similarly as a predefined block. If both cannot be placed, then a new set of locations is searched for.

The three facts at the top of the page represent the internal representation of a single cargo item. The serial number ("DRY006") is the link. The data represented carries all of the data needed not just by the system, but also by the user before and after loading.

Ship cargo locations are defined internally as shown below. The cell number ("6F13") is the unique identifier. The two lists at the end of the fact contain constraint data and preference data. By expressing a preference for a particular set of cargo types ["DS","SEAC"] into a specific location, the cell becomes 'greedy' and tries to attract those types of cargo. The limitations list,

["TEU","ISO"] prevents 'un-wanted' cargos. Various other data about the ship that affects load planning are also stored.

In all cases of cargo-to-location assignment, cargo item and cell location characteristics are evaluated. By structuring the facts and rules to account for cargo needs that matched cells facilities, we created a knowledge mapping that allowed for direct pattern matches. The only thing we had to do 'extra' was to create a set of rules that handles the 'don't care' situations. (Example: a cell provides 400Hz power, but the cargo item does not need it.) The five positions at the end of cargo_info (all zeros in this case), map directly to the five positions after the "G" in the cell location shown below. This particular cargo item is a dry store container (cargo_item fact, 4th field from the end: ds). This maps directly to the preferred cargo type in cell 6F13, "DS". In this case, the cargo item and cell location would be a match.

Overall, the planning process allows the user to define the general concept of the ship's load. This is accomplished by setting a hold's parameters. A schema was developed to maintain the knowledge of the hold's capabilities as well as attributes of the hold in various configurations.

In addition to the holds themselves, a separate schema was developed to maintain data about the cargo handling equipment, access ports and hatches, and location usability based on the status of same. The user sets these parameters at anytime during the planning evolution to reflect the current condition of the ship. Rules within the system act on these conditions and subsequently modify as necessary the cell location parameters.

TALPS rules process all of the facts, within constraints set by the user and imposed by the system, and rapidly produces a certified safe load plan. Figure 5 is a highly simplified drawing of the Load Planning process. All of the Cargo data is entered or updated, all of the ship data is updated, and then the cargo is scheduled into cargo locations. After the scheduling of the cargo, the load is validated for TSS. At any point of failure, the system backtracks and starts the process again. The output is shown as a 'proposed load plan' only because the one constant in T-AVB load planning is change!

```
define cell("6F13",6,"FWD",1,3,"G",0,0,0,0,0,"DSW",1,["TEU","ISO"],["DS","SEAC"])
```

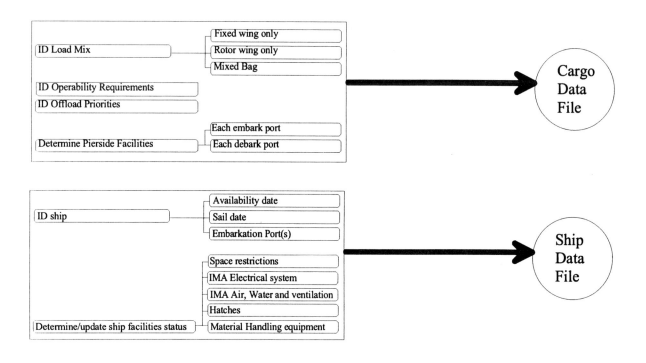

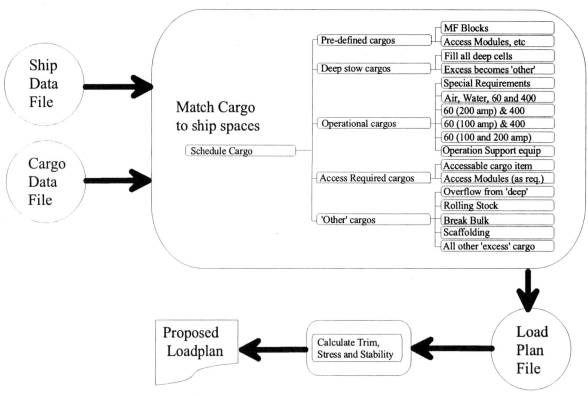

Figure 5: Simplified TALPS flow

The future of TALPS

TALPS was originally conceived as a tool to help the harried planner develop load plans for the T-AVB class of vessels. Over time, it evolved into a repository to maintain the volatile corporate knowledge of the T-AVB load planning process. TALPS has currently planned existence until 2005 at which time a Department of Defense ship-loading tool (ICODES) will be fielded. This new tool is designed to incorporate the knowledge and expertise that currently resides in TALPS as well as other ship loading applications.

Project Sponsor:

Department of Aviation, Logistics Support (ASL-34)
Headquarters, United States Marine Corps

References:

Carrico, M.A., Girard, J.E., & Jones, J.P., 1989. *Building Knowledge Systems: Developing & Managing Rule-Based Applications*, New York,: McGraw-Hill.

Cerkez, P. 1995. Knowledge Representation: An Explanation for 'Buddy', Technical Report, CS5374, Department of Computer Science, Florida Institute Of Technology, Patuxent River Campus.

Covington, M.A., Nute, D. & Vellino A., 1988. *Prolog Programming In Depth*, Glenview, Ill.: Scott Foresman and Company.

Goldberg, David E., 1989. *Genetic Algorithms in Search, Optimization & Machine Learning*, Reading MA. Addison Wesley

La Dage, John and Van Germert, Lee: 1990. *Stability and Trim for the Ship's Officer, Third Edition*, Centerville MD., Cornell Maritime Press,

Luger, G.F., & W.A. Stubblefield, 1993, *Artificial Intelligence: Structures and Strategies for Complex Problem Solving*, 2nd Ed. Redwood City Ca.: Benjamin/Cummings Publishing Co., Inc.

Rich, E., 1983, *Artificial Intelligence*, New York, McGraw-Hill.

Richards, T., 1989. *Clausal Form Logic: An Introduction to the Logic of Computer Reasoning*, Reading Mass., Addison-Wesley Publishing Co.

USMC, 1998. *Aviation Logistic Support Ship (T-AVB) Logistic Planning Manual, Revision A*, Lexington Park MD, DCS Corporation.

USMC, 1983. Feasibility, Study of the Aviation Logistics Support Ship, Washington DC: United States Marine Corps.

Natural Language Sales Assistant – A Web-based Dialog System for Online Sales

Joyce Chai, Veronika Horvath, Nicolas Nicolov, Margo Stys-Budzikowska, Nanda Kambhatla, Wlodek Zadrozny

IBM T. J. Watson Research Center
30 Saw Mill River Rd.
Hawthorne, NY 10532
{jchai, veronika, nicolas, sml, nanda, wlodz}@us.ibm.com

Abstract

This paper describes a web-based dialog system – Natural Language Sales Assistant (NLSA) – that helps users find relevant information about products and services in e-commerce sites. The system leverages technologies in natural language processing and human computer interaction to create a faster and more intuitive way of interacting with websites. By combining traditional AI rule-based technology with taxonomy mapping, the system is able to accommodate both customer and business requirements. Our user studies have demonstrated that, in the context of e-commerce, users preferred the natural language enabled navigation over menu-driven navigation (79% to 21% users). In addition, compared to a menu driven system, the average number of clicks used in the natural language system was reduced by 63.2% and the average time was reduced by 33.3%. The NLSA system is currently deployed by IBM as a live pilot and we are collecting real user feedback. We believe that conversational interfaces like that of NLSA offer the ultimate personalization and can greatly enhance the user experience for websites.

1 Introduction

With the emergence of e-commerce systems (Aggarwal, Wolf and Yu 1998; Muller and Pischel 1999), successful information access on e-commerce websites that accommodates both customer needs and business requirements becomes essential. Menu-driven navigation and keyword search provided by most commercial sites have tremendous limitations, as they tend to overwhelm and frustrate users with lengthy and rigid interactions. User interest in a particular site decreases exponentially with the increase in the number of mouse clicks (Huberman, Pirolli, and Pitkow 1998). Hence shortening the interaction path to provide useful information becomes important. Many e-commerce sites attempt to solve the problem by providing

keyword search capabilities. However, keyword search engines usually require that users know domain specific jargon so that the keywords could possibly match indexing terms used in the product catalog or documents. Keyword search does not allow users to precisely describe their intentions, and more importantly, it lacks an understanding of the semantic meaning of the search words and phrases. For example, keyword search systems usually can not understand that "summer dress" should be looked up in women's clothing under "dress", whereas "dress shirt" most likely in men's under "shirt". A search for "shirt" can reveal dozens or even hundreds of items, which are useless for somebody who has a specific style and pattern in mind. Moreover, search engines do not accommodate business rules, e.g. a prohibition against displaying cheap earrings with more expensive ones. The solution to these problems lies, in our opinion, in centering electronic commerce websites on natural language (and multimodal) dialog.

Natural language dialog has been used for call-center/routing applications (Carpenter and Chu-Carroll 1998; Chu-Carroll and Carpenter 1998), email routing (Walker, Fromer, and Narayanan 1998), information retrieval and database access (Androutsopoulos and Ritchie 1995), and for telephony banking (Zadrozny et al. 1998). The integration of natural language dialog with an e-commerce environment is a novel feature of our system. Our work goes beyond the "natural language interface" features of websites such as www.askjeeves.com, www.neuromedia.com, etc. which work in a question-answering mode and do not use dialog. When searching e-commerce sites, users often have target products in mind but do not know where to find information, or how to specify a request. Sometimes users only have vague ideas about the products of interest (Saito and Ohmura 1998). Thus, users need to be able to formulate their requests in their own words as well as revise their request incrementally based on additional information, which can be provided through natural language style of dialog. Our recent studies show that natural language dialog is a very effective medium for negotiating such contexts by understanding users' requests/intentions and by providing help/advice/recommendations to the user.

We have built a Natural Language Sales Assistant (NLSA), a system which allows customers to make requests in natural language and directs them towards appropriate web pages that sell the products. The system applies natural language understanding to interpret user inputs, arranges follow-up dialog to provide explanation and to ask for additional information, and finally makes recommendations. The NLSA prototype system is currently deployed and we are collecting real user feedback.

In this paper, we first give a detailed description of the NLSA system, in particular, the system architecture and components. We then present results from the user studies. Finally, we discuss the lessons learned and outline future work.

sends the logical form to the Dialog Manager. The PM is also responsible for obtaining the system's response from the DM. The PM applies a Response Generator to generate specific presentations based on appropriate modalities such as display tables, natural language output, GUI components, etc. An Explanation Model is also integrated to provide explanations as to what information the system understands from the interaction and why certain products are recommended. After displaying the system's response, any subsequent user input (e.g. a clarification, a correction or a new request) is again sent to the DM.

The Dialog Manager is responsible for determining the specific action(s) requested by the user and filling the parameters of the identified action (e.g. price range) through a dialog with the user. After filling in the

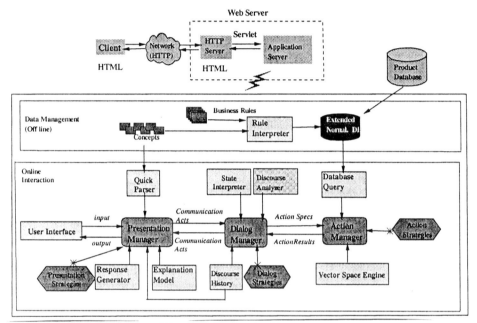

Figure 1: *System Architecture*

2 NLSA System Descriptions

NLSA includes two subsystems: data management subsystem and online interaction subsystem. It is implemented as a client-server system in a three tier architecture using Java servlets and HTTP as communication media between the client and the server.

Our architecture (in Figure 1) supports multimodal dialog in the online interaction subsystem. It is designed to support inputs from different channels and modalities including keyboard, speech input and output over a telephone or microphone, mouse input, etc. The online interaction subsystem consists of three major modules: Presentation Manager (PM), Dialog Manager (DM) and Action Manager (AM). The presentation manager uses a shallow natural language parser (Quick Parser) for noun phrases to transform the user query into a logical form, and

parameters, the DM sends the filled action template (Action Specs) to the AM for execution. The dialog manager uses both short-term conversational discourse history and long-term user history to formulate responses to the user. The Action Specs represents the results of the transformation from user requests to action plans for the action manager to satisfy the requests, for example, converting a "search for products" request into an SQL database query for a particular database engine. The DM is also responsible for receiving the Action Results from the AM; analyzing them and asking follow up questions. A State Interpreter identifies the current dialog state based on both user input and system response. When a particular state is identified, the DM applies state-based dialog strategies to arrange conversation or resolve conflicts.

The Action Manager determines the best mechanism for executing an action, given an Action Spec. Thus, for a product search request, the AM decides which information source should be looked up which information should be extracted. It uses database queries to retrieve exactly matched products or uses a traditional information retrieval technique (Vector Space Engine) to retrieve the best-matched products or information. The AM returns the retrieved information (Action Results) to the DM.

Associated with the three major modules are three kinds of strategies. Presentation Strategies select different response content for different user profiles. For example, for experienced users, the display table will include detailed technical specifications such as CPU speed, RAM size etc., while to novice users, the system displays the price and brief market messages to make it easy for the user to understand how the products relate to the user requests[1]. Dialog Strategies define the appropriate kinds of responses at different dialog states, such as the kinds of explanations to be provided to the user and the kind of follow-up questions to be asked. Action Strategies specify the databases to access under specific circumstances and the actions to take if nothing is retrieved, e.g. an approximate match between the user demands and the available products. All these strategies are designed to reflect business goals and requirements.

The Data Management Subsystem contains domain- and application-specific data, information and knowledge. With the ever-evolving business environments and customer needs, tools and processes are needed to maintain related information and knowledge so that updates to these resources can be reflected seamlessly during online interaction. This is especially true in the e-commerce domain where business information changes rapidly. Therefore, the data management subsystem addresses data, knowledge and maintenance (i.e., tools and processes). The subsystem includes the concept base, business rules and the extended database. The concept base provides knowledge about common sense concepts and the user vocabulary. Business rules are used to reflect business goals and decisions by associating common sense concepts with business specifications. The extended database combines both product specifications (directly extracted from the product database) and common sense concepts to provide a unique information repository for information access. In the following sections, we first describe in detail the Data Management Subsystem and then the Online Interaction Subsystem.

3 Data Management Subsystem

In the NLSA, the domain knowledge is represented by concepts and business rules, which address customer needs and business requirements, respectively.

---

[1] User levels are determined by the user familiarity with notebook computers. (as shown in Figure 3).

3.1 Concepts

The vocabulary set in the NLSA is organized into concepts which represent user intentions and interests in shopping for computers. Three kinds of concepts are maintained. Entity concepts are about things or substances (such as products, accessories, etc.) that a user might be interested in. Attribute concepts represent features users are looking for in products, such as "FAST", "LIGHT", "HIGH-PERFORMANCE" etc. Purpose concepts represent the general uses or functions users are looking for in a particular product, such as "SMALL-BUSINESS", "TRAVEL", etc. Each concept contains a list of words and/or phrases implying this particular concept.

XML is used to organize and manage concepts (Bray, Paoli, and Speberg-McQueen 1998; Radev et al. 1999). The following is a fragment of the representation and content of the concept <Advanced-Graphic-Capability>:

```
</ENTRY><ENTRY NORMAL_FORM = "AGP", SCALE = 0,
SUPERLATIVE = 0>
    <NOVICE>Is 3-D graphics performance, which
speeds online gaming and graphic design,
important to you?</NOVICE>
    <EXPERT>Are you interested in having an
Advanced Graphic Port for improved 3-D graphics
performance? </EXPERT>
    <NL_FORM>Advanced Graphics Port</NL_FORM>
    <DEF><![CDATA[hd_min >= 6.4 & resolution is
1024x768]]></DEF>
    <WORD>agp</WORD>
    <WORD>graphics</WORD>
    <WORD>game</WORD>
    <WORD>3-D</WORD>
    <WORD>multimedia</WORD>
    <WORD>...</WORD>
</ENTRY>
```

Each concept has different attributes to indicate if the concept is scalable or superlative. Quick Parser (Section 4.2) is provided to identify relevant concepts from the user natural language input (see the example in Section 4.2). Concepts with different attributes lead to different dialog flows during the user interactions.

3.2 Business Rules

Business rules are mappings between concepts and business specifications. Business specifications are values and business terms that are used by the business to describe their merchandises. For example, in the computer sales domain, the specifications could be different models of computers, processor speed, memory size, hard disk size, price, etc. In terms of these specifications, business rules give definitions to the concepts from the business point of view, such as how they position various models and how those models are marketed for different segments of consumers.

Business rules have the following structure:

```
CONCEPT ::= eval(ATTR) = CONST_VALUE &
            eval(ATTR) in RANGE &
            not(eval(ATTR))
```

For example,

```
<Advance-Graphics-Capability> ::=
eval(hard_disk_min) > 6.4 GB &
eval(resolution) = 1024x768
```

This rule interprets the "Advanced-Graphic-Capability" concept as a combination of minimum hard disk of 6.4 GB and resolution of 1024x768.

During the online interaction, business rules are used to translate identified concepts into business specifications. Thus, the relevant database query can be generated based on business specifications.

3.3 Maintenance

Concepts and business rules are not static. When new products or features are introduced or when new words or phrases are discovered during deployment, concepts and/or business rules need to be updated accordingly. Currently, we have designed and implemented a semi-automated tool for this purpose. The tool automatically extracts significant keywords from logs of user queries and allows manual updates of business rules through an editing interface. The automatic extraction phase applies unigrams, bigrams and trigrams on a collection of user input and uses a parts-of-speech filter and a simple noun phrase grammar to extract the significant keywords. Figure 2 shows a snapshot of the interface where automatically identified keywords (based on bigrams) can be added to existing concepts.

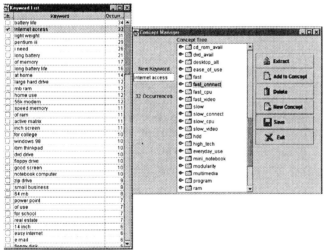

Figure 2: *Editing Interface for Concept Management*

4 Online Interaction Subsystem

The online interaction subsystem addresses the end-to-end interactions between the user and the system. It consists of the Dialog Manager arranging the content of interactions, the Presentation Manager separating content from presentation in the front end and the Action Manager performing database access and business transactions in the back end. The online interaction subsystem is designed to be domain independent. Thus the change of the application domain would only require customization of the data management subsystem.

4.1 Presentation Manager

The Presentation Manager is responsible for interpreting user input and displaying system responses. The Presentation Manager contains user interfaces, a noun phrase parser (i.e., the Quick Parser), a response generator and an explanation model.

One of the major advantages of web-based dialog systems is the addition of a new dimension for information presentation. Through a combination of UI components (such as radio buttons, forms, links, etc.) and the natural language dialog, much more information can be communicated between the user and the system in comparison to a traditional spoken dialog system. Thus, with the reduced number of turns (interactions), the user can get instructions, examples, explanations, and ideas of limitations of the system. A snapshot of a user interface (for user initial request) is shown in Figure 3.

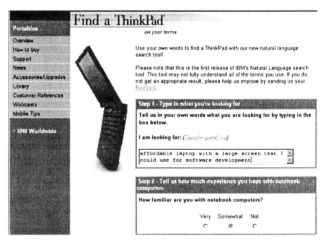

Figure 3: *A Snapshot of Initial User Interface*

4.2 Quick Parser

A shallow semantic parser is applied to identify semantic and syntactic information of interest from the user textual input. More specifically, based on a collection of regular expressions, a noun phrase grammar and concepts, the parser identifies special named entities (such as CPU speed, processor type, etc.), head of the noun phrase and concepts for further processing. The parser is implemented as a finite state cascade. It translates natural language strings into a well-formed XML message called the Logical Form (LF). The Logical Form is then passed on to the Dialog Manager. For example, if the user input is: "nice travel companion for $2000-3000 with at least 400Mhz Pentium processor", the parser will generate the following logical form in the XML format:

```
<LF>
<NP>
<ATTRIBUTE><SPECS>nice</SPECS></ATTRIBUTE>
<HEAD><SPECS CONCEPT="PORTABILITY"
SCALE="weight">travel companion</SPECS></HEAD>
<PP>
<PREP VALUE="for"/>
<NP>
<ATTRIBUTE><SPECS
TYPE="BASE_PRICE">gt2000</SPECS></ATTRIBUTE>
<HEAD><SPECS TYPE="BASE_PRICE">lt3000</SPECS></HEAD>
</NP>
</PP>
<PP>
<PREP VALUE="with"/>
<NP>
<ATTRIBUTE><SPECS
TYPE="CPU_SPEED">gt400</SPECS></ATTRIBUTE>
<ATTRIBUTE><SPECS
TYPE="CPU_BRAND">Pentium</SPECS></ATTRIBUTE>
<HEAD><SPECS>processor</SPECS></HEAD>
</NP>
</PP>
</NP>
</LF>
```

The shallow parser does not aim at a complete linguistic analysis; it merely extracts some information from the user's input that is useful for the dialog management. The parser uses several external resources, each configurable to adapt to different domains of application. Adaptation to new domains will only require updating of these resources without modifying the code.

4.3 Dialog Manager

The Dialog Manager maintains the representation of the dialog state and the dialog history, and arranges follow up interaction (such as asking for more information, providing feedback and confirmation, etc) based on those representations. Research in dialog systems presents a variety of ways to model dialog state and dialog history. These typically include a representation of the user's intentions, beliefs and focus of attention. The models depend on linguistic phenomena that are to be handled by the system such as misunderstandings, interruptions, deictic and anaphoric expressions. A similar representation can be found in LINLIN where the dialog history is a tree with three levels corresponding to the whole dialog, discourse segments and speech acts (Jonsson, 1997).

In NLSA, the dialog state is represented by a combination of the current utterance, the current system response and the interaction history. More precisely, it takes into consideration the following questions: Has the user specified any preferences for computer features? Is there any ambiguity detected in user input? Are there any concepts identified by the Quick Parser from the current utterance? Are there any conflicting constraints detected from a history of utterances. Are there more than three products recommended to the user in the previous interaction? The combination of answers to those questions forms the dialog state for that particular interaction. The dialog history is a tree representation that contains the dialog state at each point of interaction.

The Dialog Manager applies a mixed initiative strategy to arrange different follow-ups. The system first allows the user to take the initiative to specify what they are looking for in their own language. Based on the interpretation of the user input, the system then takes over the initiative to request for specific information.

An example (in British English) is the following:

U_0: I'm looking for a piano.
S_0: I'll find you a notebook if you tell me what your notebook needs are.
U_1: I'm looking for a laptop less than 500 pounds.
S_1: Display: a table of most popular models
  Reply: The price range for Thinkpads is between 799 and 2389 pounds. You may specify a value with the range or continue your search by specifying other features you are looking for.
U_2: I want something easy to carry and inexpensive.
S_2: Display: We have found several notebooks based on your search criteria: Ultraportability: models which weigh less than 3 kilograms, Low price: affordable models which sell for less than 1500 pounds, followed by a table of six products satisfying these criteria).
  Reply: Do you need a large hard disk capacity for backup data or storing large files?
U_3: No, I want something top-of-the-line.
S_3: Display: We didn't find a product that matches your terms perfectly, but we have list the closest match to your request. (Display two tables: one table satisfies the extreme-performance criteria with weights of products sorted from lightest to the heaviest; the other table satisfies the low price criteria with weights of products sorted from lightest to heaviest).
  Reply: Battery life is important to frequent travelers. Is long battery life important to you?
  ....

Depending on the dialog state and the dialog history, the Dialog Manager uses different follow-up responses. For example, if nothing from the domain of interest is interpreted from the user input (U_0), the system will give some suggestions and direct the user to restrict their queries to notebook related questions (S_0). If the user asks a question which is identified as out of the available product range (U_1), the system will first explain to the user the valid range and then will prompt the user to re-formulate his/her request (S_1). If more than three products are recommended in the previous interaction, the system will ask the most discriminating question to narrow down the number of products to recommend (S_2). When the user request causes some conflicts with previous requests in the dialog history (U_3), the system will engage in a sub-dialog with the user to explain the conflicting situation, provide suggestions and help users to reformulate their constraints (S_3). In a user study we conducted, we found that conflicting requirements occurred more than 40% of the time. Therefore, for dialog systems like ours, it is crucial that the source of conflict is identified and that the system can provide sensible feedback in such situations.

4.4 Action Manager

The Action Manager deals with the back end product retrieval and business transactions. The Action Manager uses the Action Strategies that specify different actions based on the Action Specs sent by the Dialog Manager. When a valid SQL query is presented in the Action Specs, an access to the extended database takes place and products matching the query are retrieved. When the user preferences for features are included, a sorting algorithm is applied to yield a ranked list of products.

When a valid SQL retrieves zero products from the database due to conflicting constraints, the Action Manager will notify the Dialog Manager that the constraints cannot be simultaneously met. It then resolves the conflict by using a vector space based on similarity measure between constraints (i.e., specifications and concepts) from the user input and constraints indexed to each product. The top similar products will be retrieved.

5 NLSA Evaluation

To better understand the user language and design system responses, we conducted an online user market survey prior to the deployment of the system. Furthermore, we conducted three user studies to objectively evaluate the usability of the prototype and to better understand the user needs.

5.1 Market Survey

In the market survey, participants were first given three questions: "What kind of notebook computer are you looking for?", "What features are important to you?", and "What do you plan to use this notebook computer for?" By applying statistical techniques (n-gram models) and a noun phrase grammar on a collection of user natural language responses, we extracted significant keywords and phrases that express user intentions and interests in shopping for computers. Then, participants were asked to rank 10 ten randomly selected technical terms (from 90 computer related terms) in terms of familiarities. This study allowed us to group technical terms into different complexity groups and better formulate system responses to different user groups. Over a 30-day period, we received 705

survey responses. From the natural language responses, we learned 195 keywords and phrases and included those in the vocabulary set for the deployed system.

5.2 User Studies

The studies were designed to reveal how successful the prototype system fared at meeting the users' expectations within the following areas: system flow, ease of use, validity of the system response, and user vocabulary.

The first user study was a proof of concept for dialog-based systems in an e-commerce environment. The study compared the first version of the prototype system to a fully developed menu driven system. The study (Chai, et al., 2000) showed that comparing NLSA navigation with the menu driven navigation in finding products, the number of clicks (a click was counted when the user clicked on a submit button, a radio button or a link, etc. to take action) was significantly reduced by 63.5% and the amount of time spent was significantly reduced by 33.3. Less experienced users preferred the NL enabled navigation much more than the experienced users. Overall, respondents preferred the NL dialog based navigation (NLSA) to the menu driven navigation two to one (2:1). Respondents thought the NLSA was extremely easy to use, and they were comfortable and confident with the resulting information it provided. Users liked the fact that they could express their needs in their "own jargon" instead of the foreign "computer jargon". There was also the perception that with the NLSA model, the computer did all the work for them instead of them doing all the work for the computer (as in the menu-driven model).

The second and the third user studies were conducted to evaluate the current version of the prototype with regards to the ease of navigation, clarity of terminology and their level of confidence that they could find the product they were looking for. In both studies, participants commended an interactive site where user's inputs can be interpreted and were very receptive to the natural language, dialog-based search site. The study clearly showed that dialog-based searches were preferred over non-dialog based searches[1] (79% to 21% users). The users liked the fact that the system narrowed down the search as they proceeded, provided that it was responsive and geared to users' specific needs. Participants in both studies shared the opinion that a system that worked for the user was better than a system that made the user work. When the NLSA worked according to design, it left the user with the feeling that the system was easy and the search was narrowed with relatively little effort. Table 1 sums the ratings (1 – least desirable, 10- most desirable) from the two studies for different categories of users.

The studies pointed towards improvements in the area of

---

[1] Where dialog meant either the radial selection or typed inputs

system responsiveness including tuning up of the follow up questions, prompts and explanations to the user's input. To a large extent, the success of a dialog system has been shown to depend on the kind of questions asked and the type of feedback provided. The types and nature of the questions asked throughout the NLSA were based on features and functionality of a computer. The studies conclude that asking user questions about lifestyle and usage of computer to solicit feedback would have been a more user-friendly line of action. Users' confidence in the system decreases if the system responses are not consistent with the user's input. The system feedback and the follow up questions should manage a delicate balance of exposing system limitations to the user but at the same time making sure the user understands the degree of flexibility and advantages of using a dialog system.

	Small Business		Consumers	
	Study 2	Study 3	Study 2	Study 3
Overall Rating of the Site	5.8	6.5	7.5	7.7
Level of Confidence	7.8	6.5	7.6	7.6
Ease of Use and Navigation	8.2	7.6	8.1	8.4
Clarity of Terminology	6.0	6.9	7.6	7.1

Table 1: *Comparison of Study 2 & Study 3 Ratings.*

Even though most users preferred the NL dialog based navigation, the study also showed the utility of menu driven searches. Some users definitely liked the ability to select options from a menu, specifying that the multiple-choice method was easy. There were also users who liked having questions asked of them. Typically, such users were either not comfortable with their typing ability or unable to express what they were looking for without additional external cues. More results can be found in a separate paper focusing on user studies (Chai, et al. 2001).

5.3 Deployed Pilot

Prior to the deployment of the system as a pilot, in addition to the usability user studies, a set of rigorous system testing (including express testing and server load balancing testing) was conducted to test the robustness and stability. The pilot is running on an IBM Websphere server with the servlet engine. The backend product data is stored in a DB2 database. Real-time data propagation (from the product database to the extended database used by the NLSA) is supported through staging servers. During the pilot (launched in December 2000), we are collecting information about real user interactions. In particular, we keep logs of user natural language inputs, logical forms generated by the system, system responses, SQL database queries and user feedback (in the form of questionnaire

about the pilot). We believe this information will help us further evaluate and improve the system.

6 Conclusions

This paper describes a system that provides natural language dialog capabilities to help users access e-commerce sites and find relevant information about products and services. The system leverages technologies in natural language processing and human computer interaction to create a faster and more intuitive way of interacting with websites. By combining traditional AI rule-based technology with taxonomy mapping, the system is able to accommodate both customer needs and business requirements. Our studies showed that dialog-based navigation is preferred over menu-driven navigation (79% to 21% users). In addition, our studies confirm the efficiency of using natural language dialog in terms of the number of clicks and the amount of time required to obtain the relevant information. Comparing to a menu-driven system, the average number of clicks used in the natural language system was reduced by 63.2% and the average time was reduced by 33.3%.

In these studies we learned that the current internet keyword search engines have created a "search culture" which is widely accepted by most internet users. As a result, many users are accustomed to typing keywords or simple phrases (the average length of a user query was 5.31 words long with a standard deviation of 2.62). Analysis of the user queries reveals the brevity and relative linguistic simplicity of their input; hence, shallow parsing techniques seem adequate to extract the necessary meaning from the user input. Therefore, in such context, sophisticated dialog management is more important than the ability to handle complex natural language sentences.

From a historical perspective, users have experienced different interaction styles ranging from command-driven and form-fill applications to question-answer sequences, menus and natural language dialog interaction. Although naturalness is one of the winning points for natural language dialog, it also faces serious challenges. For novice users, a conversational system by itself may be overwhelming and it may indeed be quicker to use a menu-driven system. For an experienced user, on the other hand, the amount of typing may be a drawback and browsing may be the best and quickest way to navigate. Ultimately, in order to satisfy different user needs, the natural language dialog navigation and the menu-driven navigation should be combined. While the menu-driven approach provides choices for the user to browse around or learn some additional information, the natural language dialog provides the efficiency, flexibility and natural touch to the user's online experience.

Moreover, in designing NL dialog based navigation, it is important to show users that the system does understand his/her requests before giving any recommendation or relevant information. Users remarked in our studies that they appreciated the recommended results because the system offered some explanation. This feature allows the user to "trust the system." Good navigation aids can be provided by summarizing the user's requests by paraphrasing it using context history, or by engaging in meaningful conversations with the user. Our studies found that robust natural dialog had a very big influence on the user satisfaction – almost all of the respondents appreciated the additional questions prompted by their input and the summary of their previous queries.

We believe that conversational interfaces offer the ultimate kind of personalization. Personalization can be defined as the process of presenting each user of an automated system with an interface uniquely tailored to his/her preference of content and style of interaction. Thus, mixed initiative conversational interfaces are highly personalized since they allow users to interact with systems using the words they want, to fetch the content they want in the style they want. Users can converse with such systems by phrasing their initial queries at a right level of comfort to them (e.g. "*I am looking for a gift for my wife*" or "*I am looking for a fast computer with DVD under 1500 dollars*"). Based on our results, we conclude that conversational natural language dialog interfaces offer powerful personalized alternatives to traditional menu-driven or search-based interfaces to websites. For such systems, it is especially important to present users with a consistent interface integrating different styles of interaction and to have robust dialog management strategies.

Acknowledgement

We would like to thank Catherine Wolf for the input on user testing and user interface design, Jimmy Lin for the contribution on the first version of the system and first user study, Prem Mellville for implementing tools for data management and survey analysis and our colleagues from the Conversational Dialog Systems group for illuminating discussions.

References

Aggarwal, C.; Wolf, J.; and Yu, P. 1998. A framework for the Optimizing of WWW Advertising, Trends in Distributed Systems for Electronic Commerce. *LNCS 1402*, Lamersdorf and Merz Eds.

Androutsopoulos, I., and Ritchie, G. D. 1995. Natural Language Interfaces to Databases – an Introduction. *Natural Language Engineering* 1(1):29-81, Cambridge University Press.

Bray, T.; Paoli, J.; and Sperberg-McQueen, C. M. 1998. Extensible Markup Language (XML) 1.0. Technical Report, http://www.w3.org/TR/REC-xml-19980210, World Wide Web Consortium Recommendation.

Carpenter, B., and Chu-Carroll, J. 1998. Natural Language Call Routing: A Robust, Self-organizing Approach. In *Proceedings of the Fifth International Conference on Spoken Language Processing.*

Chai, J.; Lin, J.; Zadrozny, W.; Ye, Y.; Budzikowska, M.; Horvath, V.; Kambhatla, N.; and Wolf, C. 2000. Comparative Evaluation of a Natural Language Dialog Based System and a Menu Driven System for Information Access: a Case Study. In *Proceedings of RIAO 2000*, pp 1590-1600, Paris, France.

Chai, J.; Horvath, V.; Kambhatla, N.; Nicolov, N.; and Stys-Budzikowska, M. 2001. A conversational Interface for Online Shopping. To appear in *Proceedings of the First Human Language Technology Conference.*

Chu-Carroll, J., and Carpenter, B. 1998. Dialog Management in Vector-based Call Routing. In *Proceedings of the 36th Annul Meeting of the Association for Computational Linguistics.*

Huberman, B. A.; Pirolli, P. L. T.; Pitkow, J. E.; and Lukose, R. M. 1998. Strong Regularities in World Wide Web Surfing. *Science*, Vol. 280.

Jonsson, A. 1997. A model for habitable and efficient dialog management for natural language interaction. *Natural Language Engineering*, 3(2/3):103-122.

Muller, J., and Pischel, M. 1999. Doing Business in the Information Marketplace. In *Proceedings of the 1999 International Conference on Autonomous Agents*, Seattle, USA.

Radev, D.; Kambhatla, N.; Ye, Y.; Wolf, C.; and Zadrozny, W. 1999. DSML: A Proposal for XML Standards for Messaging Between Components of a Natural Language Dialog System. In *Proceedings of the AISB'99 (Artificial Intelligence and Simulation of Behavior) Workshop on Reference Architecture and Data Standards for NLP.* Edinburgh, England.

Saito, M., and Ohmura, K. 1998. A Cognitive Model for Searching for Ill-defined Targets on the Web – The Relationship between Search Strategies and User Satisfaction. In *Proceedings of 21st International Conference on Research and Development in Information Retrieval*, Australia.

Walker, M.; Fromer, J.; and Narayanan, S. 1998. Learning Optimal Dialogue Strategies: A Case Study of a Spoken Dialogue Agent for Email. In *Proceedings of 36th Annual Meeting of the Association for Computational Linguistics and 17th International Conference on Computational Linguistics*, Montreal, Canada.

Zadrozny, W.; Wolf, C.; Kambhatla, N.; and Ye, Y. 1998. Conversation Machines for Transaction Processing. In *Proceedings of the Fifteenth National Conference on Artificial Intelligence (AAAI) and Tenth Conference on Innovative Applications of Artificial Intelligence Conference (IAAI)*, Madison, Wisconsin, USA.

Interchanging Agents and Humans in Military Simulation

Clinton Heinze[1], Simon Goss[1], Torgny Josefsson[1], Kerry Bennett[1],
Sam Waugh[1], Ian Lloyd[1], Graeme Murray[1] & John Oldfield[2]

1   Defence, Science, and Technology Organisation
    506 Lorimer Street, Fishermen's Bend,
    Victoria, Australia
    firstname.lastname@dsto.defence.gov.au

2   Royal Australian Air Force
    Evaluation Analysis & Standards Flight, 92 Wing,
    RAAF Base Edinburgh, South Australia, Australia
    john.oldfield@defence.gov.au

Abstract

The innovative reapplication of a multi-agent system for human-in-the-loop (HIL) simulation was a consequence of appropriate agent oriented design. The use of intelligent agents for simulating human decision making offers the potential for analysis and design methodologies that do not distinguish between *agent* and *human* until implementation. With this as a driver in the design process the construction of systems in which humans and agents can be interchanged is simplified. Two systems have been constructed and deployed to provide defence analysts with the tools required to advise and assist the Australian Defence Force in the conduct of maritime surveillance and patrol. The systems both simulate maritime air operations. One utilises intelligent agents to provide models of tactical decision making, the other provides the same environment but provides a set of user interfaces to allow air force flight crews to participate in human in the loop simulation by replacing the intelligent agents. The experiences gained from this process indicate that it is simpler, both in design and implementation, to add humans to a system designed for intelligent agents than it is to add intelligent agents to a system designed for humans.

Introduction

The modification and development of existing constructive[1], multi-agent military systems by the Australian Defence Science and Technology Organisation (DSTO) to provide the Royal Australian Air Force (RAAF) with human-in-the-loop (HIL) capability is reported in this paper. It extends applications developed and described earlier [1,2], and commences the process of integrating intelligent agent developments [8] with HIL systems research [3]. The applications described here differ in purpose from most other deployed HIL simulations in that they are used for exploration, evaluation and development of tactics and procedures rather than for training [15].

The innovative use of an existing multi-agent system for HIL simulation was a consequence of appropriate agent oriented design. The use of intelligent agents for simulating human decision making offers the potential for analysis and design methodologies that do not distinguish between agent

and human until implementation [14]. With this as a driver in the design process the construction of systems in which humans and agents can be interchanged is simplified. Two systems using the same base architecture are used to support operations research:

- The original system that utilises intelligent agents for modelling all of the military personnel within a scenario. This is conceptually identical with the systems reported by Tidhar et. al. [1] although applied to different aircraft and missions.

- The new system that removes the intelligent agent for a particular aircraft of interest and provides user interfaces that allow the actual crew of that aircraft to fly simulated missions for the purpose of validating and developing tactics.[2]

The use of intelligent agents to military simulation is maturing. For several years intelligent agents have been applied to constructive military simulation. Architectures, methodologies and programming patterns in support of this development are improving.

The incorporation of intelligent agents into HIL simulation is generally post-hoc engineering of large legacy systems or the injection of entities into a large distributed simulation via an interface [10]. Agents have requirements on systems that are not apparent in mainstream HIL simulations. Difficulties associated with the successful incorporation of intelligent agents into extant systems are often associated with a failure to recognise the specific requirements that agents will place on the system [9,16]. These problems can be alleviated by careful design of new systems or by costly remediation of existing systems.

This paper provides a case study of a deployed HIL simulation used for development of tactical procedures for a maritime surveillance aircraft. An existing constructive simulation that used intelligent agents to model all human components was modified. The modifications provide user interfaces that allow air force personnel to replace the agents that previously modelled them. *The experiences gained from this process indicate that it is simpler, both in*

---

[1] The simulation community uses the term *constructive* to designate those systems that contain no human interaction.

[2] There is a phase of significant duration in an acquisition or mid-life refit programme where military units are in a work-up mode in anticipation of delivery of platforms with enhanced capability that makes them effectively 'first of kind' and requires development of new or significantly altered tactics, operating procedures, and doctrine.

design and implementation, to add humans to a system designed for intelligent agents than it is to add intelligent agents to a system designed for humans.

The following section details the domain of application of this technology, that of maritime patrol and surveillance by the RAAF. Operational analysis that incorporates both constructive and HIL simulation can offer significant savings to the Air Force. Savings are realised both in mission performance and in support costs with respect to fuel used and time to complete a mission. By far the biggest savings are realised in extending the life of type of an aircraft through smarter operation.

Maritime Patrol and Surveillance Tactics

Air Operations Division (AOD) of the DSTO supports the RAAF's Maritime Patrol Group (MPG) in developing new tactics and 'concepts of operation' for the upgraded AP-3C Orion Maritime Patrol Aircraft (see Fig. 1). The Orions are used by the RAAF in peacetime for maritime search, surveillance and operations in and around Australian territorial waters.

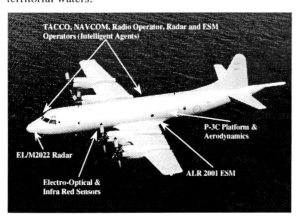

Figure 1. *The various sensors and human operators that are modelled in this work superimposed on a photograph of an AP-3C Orion maritime patrol aircraft.*

The Orions are in an extensive upgrade program that includes new sensors and avionics that significantly improve the capability of the aircraft. Because MPG have no previous operational experience with some of these new sensors, AOD's operational analysts work closely with them to baseline the expected mission performance of the aircraft in typical mission profiles and scenarios, and to develop new, integrated flying and sensor employment policies that allow the aircraft to function at its full mission potential.

The requirement from the RAAF was for AOD to investigate the effectiveness of flying tactics and sensor employment policies as a function of weather conditions, geography and other factors that impact on mission effectiveness. To meet these requirements aspects of the domain are modelled:

- A detailed physical model of the aircraft, it's sensors, including flying characteristics, fuel consumption and sensor performance.

- The tactical decision making processes on board the aircraft representing the human operators, and crew workload (including the type and amount of information available at any given time), the sensor data-fusion process and chain of command.

- The environment, including weather and sea state.

- Several types of ships.

An example mission with some of the factors that need to be considered in tactical decision making is outlined below:

Typical AP-3C Scenario

An AP-3C Maritime Patrol Aircraft is tasked to find and monitor the movements of a target whose location is not precisely known. In this situation the aircraft will fly a predefined search pattern over the region of ocean that the target is suspected of being located within. The aircraft will use its various sensors such as the radar, the ESM (Electronic Support Measures: for detecting the radar transmissions of other ships and aircraft) and infra-red optical sensors to try and locate and classify all possible ships in the region in order to find the target. The radar operator and the ESM operator perform their duties trying to detect and classify various 'contacts' on their sensors. Typically these two operators have hundreds of 'contacts' on their sensors at any given time. The protocol for using the radar and ESM sensors (they have many different modes) depends on a number of factors such as weather conditions, altitude, target type, the presence or otherwise of other ships and aircraft and whether the aircraft wants to advertise its position to the target it is looking for. Contacts that cannot be eliminated at this stage are passed up to the Sensor Employment Manager (SEM) who performs data-fusion duties, such as associating data from the two sensors if they are deemed to be from the same source, and who directs the use of different sensor classification techniques. The SEM passes on information about contacts that may possibly be the target to the Tactical Coordinator (TACCO). The TACCO decides which contacts need further investigation and in which order, either by flying closer or changing aspect for different sensor classification techniques. The TACCO must balance many competing factors, including minimising the amount of unnecessary flying distance in order to complete the mission as soon as possible (in effect solving 'travelling-salesman' type problems) and not concentrating on identifying one suspicious contact at the expense of others.

The TACCO and SEM are always on the alert for 'suspicious' behaviour that may single out one unknown contact as the target. In effect 'suspicious' behaviour means a reaction or response from the contact that is consistent with a particular goal specific only to the target (such as remaining covert). For instance, an ESM contact identified as a powerful but unknown navigation radar on a ship may be lost just prior to the same contact being picked up on the radar sensor and classified as a relatively small ship. This may be due to a target (with a low radar signature) switching off its own surveillance radar upon detecting the radar transmission of the AP-3C aircraft.

A system capable of simulating scenarios of this type was required. Decisions about the nature of the constructive simulation were guided by previous experience with fighter combat, strike missions, and airborne early warning and control.

Several components were candidates for reuse from

previous developments. Additionally the aircrew of MPG expressed interest in having the ability to interact with a simulation as it ran, and using the simulation as a tool for exploring tactics. This was in part driven by exposure to the tools used by analysts in validation sessions for air mission models. This need arose through the lack of a simulation facility within the MPG to account for the upgraded system. Opportunities arose through insights gained from the development of tactical development environments for other projects currently being undertaken at AOD. Thus there was an expressed requirement for two systems:

- a constructive operations research focussed system that could be used to process many thousands of runs of many scenarios to carefully evaluate tactics and procedures; and

- an interactive HIL system capable of providing the flight crews the opportunity to review, replay, interact with and participate in a small number of scenarios.

Simulation Framework

The components common to both systems are detailed here. The details of the intelligent agents and the HIL user interfaces discussed in the section following this.

BattleModel

In light of previous experience with constructive simulation, the 'BattleModel' simulation framework was chosen as the primary modelling environment for this work. BattleModel is a simulation framework developed by the DSTO. The details of the framework and its suitability for agent based modelling of military decision-making have been documented [13]. BattleModel was designed several years ago to conduct constructive simulations in support of operations research. A strong design requirement was that BattleModel support the integration of intelligent agents. (The support of HIL simulation was not considered a priority.)

AP-3C Orion

The aircraft itself is modelled to the extent that it has the same manoeuvring characteristics of the AP-3C including the same fuel consumption, climb and descent rates and cruise performance as a function of weight and altitude. The sensor suites modelled in this scenario include a high fidelity radar model originally built by the Surveillance Systems Division of DSTO [12]. This model includes all the radar tracking and radar imaging modes available on the AP-3C Elta radar. Further systems modelled on the aircraft include the ESM electronics, visual model and Electro-Optical sensor.

Weather and the Environment

The weather and environmental conditions in the area significantly influence mission effectiveness. The presence of certain cloud formation and thunderstorm activity severely constrains where the aircraft can fly and affects sensor performance – particularly visual detection and classification range. Strong winds and rainfall have some effect on the radar tracking capability but it mainly affects visual classification ranges and the performance of the various classification modes on the radar. The sea state and the size and direction of the swell also affects the capability of the radar to identify contacts. Sufficiently detailed models of the weather and the sea and land environment provide the inputs into the sensor performance models and into the tactical decision making of the agents.

Ships

The types of military and commercial ships found in the Australian region are modelled. These provide the surface radar contacts for which the Orion will search. The ships are fitted with suitable radio transmitters and radars providing the ability to model the ability of the Orion to detect the ships by radar, or to detect their electronic emissions by ESM.

Intelligent Agents and System Design

The first system to be implemented was the constructive simulation. Models of the aircraft, ships and related subsystems, the weather and environment were engineered. Intelligent agents were used to model all of the human players in the system. From a design and implementation perspective this was similar to previously developed intelligent agent systems [1]. The acquisition of the knowledge required to construct these systems involves familiarisation with AP-3C tactical procedures documentation, debriefing of flight crew and the regular participation of DSTO staff in operational missions on board the aircraft.

The second system was the interactive or HIL variant. This reused most of the components of the first systems but replaced the agents used to model the AP-3C crew and replaced them with user interfaces and a HIL capability.

System Design

The design of BattleModel and all subsequent AOD simulations have built upon experiences with agent oriented systems. This experience has led to a view of system development that does not distinguish between the human acting in the world or the agent acting in the simulation. In a software engineering sense this tends to merge the business domain model, the use cases and the system architectural design [14]. This approach was taken because explicit knowledge representation with agents closely matches the knowledge acquired from RAAF personnel. Constructing agents that, at a knowledge level, closely resemble the humans that they model reduces the software engineering effort by closing the gap between knowledge engineer and software engineer [7].

Agent Oriented Design

The development described in this paper incorporated the modelling of three related, but different, application systems. Figure 2 illustrates the modelling similarity when each activity is represented with the symbology of the Unified Modeling Language (UML) and use case symbology. The lowest row gives a standard application of UML as we used in the development of Human-in-the-Loop simulations. The top row corresponds to domain or business modelling of real-world defence operations for the documentation of concepts of defence operations. The process of applying and testing techniques and methodologies from the knowledge acquisition community (such as cognitive systems engineering and cognitive work analysis) to software engineering, is ongoing. The middle row is an extension to the UML to include the modelling of intelligent agents as actors within the design scope of the system (see also Heinze, Papasimeon and Goss [14]).

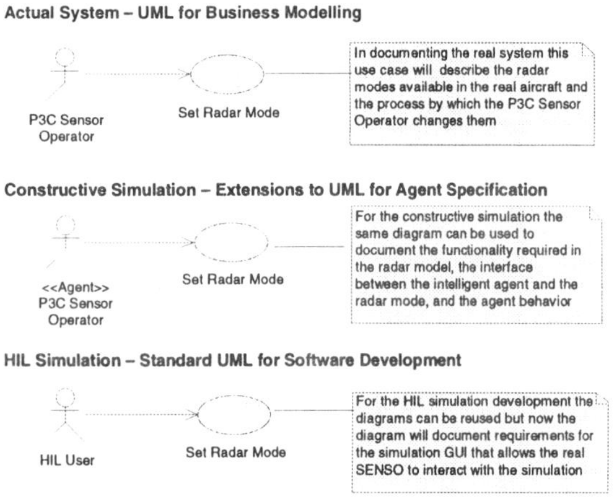

Actual System – UML for Business Modelling

P3C Sensor Operator — Set Radar Mode — In documenting the real system this use case will describe the radar modes available in the real aircraft and the process by which the P3C Sensor Operator changes them

Constructive Simulation – Extensions to UML for Agent Specification

<<Agent>> P3C Sensor Operator — Set Radar Mode — For the constructive simulation the same diagram can be used to document the functionality required in the radar model, the interface between the intelligent agent and the radar mode, and the agent behavior

HIL Simulation – Standard UML for Software Development

HIL User — Set Radar Mode — For the HIL simulation development the diagrams can be reused but now the diagram will document requirements for the simulation GUI that allows the real SENSO to interact with the simulation

Figure 2. An example use case diagram showing the actual system, the agent based simulation and the HIL simulation. This diagram emphasises the reusability of system documentation and design that is available with attention to modelling choices.

The fundamental similarity between the actual system operated by an actual crew, a simulated system operated by simulated crew, or a simulated system operated by an actual crew enabled selection of modelling and documentation techniques that could be reused across this spectrum. Use of comparable tools and languages, together with the ability to re-use modelling and documentation over a number of development projects, reduces development time and allows for efficient focusing of resources.

A fundamental premise of this article is that it is easier to add humans to a system designed for intelligent agents (ie, to an environment designed for constructive simulations), than it is to add intelligent agents to a system designed for humans (ie, to an environment designed for HIL simulation). This premise has been formulated following experiences of attempting to inject intelligent agents (computer generated forces [CGFs]) into simulations that incorporate a human flying an aircraft (stationary cockpit platform with realistic consoles, controls and communications) within a virtual world. Though there are

many engineering challenges in immersing intelligent agents into such HIL simulators, an indicative problem area is the construction of things and spaces that can be understood and acted upon by agents. Much HIL simulation development is focused on constructing an information environment of relevance to the human perceptual and action system. Projected visualisations (rendered scenes provided by graphics engines) are quite realistic with near-real-time changes of the environment through which the pilot navigates, and with identifiable symbology of 'things' in this environment (eg, other planes). Communications are representative of human voices and human languages. In summary, the back-end graphical and voice databases of these simulators do not provide a structured representation for ready access by reasoning agents. There are thus significant issues associated with ensuring that intelligent agents that must interact with terrain and objects in the scenario also have the ability to take in relevant information and act in an appropriate manner accordingly. One manner of achieving this is to program agents to perceive and act in a human-like manner. Another is to construct a parallel system that gives an agent-compatible environment. In either case, considerable development work is required because the application programming interface (API) for humans cannot be used by intelligent agents.

In contrast, relatively lower costs, resources and development time are required to allow a human immersion within a system that has been primarily designed for agent play. At the implementation level, humans and intelligent agents connect to the rest of the simulation through exactly the same API. This allows a "plug-and-play" philosophy with respect to interchanging agents and humans. The visual (a graphical user interface) and other databases of relevance to human perceptual and action requirements are readily constructed for 'plug-in' together with the human. Such a system also shows potential for some members of a AP-3C crew to be real, and some to be intelligent agents. Work is currently being directed to investigate this concept.

Intelligent Agents

The tactical decision making component was modelled using individual intelligent agents (implemented in the dMARS language [5]) for each crew-member that has a significant role in the tactical decision making process. intelligent agents were chosen because of the requirement to model decision-making based on a degree of awareness of the environment or tactical situation the aircraft finds itself in. Maritime surveillance tactics, as with almost all tactical decision making, rely on making an assessment of the current situation based on fusing data from different sensors and also on making assessments of the intent of other entities.

The construction of the models of the AP-3C crew was in and of itself a considerable challenge. The task of modelling military decision-making in a manner that allows for the explicit representation of tactical options to support evaluation and development is made more difficult because of the nature of the specific domain. The AP-3C intelligent agent development differed from previous systems (see Tidhar et. al. [1] for a description of these) because it involved the modelling of an aircraft with several interacting crew. Issues of teamwork, communication, and cooperation are more significant.

The AP-3C crew agents are based upon an existing agent design that characterises decision making as a four stage process of situation awareness, situation assessment, tactics selection, and tactics implementation. The basic design was extended to provide a flexible way of modelling different tactical options so that different tactics could be simply tried and evaluated. The dMARS -Agent formalism is particularly suited to modelling this type of situation awareness based behaviour. Additionally, the plan language which expresses procedural knowledge affords knowledge acquisition and validation advantages [6] (See Fig. 3).

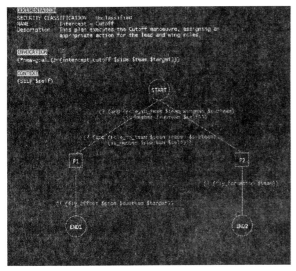

Figure 3. A dMARS plan. Plans are graphical representations of actions to perform and goals to adopt. With attention to design, plans can be understood by subject matter experts. This bridges the gap between the domain expert and the software engineer [11].

In terms of the tactical decision making process, six of the crew members on the aircraft are modelled (using Intelligent Agents technology) to the extent that the type of information, the amount of information and the communications and chain of command on the aircraft are accurately reproduced [4,17].

The advantages of using Intelligent Agents for this are two-fold. Firstly, the roles and area of responsibility of each individual crew member can be incorporated into each agent individually which facilitates modification of tactics and monitoring of workloads[3]. Secondly, the execution of the tactical model can be displayed graphically and understood by a non computer programmer. This allows actual aircrew to validate the existing tactical model and also to determine not just what decisions were made but also why they were

made.

The agents receive information from the simulation, reason about it and make tactical decisions that alter the aircraft states – or send message to other agents. The agents receive only that subset of data that would be available to the real crew member that they model and efforts are to use knowledge representations within the agent that match to those used by air-crew.

HIL Interface

For the interactive variant the agents that modelled the crew of the AP-3C were removed and interfaces that allowed for HIL participation were added. Figure 4 shows the high level plan view that is presented to the AP-3C crew. Added to this are interfaces that allow them to control the AP-3C by changing its course, altitude, or speed, and to control the radar.

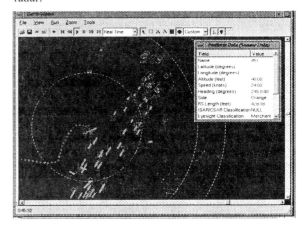

Figure 4. A screen capture of the main plan view of the battle-space. The squares surround ships that are potential Targets of Interest for the Orion. This view does not reflect the radar or situation displays that might be found on a real aircraft but provides the necessary level of information for evaluating tactical options.

The commands available to the crew using the interactive AP-3C are identical to the set available to the agents. This allows for reuse of all of the other components of the system. The interactive simulation is not intended to replicate the AP-3C's on-board displays as it is designed to provide the crew with a display for considering tactics and not practicing procedures[4].

Studies and "CONOPS" Development

In this work the 'BattleModel' is used both for faster than real-time constructive simulations of missions, with the Intelligent-Agents making the tactical decisions, and also interactively or "crew-in-loop", where tactical decisions are made by actual crew members. The constructive mode is

---

[3] This approach enables crewing options to be explored by simulation in AOD work for other platforms.

[4] A suitable lack of fidelity is in fact highly desirable to keep the simulation and exploration of tactical options at the function level and separate from the specific interfaces of the deployed aircraft.

used to gather information on several hundred simulated missions for statistical analysis and robustness tests of various tactics[5].

Figure 5 illustrates the tactical development cycle used by the RAAF and where BattleModel fits into the process. Initial tactics, mission profile and measures of effectiveness are supplied to AOD for initial modelling and analysis at the top of the cycle. Constructive simulations of hundreds of missions are then performed using BattleModel for a given tactic or environmental condition. The outcomes of these missions are then analysed, both statistically and individually to determine the drivers of mission effectiveness and identify worst-case-scenarios. These results are then presented to the RAAF for evaluation and analysis. The initial tactics are then refined further using the HIL mode based on the modelling results and subsequently input into another iteration or round of modelling. Once the tactics are deemed suitably mature they become operational.

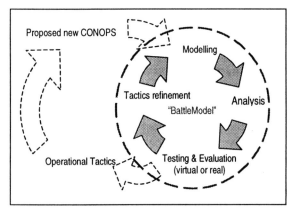

Figure 5. The tactical development cycle used by the RAAF illustrating where BattleModel fits into the process.

In the context of Figure 4 the AP-3C BattleModel is used to provide data for the modelling phase and the interactive simulation is used to test and evaluate the tactics and to refine them for further modelling.

Application Deployment

The deployment of this system within the tactical development program outlined above, currently involves three DSTO analysts and several RAAF officers on a full-time basis. Fifteen DSTO scientists, commercial software engineering contractors and several RAAF 92WG AP-3C aircrew are also involved to various degrees on a casual basis. The initial development and deployment of this system required approximately eleven staff-years of DSTO scientist and analyst effort over a three year period and approximately AU$380K for software engineering support and associated hardware. Approximately three staff-years of effort was devoted to the design, development and testing of the intelligent agent module.

---

[5] Faster than real time studies are essential: varying 8 parameters across three variables within typical scenarios requires three years to complete if constrained to real time performance.

With the system currently deployed at DSTO Melbourne, regular three-day workshops are held on a half-yearly basis with the schedule to be increased considerably with a further deployment at RAAF Edinburgh in 2001. The HIL applications of the system are required to execute in real-time and hence require several hours to complete a single mission. Although complete missions are not always required this typically limits the system to three or four missions per day.

The agent based applications are not limited to execute at real-time and hence are only hardware limited. These applications execute at approximately 5 X real-time on SGI Origin 200, 4 processor, 360MHz R12K machines with 2GB memory. Approximately 40% of this CPU time is directly attributable to the agent's process. Typical support studies for the tactical development program requires statistical evaluation of approximately a dozen agent controlled scenarios with approximately 100 missions simulated in each scenario. Total CPU time (per Origin 200) is of the order of 500 hrs for a given study.

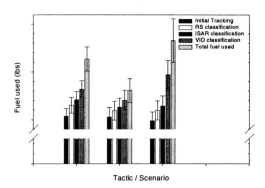

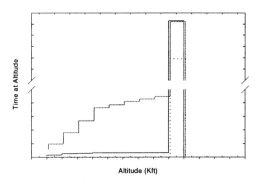

Figure 6. Typical results from "AP-3C BattleModel", the constructive simulation. These types of graphs detail time of flight, fuel used, altitudes maintained and other measures of performance that are used to compare tactics and to determine standard operating procedures.

The operations research and analysis of tactics is carried out by a process of specifying tactics, measures of effectiveness, scenarios, and conducting extensive simulation. Typically existing tactics are base-lined and suggested improvements or variations evaluated relative to the baseline. In this way, measures such as time of flight, fuel used, or time at a specific altitude can be used to evaluate tactics.

By parameterising the tactics search of a range of tactics is possible. Typical scenarios run much faster than real time allowing many more instances to be looked at than is possible with a HIL facility. Results are obtained, analyses conducted and the findings reported to the operational squadrons or the MPG (see Fig. 6). The system deployment results from the tactical development program are national security classified and cannot be discussed further.

Unusual, suspect, promising, or otherwise interesting combinations of tactics and scenarios can be examined in detail in the HIL facility. Furthermore, the HIL facility can be used to reduce the search space by characterising and constraining the types of tactics that need to be considered by exploratory investigation by experienced AP-3C crews. Thus the human in the facility performs a valuable *pre-analysis* role in defining the types of scenarios that might be of interest and the range of tactics that might be explored and then *post-analysis* in validating the usefulness of tactics and the behaviour of the agents.

The interactive or HIL mode is used to test and evaluate new tactics in a realistic environment and to refine existing tactics based on statistical analysis of constructive simulation results. In this mode, the tactical picture is projected onto a large screen showing the current sensor information (radar, ESM contacts, aircraft location and state etc) superimposed on to a geographical map of the region. This allows the crew to focus on developing and evaluating higher-level tactical procedures (see Figure 7) rather than on low-level interactions with individual controls.

Figure 7. Six RAAF AP-3C crew members from Maritime Patrol Group forty six minutes into a simulated mission using the interactive AP-3C simulation with its HIL mode to evaluate some maritime search and classification tactics.

The simulations are housed within a facility at DSTO (see Figure 7). Within this facility AP-3C crews can simulate missions and explore tactical options. The interactive simulation can record, replay, and re-run allowing specific missions to be studied, reviewed, and alternate tactics explored and evaluated. Typically two crews will alternate missions lasting many hours over a period of several days. During this time proposed tactics can be reviewed, checked against a variety of scenarios, and otherwise evaluated.

Maintenance and Future Development

The current implementations of the constructive and the Interactive AP-3C simulations are maintained and run by DSTO directly with strong infrastructure and financial support from the RAAF due to the priority nature of this work. AP-3C crews spend time at AOD on a regular basis – refining their concepts and following the results of operational studies. The interactive nature of the process has tightened organisational links between AOD and the MPG and has fostered strong cooperation.

A proposal to transition the technology from the defence scientist to the operational flight crew is currently being considered. If accepted this would see the technology transferred from DSTO into the squadron where it could be used regularly by operational crews for tactical development. It is important to distinguish this system from training simulators that exercise procedures and skill based reactions of operators. These simulations systems are for the development of tactical procedures and the trialing of concepts and hence do not have the expensive development and maintenance costs associated with the high-end graphics of training simulators.

Future developments in agent languages are expected to feed the AP-3C project. These include technological improvements in agent languages; methodological improvements in the software engineering, development and maintenance of these systems, and knowledge engineering aspects that provide techniques for closing the gap between the conceptualisations of the domain held by the domain experts and the explicit representations within the computational system. Currently DSTO is undertaking research and development in support of the existing agent developments such as that described here and the systems that are expected to enter service throughout the next decade. It has been possible to rapidly develop and commission new operational systems that are at the leading edge of agent development but where the risk is mitigated by maintaining a strong coupling between research and development and the operational systems.

The next two advances being pursued by the development group lie in the areas of modelling teams and command and control and the mainstreaming of the technology. The former should allow for easier modelling of socially complex scenarios whilst the latter will allow agent technologies to be deployed directly into operational air force units.

Concluding Remarks and Lessons Learned

Defence organisations are primarily concerned with developing and maintaining the capability to conduct successful and efficient military operations. These operations rely heavily on the performance of the available defence systems and the expertise of the humans operating them. Modelling and simulation of these operations is a priority for defence organisations in evaluating existing and proposed defence systems. Modelling the human operators is critical to conducting such evaluations.

A combination of constructive and interactive technologies has allowed DSTO to supply advice about the tactical operational performance of the AP-3C Orions to MPG. The HIL system allows the AP-3C crews to gain familiarity with the system and to explore, prototype and workshop tactics that can then be studied in-depth using intelligent agents, as substitutes for the crew, in constructive simulations that cover thousands of scenarios. This method has caused crew to reflect on procedures and come to insights about their own performance not otherwise available to them. This promotes 'double loop' organisational learning [18].

The ability to *plug-and-play* intelligent agents and humans within the same basic system has dramatically improved the ability of DSTO to obtain valuable input from the air force. The system has provided a clear means of validating the behaviour of agents and has value in knowledge acquisition.

Significant savings in dollars and aircraft life can be obtained if tactics can be evaluated and refined with modelling and simulation. By maintaining systems that explicitly model flight crew and their tactical decision making with intelligent agents it has been possible to rapidly develop HIL equivalents. These systems provide valuable advice to the operators of military aircraft and provide mechanisms for validation, exploration, and evaluation of tactical procedures. By including the operational crews in the development of simulation improvements in knowledge acquisition and validation of the intelligent agents have been realised.

Acknowledgments

The authors would like to thank Martin Cross, Tracy Truong, Arvind Chandran from DSTO and Gil Tidhar, Phil Dart, Mario Selvestrel, and Darryl Hunter, from Kesem International who assisted with the development of these systems. Without the strong and active support of the Orion flight crews of No. 92 Wing of Maritime Patrol Group this work would not have been possible. The authors would also like to acknowledge the financial support from MPG the support of David Glenny, the responsible Research Leader.

References

1. G. Tidhar, C. Heinze, S. Goss, G. Murray, D. Appla, and I. Lloyd. Using Intelligent Agents in Military Simulation or "Using Agents Intelligently". In Proceedings of Eleventh Innovative Applications of Artificial Intelligence Conference. Deployed Application Case Study Paper, Orlando, Florida, 1999.

2. G. Tidhar, C. Heinze, and M. Selvestrel. Flying Together: Modelling Air Mission Teams, Applied Intelligence, vol. 8, pp. 195-218, 1998.

3. D. McIlroy, C. Heinze, D. Appla, P. Busetta, G. Tidhar, and A. Rao. Towards Credible Computer Generated Forces. In Proceedings of Second International Simulation Technology and Training Conference, (SimTecT ' 97), Melbourne, Australia, 1997.

4. AP-3C Tactical development workshop, held at AOD, AMRL Fishermens Bend, Melbourne, May, 2000.

5. d' InvernoM. and Kinny, D. and Luck, M. and Wooldrige, M., 'A Formal Specification of dMARS', In proceedings of the Fourth International Workshop on Theories, Architectures and Languages, 1997.

6. Georgeff, M. P. and Lansky, A. L., 'Procedural Knowledge', Proceedings of the IEEE Special Issue on Knowledge Representation, volume 74, pages 1383-1398, 1986.

7. C. Heinze, B. Smith, and M. Cross. Thinking Quickly: Agents for Modeling Air Warfare. In Proceedings of Australian Joint Conference on Artificial Intelligence, AI ' 98 Brisbane, Australia, 1998.

8. McIlroy, D. and Heinze, C., 'Air Combat Tactics Implementation in the Smart Whole AiR Mission Model (SWARMM)', In Proceedings of the SimTecT Conference, 1996, Melbourne, Australia.

9. Jones, R. M. and Laird, J. E. Constraints on the design of a high-level model of cognition. In *Proceedings of Nineteenth Annual Conference of Cognitive Science*, 1997

10. Tambe, M. and Jones, R. M. and Laird, J. E. and Rosenbloom, P. S. and Schwamb, K., 1994. Building Believable Agents for Simulation Environments: Extended Abstract. In *Collected Papers of the SOAR/IFOR Project*, Information Sciences Institute, University of Southern California, pages 78-81. Marina del Ray, CA.

11. Rao, A. S., 'A Unified View of Plans as Recipes', Contemporary Action Theory, ed. Holmstrom-Hintikka, G. and Tuomela, R., Kluwer Academic Publishers}, The Netherlands, 1997.

12. Detection Performance Prediction Model for the EL/M2022 Maritime Surveillance Radar System (U)Antipov, B. Reid, J. Baldwinson; DSTO –TR-0870 (CONFIDENTIAL), 1999

13. C. Heinze, D. Appla, and I. Lloyd. "The BattleModel". In Proceedings of Special Interest Group on Artificial Intelligence (SIGAI' 97), Fishermens Bend, Australia, 1997.

14. Heinze, C., M. Papasimeon, and S. Goss. Specifying Agent Behaviour With Use Cases. In Proceedings of Pacific Rim Workshop on Multi-Agents, PRIMA 2000.

15. Tidhar, G., Murray, G., and Steuart S., 'Computer-Generated Forces and Agent-Oriented Technology', In Proceedings of the Australian Joint Conference on Artificial Intelligence Workshop on AI in Defence, 1995, Canberra, Australia.

16. Wooldrige, M. J. and Jennings, N. R., 'Pitfalls of Agent-Oriented Development', In 'Proceedings of the 2nd International Conference on Autonomous Agents (Agents-98)', Minneapolis, USA, 1998.

17. Transcript of 92 Wing P-3C Tactical Walk-Through. T. W. Josefsson and S. Goss (editors), DSTO-IPIC-0027, 1999.

18. Senge, P., The Fifth Discipline: The Art and Practice of the Learning Organisation. Random House Publishers, Australia, 1998.

The RadarSAT-MAMM Automated Mission Planner

Benjamin D. Smith   **Barbara E. Engelhardt**   **Darren H. Mutz**

Jet Propulsion Laboratory
California Institute of Technology
4800 Oak Grove Drive
Pasadena, CA 91109
{firstname.lastname}@jpl.nasa.gov

Abstract

The RadarSAT Modified Antarctic Mapping Mission (MAMM) ran from September to November 2000. It consisted of over 2400 synthetic aperture radar (SAR) data takes over Antarctica that had to satisfy coverage and other scientific criteria while obeying tight resource and operational constraints. Developing these plans is a time and knowledge intensive effort. It required over a work-year to manually develop a comparable plan for AMM-1, the precursor mission to MAMM. This paper describes the automated mission planning system for MAMM, which dramatically reduced mission-planning costs to just a few workweeks, and enabled rapid generation of "what-if" scenarios for evaluating mission-design trades. This latter capability informed several critical design decisions and was instrumental in accurately costing the mission.

Introduction

The Modified Antarctic Mapping Mission (MAMM) executed from September through November of 2000 onboard RadarSAT, a Canadian Space Agency (CSA) satellite. This joint NASA/CSA mission is a modified version of the First RadarSAT Antarctic Mapping Mission (AMM-1) executed in 1997 (Jezek *et al*, 1998). The objective of AMM-1 was to acquire complete coverage of the Antarctic continent, whereas the objective of MAMM is to acquire repeat-pass interferometry to measure ice surface velocity of the outer regions of the continent, north of latitude –80 degrees. The mission objective is to perform synthetic aperture radar (SAR) mapping of the Antarctic over three consecutive 24-day repeat cycles.

Planning SAR mapping missions is a time- and knowledge-intensive process. RadarSAT has a SAR instrument that can be commanded to acquire data in any one of several rectangular swaths parallel to its ground track. The spacecraft can also downlink acquired data to ground receiving stations when its ground track passes over them. The planning problem is to select a set of swaths and downlinks such that the swaths cover the desired region of Antarctica and satisfy science requirements, and the combined acquisition and downlink schedule meets the operational and resource constraints imposed by the RadarSAT Mission Management Office (MMO). The driving operational constraints are the limited on-board tape recorder (OBR) capacity and downlink opportunities,

which together constrain the amount of swath data that can be acquired and saved on the OBR between downlinks.

The AMM-1 mission demonstrated the need for an automated planning capability. The schedule for AMM-1 consisted of 850 acquisitions (swaths) over 18 days, and took over a work-year to develop manually. Despite repeated checking, this plan violated operations constraints that were not detected until the final MMO review. This inability to detect all the operations and resource constraint violations during the planning process required expensive and disruptive last-minute revisions.

This experience led to the development and use of an automated mission planning system for MAMM. The system takes a set of swaths selected by the human mission planner, automatically generates a downlink schedule, then expands the swaths and downlinks into a more detailed plan that it checks for operations constraint violations. With this system MAMM developed its 24-day mission plan containing 818 swaths in a matter of weeks, as compared to the work-year required to develop a comparable mission plan for AMM-1.

In addition to reducing the plan development effort, the MAMM planner also provides resource tracking and other plan details that enable accurate costing and feasibility estimates. The MAMM planner also enables "what-if" studies that were not possible under AMM-1. The planner quickly generated detailed variations of the baseline plan for different ground station availability assumptions. These study plans were instrumental in selecting ground stations and making other decisions about mission alternatives.

The rest of this paper describes the automated planning system that was constructed for MAMM based on the ASPEN planning environment (Chien *et al.* 2000).

Mission Planning Problem

The objective of MAMM is to acquire repeat-pass SAR interferometry of Antarctica north of –80 degrees latitude to measure ice surface velocity of the outer regions of the continent.

For mission planning purposes, RadarSAT has two commands: (1) acquire SAR data in one of several rectangular swaths parallel to the spacecraft ground track and either save it to the onboard recorder or downlink it in real time as it is being acquired; and (2) playback and

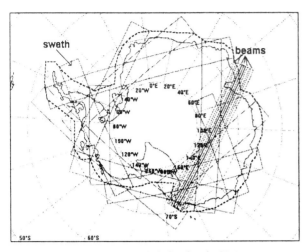

Figure 1: Swath Selection in SPA.

Data can only be downlinked when a ground station is in view
All recorded data must be downlinked
OBR playback may only occur during downlink
SAR acquisitions cannot overlap
Cannot transmit RTM data when recorder is in record, spin-up, or spin-down modes
Data takes shall be no shorter than 1.0m
Adjacent data takes shall be at least 5.25s apart when beams are changed
Data takes shall be at least 11s apart when beams are not changed.
OBR takes 10s to spin up, consumes 10s of tape
OBR takes 5.5s to spin down, consumes 5.5s tape
OBR transitions to idle between takes iff OBR data takes are > 30s apart, else continues recording.
There will be <= 6 OBR transactions per orbit
SAR shall be on at most 32.0 minutes per orbit

Table 1: Selected Operations Constraints

downlink the SAR data on the recorder. The mission-planning problem is to select a subset of the possible swaths and downlink opportunities (real-time and playback) such that the resulting schedule satisfies the scientific requirements and the operating constraints.

A data acquisition command specifies the start time, duration, downlink mode, and beam. The downlink mode determines whether the data is saved to the onboard recorder (OBR) or downlinked in real-time (RTM). The beam controls the incidence angle of the SAR instrument and determines which of several swaths parallel to the spacecraft ground track is acquired. The incidence angles of adjacent beams are separated by a few degrees and acquire data in rectangular swaths that partially overlap those of adjacent beams. Several swaths typically cover any given ground region, although those swaths are often in different orbits and/or different beams.

The playback command plays back and downlinks all the recorded data on the tape, then erases the tape.

Downlink (playback or real-time) may only occur when the spacecraft ground track crosses within range of a ground receiving station (the station is *in-view*). The spacecraft may downlink playback data while also downlinking data being acquired in real-time. The station in-view periods are called *masks* and are specified in a mask file provided by the RadarSAT Mission Management Office (MMO).

In addition to the above, the mission plan must obey operations constraints imposed by the RadarSAT Mission Management Office (MMO), some of which are shown in Table 1. These primarily consist of resource constraints, set-up times between data acquisitions, tape recorder and SAR instrument operating constraints, and downlink policy rules. The resources are onboard recorder capacity, tape transactions (number of times the tape has been started and stopped), and SAR instrument on-time per orbit. The relevant device states referenced by the operations constraints are the tape mode (idle, spinning up, recording,

spinning-down, playback) and the SAR beam (one of sixteen).

The Planning Process

The mission planning process is an iterative one. The mission planner develops several plan versions before arriving at the final mission plan. Each version is reviewed against scientific, cost, and risk criteria. This analysis informs the approach for developing the next iteration, sometimes drastically. MAMM generated four revisions before arriving at the fifth and final mission plan. The process for generating an individual plan consists of the following four steps. The resulting plan is a time-ordered list of data acquisition requests and downlink session requests.

1. **Select SAR swaths** that cover the desired target regions in Antarctica and satisfy other scientific requirements. The swaths are selected from all the swaths that intersect the target region during one 24-day repeat cycle. This step is partially automated by a tool developed by the Canadian Space Agency called SPA [7] that identifies the available swaths for each beam as shown in Figure 1 by propagating the spacecraft orbit. The user selects the desired (sub-)swaths, and SPA generates a swath request file. SPA does not check operations constraints or ensure that the swaths can be downlinked, so there is no guarantee that the selected swaths comprise a valid mission plan.

2. **Create a downlink schedule.** The downlink schedule specifies which station masks (downlink opportunities) will be used to downlink the data acquisitions, and specifies for each acquisition (swath) whether it will be downlinked in real-time or stored to the data recorder. The schedule must obey resource and operations constraints. In particular, real-time acquisitions must

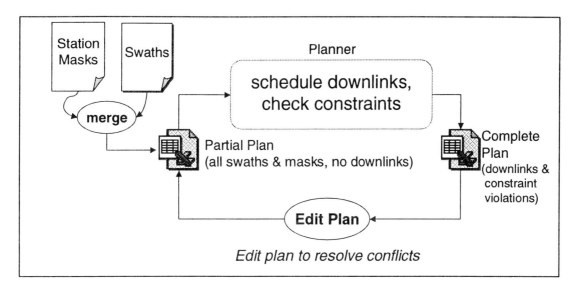

Figure 2: System Data Flow Architecture

occur during a downlink session, and playback sessions must be scheduled during masks that are long enough to downlink all the data on the onboard recorder. The schedule should also try to maximize objective criteria—certain stations are more reliable or have lower costs than others; and resource costs make real-time takes preferable to recorded ones.

3. **Compute resource usage and check for constraint violations.** Determine whether the composite acquisition and downlink plan violates any operations constraints. Checking resource-related constraints requires computing usage profiles for each resource (OBR storage, SAR on-time).

4. **Address violations.** If the schedule violates operations constraints, cannot downlink all of the acquisitions, or is of insufficient quality return to Step 1 and modify the selected swaths to correct the problems. Modifications include changing the swath start-time, swath duration, and/or beam; or selecting an alternate swath that covers the same target area.

Part of what makes the mission-planning problem difficult is the interaction between swath selection (Step 1) and downlink scheduling (Step 2). The ground stations are rarely in view when the satellite is over the desired regions of Antarctica, which means many of the acquisitions have to be recorded and downlinked later. Since playing back data for downlink erases the tape and the in-view periods are shorter than the tape capacity, the swaths selected for a given orbit must fit within the downlink opportunities near that orbit. If the scientifically desired swaths do not fit, an alternate swath must be selected. The alternate may be in a different orbit, which could force swath reselection for that orbit as well.

Replanning During Operations

Planned SAR acquisitions can be lost during operations due to spacecraft and ground station anomalies. Lost acquisitions are rescheduled using the same mission planning process on a smaller scale: select alternate swaths that covers the missed target regions (Step 1), revise the downlink schedule to accommodate them (Step 2), and make sure the resulting schedule is consistent with the operations constraints (Step 3). If conflicts are found, return to Step 1 and select different swaths. In order to minimize schedule disruption, the selected swaths must not overlap acquisitions already in the schedule, and existing acquisitions cannot be moved to make space for the new ones.

Rescheduling several swaths, as can happen with a major anomaly, is a time- and knowledge-intensive task. In addition, mission time-pressures demand that new plans be generated very quickly in order to exploit the next acquisition opportunity, usually within 24 to 36 hours. AMM-1 required a staff of four working from pre-generated contingency plan segments in order to generate plans within these time pressures.

Application Description

The mission planning application automates Steps 2 and 3. The other steps were intentionally not automated since they involve swath selection, which requires human scientific judgment.

The human mission-planner selects a set of swaths (Step 1) using a swath selection and coverage analysis tool called SPA, which CSA developed for RadarSAT missions. The swath input specifies the time, duration, and beam of each swath. These are passed to the planning system along with downlink priority policy and a mask file, provided by the RadarSAT Mission Management Office (MMO), that specifies the *in-view* periods for each ground station.

The mask and swath files are combined into a single file and passed to the ASPEN planning system, which is described in more detail below. The planner generates a downlink schedule for the swaths (Step 2), and then expands the resulting swath-and-downlink schedule into a more detailed plan that includes support activities such as tape on/off transitions and beam switches, and tracks resource usage. This provides the additional details referenced in the operations constraints. ASPEN checks the plan for constraint violations (Step 3), and finally converts it from ASPEN format to an excel spreadsheet format preferred by the mission planners.

The spreadsheet provides a time-ordered list of acquisition, playback, and downlink commands; identifies the swaths that violate constraints or cannot be downlinked; and provides resource profiles. It also summarizes plan metrics such as resource usage totals, ground station connect time (for costing), and the number of real-time and recorded acquisitions.

Based on the report files, the human mission planner modifies the selected swaths as needed to resolve the conflicts or improve schedule quality (Step 4).

Figure 2 summarizes this flow of information (Step 1- 4) graphically. This check-and-edit cycle is repeated until a conflict-free plan is generated. This rapid feedback allows the user to generate a conflict-free plan much more quickly than is possible by hand. Maintaining the human planner in the loop enables the use of human scientific judgment in selecting swaths.

The MAMM planning system is implemented in C++ and runs on a SUN Ultra/60 workstation. The conversion utilities (from SPA to ASPEN, and from ASPEN to Excel) were written in Perl.

The ASPEN planner

The core of the MAMM planner is ASPEN (Chien *et al.* 2000), an automated planning and scheduling system developed at the Jet Propulsion Laboratory. The ASPEN planning environment consists of a domain modeling language, an incremental constraint tracking facility (the plan database), interfaces for planning search algorithms, and a library of planning algorithms that exploit the plan database capabilities via those interfaces. The plan database records a partial plan and the constraints that are satisfied and violated by that plan. The plan database supports several plan-modification operators, an operation for incrementally propagating the constraints following modifications, and interfaces for accessing the constraint and plan element information in the database. Search algorithms use these capabilities to determine how to modify the current plan. For a given application one can select one of the general-purpose algorithms in the library or develop a new application-specific algorithm.

The MAMM planner encodes the operations constraints in the ASPEN domain modeling language. It uses a domain-specific planning algorithm to schedule the downlink activities and expand the swath and downlink requests into a more detailed schedule. The planning algorithm then calls the constraint update operation to determine which domain constraints are violated. This structure is shown in Figure 3.

When ASPEN terminates it saves the plan and constraint violation information to a file, which is then converted into an Excel spreadsheet format preferred by the mission planners. This is a time-ordered list of swath, mask, and downlink activities, with one row for each activity. There is one column for each resource. The value of that column for each activity (row) is the value of that resource at the end

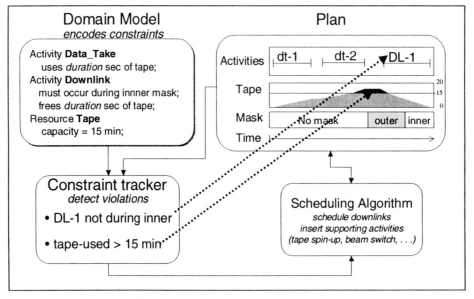

Figure 3: ASPEN planning components

of that activity. The last column holds a list of the operations constraint violations in which that activity is involved. A table maps ASPEN conflicts to corresponding high-level operations constraints, and it is these high-level constraints that are reported in the spreadsheet.

Knowledge Representation

The RadarSAT operations constraints are expressed in the ASPEN domain modeling language. The elements in this language are activities, states, resources, and constraints. An activity is an action the spacecraft can perform, such as a data take or beam switch. Activities have a start time and duration and may overlap each other. A resource represents a physical or logical resource of the spacecraft, such as the onboard recorder tape or instrument on-time. A state represents a physical or logical state of the spacecraft, such as the current SAR beam or whether a given ground station is *in-view* or *not-in-view*. Each state and resource is represented as a *timeline* that shows how it evolves over time.

The activities, states, and resources are related by *constraints*. These can be temporal constraints among activities (a tape spin-down must immediately follow a data take), resource constraints (a data take uses d seconds of OBR tape, where d is the duration of the data take), and state constraints (the SAR instrument must be ON during a data take). The MAMM operations constraints were encoded in terms of these constraints.

Figure 4 shows how some of the MAMM domain knowledge was encoded in ASPEN. Figure 5 shows a sample plan fragment with each of these elements. The full ASPEN domain model has 6 resource timelines, 7 state timelines, and 27 activity types as summarized in Table 2.

```
Activity OBR_Data_Take {
    reservations =
      obr_storage use duration,
      obr_state must_be "record";
};
Activity spin_up {
  Duration = 1300;
  Reservations =
        obr_storage use duration, // consumes tape
        obr_state change_to "record";
};
Resource obr_storage {
  Type = depletable;
  Capacity = 91600; // 15.5 minutes = 91600 seconds
};
State obr_state {
    States = ("idle", "playback", "record");
    Default_state = "idle";
    Transitions = ("idle"-> "playback", "idle"->"record"
                    "playback"->"idle", "record"->"idle");
};
```

Figure 4: ASPEN Domain Modeling Example.

Activity (27)	Acquire_data
	Acquire_OBR_data
	Acquire_RTM_data
	Downlink
	Downlink_RTM
	Downlink_OBR
	State changers (x 11)
	Mask timeline setter (x 10)
State (7)	Mask (x 5 stations)
	Beam
	OBR mode
Atomic Resources (2)	SAR-in-use
	OBR-in-use
Depletable resources (4)	SAR-on-time
	OBR storage
	Tape transactions
	Data_not_downlinked

Table 2: MAMM Domain Model Summary

Scheduling Algorithm

The MAMM planner uses a domain-specific planning algorithm to control the plan database. The initial plan consists of a set of swath request activities and station mask activities. The algorithm first adds the mask activities to the database. The state constraints on these activities set the state timelines for each ground station. The planner then adds the swaths to the database and decides how to downlink them.

The downlink-scheduling problem is a constrained assignment problem. Each swath must be assigned exactly one 'mode' (real-time or recorded) and exactly one downlink opportunity. That assignment must satisfy the domain constraints—specifically, recorded swaths must not exceed the tape capacity between downlinks and the downlink opportunity must be longer than the amount of recorded data; real-time swaths must be taken while a real-

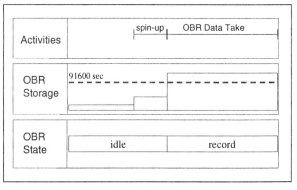

Figure 5: Plan Fragment using activities, states, and resources defined in Figure 2. Each box on the timeline is a *timeline unit* and represents the value of that state or resource over that time period.

time capable station is in-view.

The system employs a greedy algorithm to solve the downlink-scheduling problem. In each iteration it makes the best feasible assignment. If no assignment is possible, it backtracks. Since there may be no way to downlink all the selected swaths, it limits its backtracking to a two-orbit window. If no feasible solution can be found in that window, it selects a feasible schedule that downlinks the most data, and reports the lost data as a constraint violation.

Once the algorithm has assigned to each swath a downlink mode and downlink opportunity, it reflects these assignments in the plan database. It grounds the 'downlink mode' parameter of each swath to OBR or RTM accordingly, and creates a downlink activity for each mask that was assigned to one of the swaths.

At this point the plan consists solely of swath, mask, and downlink activities. The planning algorithm then performs a limited expansion and grounding of the plan. In each iteration it selects a value for an ungrounded activity parameter, or adds an activity to satisfy an open temporal constraint. For example, if activity A is in the plan and has an open constraint that it must be before activity B, the planner will add an activity instance of type B just after activity A. At the end of this phase, the plan contains all of the activities needed to acquire and downlink the requested swaths. The resource and state timelines have also been computed based on the state and resource constraints made by the activities in the plan.

Finally, the algorithm invokes ASPEN's constraint tracker to identify *conflicts*: violations of constraints in the domain model. These consist of temporal violations (e.g., data take activities are too close together), resource violations (e.g., exceeded tape capacity), and state violations. The algorithm does *not* attempt to fix the constraints, even though that is within ASPEN's capabilities. The conflict resolution is intentionally left to the human mission planner since it involves swath-selection changes that require human scientific judgment.

Planner Use and Benefits

A development version of MAMM was released to the MAMM mission planners in February of 2000 for initial planning and evaluation, and was officially deployed in April. The MAMM mission planners used the system from March through July to develop the MAMM mission plan as well as several draft plans and trade-study plans.

The plan development effort for MAMM using the automated system was about one sixth of the manual planning effort for AMM-1. The two missions were comparable: MAMM contained 818 acquisitions over 24 days (repeated three times), and AMM-1 contained 850 acquisitions over 18 days. The MMO review of the final MAMM plan detected no constraint violations, and the plan executed flawlessly on RadarSAT from September to December of 2000. In addition to reducing plan development costs, the system's ability to provide detailed

Version	Date	Iterations	Workweeks
1	3/6	3	2
2	4/12	2	2
3	4/27	2	2
4	6/8	4	3
Final	6/19	1	1
TOTAL		12	10

Table 3: MAMM plan development effort.

resource usage information and to rapidly generate downlink schedules for different station availabilities and station priority policies were instrumental in evaluating mission alternatives, costing the mission, and negotiating resource quotas.

Based on the overwhelming success of this planning system, efforts are now underway to make it available for evaluation at the Alaska SAR Facility (ASF), whose charter includes developing RadarSAT data acquisition plans to satisfy the observation requests of a large scientific community.

Mission Plan Development

The MAMM mission designers used the automated planner to develop a series of four draft plans and the final mission plan. Each draft was reviewed against scientific, cost, and risk criteria, and the results determined the swath selection strategy for the next version. The average development time for each plan was about two workweeks. Roughly 60% of that time was spent in the initial swath selection, 10% in using the automated planner (setting up runs, learning how to operate it, and getting the results), and 30% revising the swaths to eliminate constraint violations detected by the planner. Constraint violations were removed in between one and four check-and-edit iterations. Table 3 summarizes the development times for each of the plan revisions.

The total development time for all MAMM plans was 10 workweeks. By comparison, mission planning for AMM-1 required over a work-year, with individual plans taking 3-4 months (12-16 workweeks) to develop. Overall the automated planning system reduced planning effort from over a work-year to 10 workweeks, or a factor of six.

If one includes the development time for the automated system, the automated approach is still 25% less effort than the manual one. The total planning and development effort for MAMM was about 9 work-months (6.75 to develop the planner, and 2.5 to develop the plans) as compared to over 12 work-months for AMM-1. If the system is adopted by ASF those development costs will be amortized over future missions, yielding even greater cost-savings.

Costing and Trade Studies

In addition to reducing development costs, the automated system provided valuable information for the plan evaluation phases. For each plan it provided detailed resource and summary information that informed the cost and risk assessments. It also automatically generated "what-if" variations of draft plans for evaluating mission alternatives. The mission designers and project managers perceived both of these capabilities as highly beneficial, and the information was directly used to estimate ground station costs and negotiate RadarSAT resource quotas.

Some of the specific questions it was used to answer during the mission design process are as follows.

1. Determine the resource requirements for purposes of costing the mission and negotiating spacecraft resource allocations with the CSA.

This question was addressed with summary statistics that the system generates for each plan. These include total on-board recorder usage, SAR on-time, and total downlink data time broken down by station. This first two were invaluable in negotiating on-board resource allocations. The downlink durations by station were used to estimate ground station costs, forecast usage levels, and to schedule downlink sessions. The detail and early availability of these schedules greatly simplified this process over AMM-1.

2. How do different downlink scheduling policies impact the mission plan?

This question was addressed by performing what-if simulations using the ASPEN system. Since downlink station priorities were one of the parameters of the downlink generation algorithm, the plan was expanded and downlink schedules generated using four different possible priority systems. ASPEN supplied the data to reach a decision on the priorities and significantly impact the mission negotiations during the early stages.

3. What is the impact of not using certain ground stations?

This question was addressed using what-if scenarios in which ASPEN was not allowed to downlink data to certain stations. This was accomplished by simply excluding the masks for those stations from the input file—the station was never in-view, and therefore never available for downlink. This enabled a closer examination of the impact of removing a ground station on the other stations and on the science collection in general. Using this information, the mission identified an unnecessary ground station early in the mission planning phase, and saved a significant amount of funding that would otherwise have been needed to support that station during operations.

Anomaly Replanning During Mission Operations

Spacecraft or ground station anomalies during operations can cause scheduled data acquisitions to be lost. These acquisitions can be rescheduled.

The operations re-planning staff must submit the rescheduled swaths at least 36 hours before they are executed, to provide the MMO enough time to process and uplink the requests. In most cases this means the replanning staff has to submit a new acquisition plan within 48 to 72 hours of the anomaly. To manually turn around plans within these time constraints on AMM-1 required a team of four people working from pre-generated contingency plan segments. The missed observations were placed into gaps in the original plan to minimize coverage holes. More extensive changes, such as altering the remaining (unexecuted) planned swaths were avoided to minimize the planning effort and the chance of introducing errors into the plan. Unfortunately, it was sometimes impossible to find a way to reschedule all the missed observations within that time frame using these manual procedures. These observations were simply dropped from the schedule.

For MAMM the automated planner was available during operations for identifying operations conflicts in manually generated replan schedules. The system took as input the replanned schedule, and provided a list of conflicts within minutes. This capability enabled the replanning team to quickly identify and correct any constraint violations before submitting it to the MMO for a final (and more costly) check.

Use of the system for anomaly re-planning was part of the operations procedures, was available during operations, and successfully replanned simulated anomalies during the operations rehearsals. However, it was never needed during the mission. Few anomalies occurred in the first cycle, and they only impacted acquisitions that could be manually rescheduled trivially and confidently.

Nevertheless, this capability is expected to be useful on future missions. If it had been available on AMM-1, which had 10 spacecraft anomalies and lost a primary ground receiving station early in the mission, the AMM-1 project manager estimated that the re-planning staff could have been reduced from four to one.

Development and Deployment

The automated planning system was developed using the ASPEN planning environment. ASPEN provided the domain modeling language and constraint checking facilities. The development process was fairly typical: acquire the specifications and domain knowledge (operations constraints), encode the knowledge, develop the infrastructure and then test it. The work force breakdown is shown in Table 4.

The development process was repeated over two iterations. The first iteration (R1) produced an operational system that had the most critical capabilities and operational constraints. This was used to develop a draft plan for use in making costing and feasibility estimates. That development process also provided feedback on ease of operability, needed and unnecessary capabilities, and uncovered some minor refinements to the operations constraints. Development of R2, the second and final version, was informed by the feedback from R1. The total work effort was just under 7 work months.

TASK	R1	R2	Total
Knowledge Acquisition	1.0	0.5	1.5
Knowledge Engineering	6.0	2.0	8
Scheduling & Downlink Algorithm	2.0	1.0	3
Infrastructure	6.0	2.0	8
Testing	1.0	6.0	6
TOTAL	16.0	11.5	27.5

Table 4: Application development effort in workweeks.

Difficulties

The primary difficulty was in the size of the plans. A typical 24-day MAMM input plan has over 800 swaths and 1,000 downlink masks, and expands into a plan with over 8,000 activities and 16,000 timeline units. ASPEN typically generates plans about a tenth this size in a few minutes, but these large plans require about an hour to generate. The performance degradation was a result of constraint propagation costs and memory swapping.

To reduce propagation costs we redesigned the scheduling algorithm to eliminate unnecessary "downstream" propagation. When an activity is added to the schedule and imposes a resource reservation, it forces all of the resource timeline units downstream of the activity to be recomputed. Placing activities in increasing time order, where possible, minimizes the number of downstream activities. The algorithm uses heuristics ensure the most computation-efficient ordering.

We further improved performance by re-engineering the domain model to minimize the size of the expanded plan. This reduced the expanded plan for an 818-swath input from about 12,000 activities and 20,000 timeline units to 8,000 activities and 16,000 timeline units, or about 25%. This reduced the plan size below the memory limit where swapping drove the performance to unacceptable levels.

Without these improvements a typical 800-swath plan required over 10 hours to run. With the modifications, the expanded plan was about 25% smaller and only required about an hour to process.

Lessons. Very large planning problems encounter performance issues that do not arise for more moderate problem sizes. The impact of performance tuning on development and maintenance need to be considered in projecting costs and selecting planning systems.

Maintenance

Maintenance has not yet been an issue. The RadarSAT operations constraints have been static for several years and are expected to remain so. Should maintenance be needed, the update mechanism is to modify the domain model and, if necessary, update the expansion-ordering heuristics. End-users should be able to make simple modifications to the APEN model themselves. The language is designed for non-AI experts, and such personnel have successfully developed detailed ASPEN models (Willis, Rabideau, and Wilklow 1999; Sherwood *et al.* 1998). However, major changes would probably require additional performance tuning, which would require an experienced developer.

Conclusions

Mission planning is a time- and knowledge-intensive task. It required over a work-year to manually develop the mission plan for AMM-1. We developed an automated planning system that reduced the mission planning time for MAMM, the follow-on mission to AMM-1, to just two work-months. In addition to reducing mission planning effort it also enabled rapid generation of "what-if" plans for evaluating mission alternatives, and provided resource usage information that was used for costing the mission and negotiating spacecraft resource allocations.

These analyses contributed to the quality and success of the mission, and the mission planners considered this capability an invaluable tool. Automated planning was overwhelmingly successful for MAMM, and we would expect similar successes for future RadarSAT missions.

Acknowledgements

This paper describes work performed at the Jet Propulsion Laboratory, California Institute of Technology, under contract from the National Aeronautics and Space Administration. The authors also wish to thank John Crawford, the MAMM project manager, for championing this technology; Richard Austin, the mission planner, for using the system and providing design feedback; the Canadian Space Agency for providing the RadarSAT operations constraints, and Dr. Kim Partington for his support and sponsorship during his tenure as manager of NASA's Polar Science Program.

References

Chien, S.; Rabideau, G.; Knight, R.; Sherwood, R.; Engelhardt, B.; Mutz, D.; Estlin, T.; Smith, B.; Fisher, F.; Barrett, T.; Stebbins, G.; and Tran, D. 2000. ASPEN—Automating Space Mission Operations using Automated Planning and Scheduling. In *SpaceOps 2000*. Toulouse, France.

Jezek, K.C., H.G. Sohn, and K.F. Noltimeir. 1998. The RadarSAT Antarctic Mapping Project. In *Proceedings of IGARSS '98*. p. 2462-2464.

Sherwood, R.; Govindjee, A.; Yan, D.; Rabideau, G.; Chien, S.; and Fukunaga, A. 1998. Using ASPEN to Automate EO-1 Activity Planning. In *Proceedings of the IEEE Aerospace Conference*. Aspen, CO. IEEE Press.

Willis, J.; Rabideau, G.; and Wilklow, C. 1999. The Citizen Explorer Scheduling System. In *Proceedings of the IEEE Aerospace Conference*. Aspen, CO. IEEE Press.

Emerging Applications

Scaling Up Context-Sensitive Text Correction

Andrew J. Carlson　　　　　**Jeffrey Rosen**　　　　　**Dan Roth**

Department of Computer Science
University of Illinois at Urbana-Champaign
Urbana, IL 61801
[ajcarlso, jrosen, danr@uiuc.edu]

Abstract

The main challenge in an effort to build a realistic system with context-sensitive inference capabilities, beyond accuracy, is scalability. This paper studies this problem in the context of a learning-based approach to context sensitive text correction – the task of fixing spelling errors that result in valid words, such as substituting *to* for *too*, *casual* for *causal*, and so on. Research papers on this problem have developed algorithms that can achieve fairly high accuracy, in many cases over 90%. However, this level of performance is not sufficient for a large coverage practical system since it implies a low sentence level performance.

We examine and offer solutions to several issues relating to scaling up a context sensitive text correction system. In particular, we suggest methods to reduce the memory requirements while maintaining a high level of performance and show that this can still allow the system to adapt to new domains. Most important, we show how to significantly increase the coverage of the system to realistic levels, while providing a very high level of performance, at the 99% level.

Introduction

Virtually all current day software systems that perform text processing provide some spell checking facility. Word processors, email and news readers, and even operating systems provide tools to verify that the text contains valid words. When an invalid word is discovered some form of distance measure is used to select candidate correct words from a dictionary. The shortcoming of all these spell checkers is that they fail to detect errors that result in a valid word, as in *I'd like a peace of cake*, where *peace* was typed when *piece* was intended, or *I took a walk it the park*, where *it* was typed instead of *in*, etc.

An earlier study (Kukich 1992) showed that errors that result in valid words account for anywhere from 25% to over 50% of observed spelling errors. Today, as our reliance on text processing tools increases while fewer resources are spent on editing published text - the Internet revolution has resulted in additional pressure to shorten the time from writing to publishing - this could be a significant undercount.

However, identifying and correcting mistakes that result in valid words requires awareness of the *context* in which

different words, such as *piece* and *peace*, tend to occur. The problem of characterizing the linguistic context in which even a single word tends to occur is a difficult problem and a large scale one; it might depend on particular words near the target word, the pattern of parts of speech around the target word and so on. A "knowledge engineering" approach to this problem, therefore, is unlikely to succeed. Indeed, in recent years, machine learning techniques have begun to be applied to this problem and several of them were shown to do quite well (Golding & Roth 1996; Golding & Roth 1999; Mangu & Brill 1997).

Existing work along these lines has focused on developing learning methods that are appropriate for this problem and thus concentrated on a relatively small number of words. Restricting the problem this way (to 20–40 words, depending on the study) also allowed researchers to keep the experiments manageable, given the large scale of the problem.

However, in order to be useful as a practical tool, systems addressing this problem need to be able to offer wide word coverage with reasonable performance and resource requirements. This work offers solutions to several issues relating to the *scaling up* of these systems.

First, it is clear that almost every word in English could be mistaken for some other valid word, and therefore a practical system needs to have a coverage of thousands of words. Our first step in the current work is therefore to increase the coverage of our system to roughly five-hundred words. The approach taken by most of the existing work has been to form *confusion sets* and treat the problem as a disambiguation task over the members of a confusion set. Confusion sets consist of words that are likely to be misused in place of one another. In this paper we continue with this approach. We seek to handle a number of confusion sets closer to the scale of the real problem, but without having to fine-tune parameters for each set.

Second, given that the number of features that might be required to characterize the context of a word is very large, scaling up to realistic coverage might introduce resource problems - memory and evaluation time. We suggest a way to avoid that and show its minimal effect on the performance. A related issue involved in a practical approach to context sensitive text correction is that different genres of text might have different characteristics and might use different vocabulary; this could require different characterization of the context. We show that our approach can adapt to new texts quickly and reliably.

Finally, the most important issue is performance. Research papers on context sensitive text correction have shown different algorithms that can achieve fairly high accuracy, in many cases over 90%. However, this level of performance is not sufficient for a large coverage practical system. Performing at the 90% level in a wide coverage system means that the system will make, on average, one mistake per sentence, and this would be unacceptable for most users. We suggest a way to significantly increase the performance of a wide coverage system by automatically reducing the willingness of the system to alert the user for mistakes in which it is less confident. This solution relies on the ability of the algorithm to reliably assess its confidence in the prediction, and, as we show, our approach can do that, yielding an average performance of over 99% over a large corpus, with prediction willingness of 85%.

Our algorithmic approach builds on one of the most successful approaches studied for this problem (Golding & Roth 1999), based on the SNoW learning architecture (Carlson *et al.* 1999; Roth 1998). We briefly describe how SNoW is used here, discuss some methodological issues and then interleave the scaling up discussion with the experiments performed to exhibit the performance of the system.

Context-Sensitive Text Correction

Given a body of text, possibly like this paper, we would like to scan it and locate errors resulting from the improper usage of *real words*. This task has typically been referred to as *context-sensitive spelling correction* in earlier research, but here we refer to it as text correction rather than spelling since the techniques are not limited to simple single word substitutions. Context-Sensitive Text Correction is the task of fixing spelling errors that happen to result in valid words, such as substituting *to* for *too*, *casual* for *causal* or simple word usage errors like in *"There could be any amount of reasons he didn't show up."*, where *amount* was used instead of *number*. Our definition of the task includes correcting not only "classic" types of spelling mistakes, such as homophone errors, (e.g., *peace* and *piece*) and typographic errors, as in *"I'll be ready in five minuets."* (where *minuets* was typed when *minutes* was intended), or when *from* is replaced by *form*. We can also fix mistakes that are more commonly regarded as grammatical errors (e.g., "among" and "between"), incorrect forms of pronouns, as in *"I had a great time with his."*, where *his* was typed instead of *him* or errors that cross word boundaries (e.g., *maybe* and *may be*).

Problem Formulation

We cast context-sensitive text correction as a disambiguation task (Roth 1998). Given an input sentence and a distinguished word sequence (usually of size 1) - which we call the *target* - within the sentence, we wish to predict whether the target is correct, or whether it should be replaced by some other word sequence. The ambiguity among words (or word sequences) is modeled by *confusion sets*. A confusion set $C = \{W_1, \ldots, W_n\}$ means that each word

W_i in the set is ambiguous with each other word. Thus if $C = \{hear, here\}$, then when we see an occurrence of either *hear* or *here* in the target document, we take it to be ambiguous between *hear* and *here*; the task is to decide from the context which one was actually intended.

Applying SNoW to Context-Sensitive Text Correction

Our study makes use of one of the more successful learning approaches tried on the problem of context sensitive text correction (Golding & Roth 1999). SNoW (Roth 1998; Carlson *et al.* 1999) is a multi-class classifier that is specifically tailored for large scale learning tasks. The SNoW learning architecture learns a sparse network of linear functions, in which the targets (elements in confusion sets, in this case) are represented as linear functions over a common feature space. Several update rules can be used within SNoW. The most successful update rule, and the only one used here, is a variant of Littlestone's Winnow update rule (Littlestone 1988), a multiplicative update rule that we tailored to the situation in which the set of input features is not known a priori. SNoW has already been used successfully for a variety of tasks in natural language and visual processing (Golding & Roth 1999; Roth, Yang, & Ahuja 2000; Punyakanok & Roth 2001). We refer the reader to these for a detailed description of SNoW; here we briefly describe how it is applied to context-sensitive text correction and the modifications made relative to (Golding & Roth 1999).

When SNoW is applied to context-sensitive text correction a target node is allocated to each word sequence that is a member of a confusion set. Thus, each word sequence is learned as a function of the context in which it correctly appears. A SNoW unit corresponds to a confusion set; in training, elements belonging to a unit are trained together in the sense that they compete with each other - given a confusion set element, it is viewed as a positive example to its corresponding target and as negative to the targets in its unit. At evaluation time, an element of one of the confusion sets is identified in the text, and the competition is between the targets' corresponding elements in the confusion set.

In principle, a more general approach could use a single confusion set containing all words. However, this is not practical for a general text correction system. If we ignore the confusion sets and present all examples to all targets for training, and then have all targets compete at evaluation time, we see great decreases in both computational efficiency and performance (Even-Zohar & Roth 2000).

The key difference in the architecture used here from the one used in (Golding & Roth 1999) is the fact that we use only a single layer architecture without the notion of the "clouds" used there. While, as shown there, the use of clouds improves the performance somewhat, the simplified architecture used here greatly reduces the learning time and memory requirement. We get the performance level back up in other ways, using a larger training corpus and, mainly, using the confidence level enhancements described later. In particular, that implies that we explicitly use the activation level output by SNoW, rather than only the prediction.

Experimental Methodology

This work makes used of the concept of *confusion sets* and treats the problem as a task of disambiguating the correct set member. The confusion sets acquired for this work were generated automatically by using simple edit distance in both the character space and phoneme space. We later pruned and edited the list manually. Overall, the experiments used a set of 265 different confusion sets (previous works have used between 10 to 21). 244 of the confusion sets were of size 2, 20 were of size 3, and 1 was of size 4.

The experiments were performed on data from the TDT2 English corpus that is available via the Penn treebank (Marcus, Santorini, & Marcinkiewicz 1993). The corpus includes text taken from six English news sources, which aids in the generality of our system. It includes about 1,000,000 English sentences, providing a good amount of data for most of the confusion sets we are interested in. Each experiment was run using five-fold cross-validation, where in each case 80% of the corpus was used for training and the remaining 20% was used for testing.

Clearly, determining the type of features used by the learning algorithm is crucial to its performance. The feature space needs to be expressive enough to allow good approximation of the target functions using linear functions but without excessively increasing the resource requirements. We use the type of features identified in previous research on this problem - collocations: small conjunctions (size 2) of words and part of speech (POS) tags around the target word (up to three words away from the target) and context words in a small window (five words away from the target) around the target word. POS information is added to the text using a SNoW-based POS tagger (Roth & Zelenko 1998).

To avoid a vast amount of rare features we used an eligibility mechanism during the feature extraction process, which eliminated those that occurred less than 4 times. Overall, the feature space had 647,217 features, of which 495 were labels, 549,650 were collocations, and 97,072 were context words. All of the experiments were performed using the Winnow update rule within SNoW, with the following parameters: $\alpha = 1.3$, $\beta = 0.8$, $\theta = 1.0$, and a initial weight of 0.2. Two full epochs (passes through the training sample) were used.

Scaling Up

We describe several suggestions for handling issues that arise in scaling up context sensitive text correction, along with experiments exhibiting their effectiveness.

Network Pruning

Previous work on context sensitive text correction (Golding & Roth 1999; Mangu & Brill 1997) has clearly shown that learning with a larger number of features improves the performance. We describe a method for selectively pruning the effective number of features used, as part of the learning process, and show its effectiveness in reducing the memory requirements while minimally affecting the performance. It also reduces the evaluation time, which scales linearly with the number of active features in the example.

Confusion Set	Train WSJ Test WSJ	Train TDT2 Test WSJ	Train both Test WSJ
accept, except	90.6	94.5	93.2
affect, effect	96.7	96.1	96.4
among, between	87.3	89.5	90.1
amount, number	84.8	79.0	88.5
cite, sight, site	85.1	90.1	90.1
country, county	93.8	95.2	96.1
fewer, less	90.6	91.8	92.6
I, me	98.1	98.9	98.9
it's, its	98.8	99.0	99.2
lay, lie	74.3	85.1	83.8
passed, past	95.9	97.6	97.5
peace, piece	88.7	91.7	91.7
principal, principle	91.7	93.4	94.7
quiet, quite, quit	83.7	90.7	90.4
raise, rise	94.3	93.0	95.1
than, then	97.7	98.6	98.5
their, there, they're	97.2	98.5	98.6
weather, whether	97.0	98.0	98.0
you're, your	94.5	98.3	98.3
Set Average	96.0	96.7	97.2
All Sets Average	94.5	94.6	95.7

Table 2: Adaptation Results for Specific Confusion Sets: The WSJ train / WSJ test column gives performance from using the WSJ corpus only using 80-20% splits. The TDT2 train / WSJ test column gives performance for training on TDT2 and testing on the same 20% splits of the WSJ corpus. The "train both" column gives performance for training on TDT2, then training on the same 80% of WSJ as in the first experiment, then testing on the remaining 20%. These experiments were done using 5-fold cross-validation, with a 10% eligibility ratio.

The approach is based on the intuition that we need not rely on a feature that is observed with a given target very rarely[1]. We refer to this method as *eligibility*. The key issue, we found, is that this method of pruning needs to be done on a *per target* basis, and has to be relative to the sparseness of the target representation. We define an *eligibility ratio*, such that only a specified percentage of the most active features observed have a weight assigned and participate in predictions. This is done by making a first training pass through the data, creating a histogram of feature occurrences for each target, and then eliminating the least active features until we are left with the proper number of features. Another epoch of training is then performed with the remaining features.

The experiments use eligibility ratios of 100% (no pruning), 10%, and 1%. In each experiment, we used five-fold cross-validation, running five 80%-20% splits for each confusion set, so that each example for a given confusion set appeared as a test example once and a training example four times. Overall effects of eligibility on all our confusions sets as well as the details for 19 different confusion sets are

---

[1] A second, also intuitive, option – to prune based on the *weight* of the feature is not as effective for reasons we will not address here.

Confusion Set	Examples	Eligibility Ratio					
		1.0		0.1		0.01	
		Perf	Links	Perf	Links	Perf	Links
accept-except	2910	95.7	8169	96.7	1174	94.4	85
affect-effect	3278	94.2	8202	95.3	1264	94.1	84
among-between	20458	88.5	33279	90.0	4241	85.1	340
amount-number	9134	90.0	14248	89.9	1773	86.0	147
cite-sight-site	3983	91.9	5634	92.9	866	88.7	59
county-country	11897	95.6	16242	95.4	2196	93.4	166
fewer-less	7445	92.0	14986	92.9	1861	92.0	156
I-me	74022	99.0	45906	99.2	5077	98.4	463
it's-its	57843	97.3	62437	97.8	7321	96.8	633
lay-lie	1620	84.1	4479	85.8	692	77.7	48
passed-past	8772	95.6	15328	96.0	2011	92.9	158
peace-piece	7646	95.4	12018	96.3	1476	91.7	122
principal-principle	1270	87.2	4007	86.1	721	83.0	42
quiet-quite-quit	3836	89.6	7320	91.7	1203	87.7	78
raise-rise	3773	93.6	9120	93.8	1326	90.4	94
than-then	46651	97.0	53626	98.3	6692	97.5	544
their-there-they're	85407	97.4	57138	98.2	6790	96.7	582
weather-whether	12234	98.6	17698	98.4	2081	96.7	180
you're-your	14071	97.2	13668	97.8	2616	96.1	217
Set Average	376250	96.4	21639	97.1	2704	95.4	221
All Sets Average	6117483	95.5	17932	95.2	2233	89.5	183

Table 1: Effect of Eligibility on Specific Confusion Sets: We show results for 19 confusion sets for three eligibility ratios: 100% (no pruning), 10%, and 1%. Examples indicates the total number of examples for each confusion set. Each example was presented using 5-fold cross-validation with an 80%-20% split of the data. For each ratio value, Perf indicates the accuracy for the set, and Links are the average number of links (features) per target word.

shown in Table 1. We found that the size of the networks could be reduced greatly without a significant decrease in performance. Using a ratio of around 10% seemed to be a good cutoff point for the tradeoff between performance and size. This gives us an average across all confusion sets of 2,233 features per target, a substantial reduction from the original 17,932, with a slight drop in accuracy.

Adaptation

In order for a general text correction system to be useful, it needs to be able to perform well in domains other than the one on which it was trained. This is clearly an important issue in natural language processing given the diversity of text genres in terms of vocabulary and style. For a learning system there is an additional issue. There is a clear trade-off between pruning the feature base of the hypothesis and its ability to adapt to new text (Herbster & Warmuth 1998). Intuitively, features which are rarely present in one domain could be important in another, but if they are pruned when trained on the first domain, the hypothesis will not be able to adapt its weights given the new texts.

We implemented an adaptation mechanism that is based on suggestions in (Golding & Roth 1999) and performed several experiments in order to examine the adaptation properties of our system in the presence of significant pruning (10%) and a large and diverse training corpus, the TDT2.

As a baseline, we ran experiments using 5-fold cross-validation on the Wall Street Journal corpus, using 80-20%

splits. This gave us an overall performance of 94.5% for the weighted average across all 265 confusion sets. The WSJ corpus is rather small compared to the TDT2 corpus, and so we wondered if the extra data might help a network trained on the TDT2 corpus perform better on the WSJ test data. We found that the system was able to adapt even after significant pruning of features. Using all 265 confusions sets and 5-fold cross-validation, we trained on only the TDT2 corpus and tested on the same 20% slices of the Wall Street Journal as before. This gave overall accuracy of 94.6%, which was slightly better than the 94.5% obtained by training on WSJ only. This suggests that training on a large corpus such as TDT2 countered the effects of testing outside of the training domain. Finally, we tried to boost performance on the WSJ test data by adapting our already trained system to the new corpus by training it on the other WSJ data. When we trained on the TDT2 corpus as before, then trained on 80% of WSJ, and then tested on the leftover 20% of WSJ (the same test data as before), we reached 95.7% performance over all 265 confusion sets – a significant improvement over the results obtained when just WSJ is used in the training, which are 94.5%. The results are summarized in table 2.

These results indicate that even in the presence of significant feature pruning, the system can adapt well to new domains. Moreover, it suggests that in order to enhance performance on specific domains, it is beneficial to "fine-tune" it to this domain. We emphasize that this is costless, since context-sensitive text correction requires no annotation of the text - it assumes that the text is correct and uses this

Confusion Set	Examples	Prediction Threshold					
		0.05		0.125		0.2	
		Perf	Will	Perf	Will	Perf	Will
accept-except	2910	97.9	96.4	99.1	88.1	99.6	80.1
affect-effect	3278	96.7	95.9	97.4	88.3	97.6	75.9
among-between	20458	93.0	91.1	96.3	77.6	98.2	63.1
amount-number	9134	93.0	91.2	96.2	76.8	98.0	61.8
cite-sight-site	3983	95.3	93.2	97.4	81.5	98.6	66.8
county-country	11897	96.6	96.4	97.6	89.7	98.4	77.3
fewer-less	7445	89.9	94.6	96.7	85.9	98.0	73.7
I-me	74022	99.5	99.2	99.7	97.7	99.9	95.2
it's-its	57843	98.6	98.0	99.2	94.2	99.4	87.9
lay-lie	1620	89.9	88.8	93.4	71.3	96.8	57.0
passed-past	8772	97.6	95.7	99.0	88.6	99.5	80.0
peace-piece	7646	97.9	96.4	99.1	90.3	99.5	82.4
principal-principle	1270	90.3	87.5	94.1	68.4	96.3	51.5
quiet-quite-quit	3836	94.7	92.4	98.0	78.2	99.5	63.1
raise-rise	3773	96.0	94.7	97.7	84.4	98.7	72.4
than-then	46651	98.9	98.3	99.4	94.8	99.7	88.9
their-there-they're	85407	99.0	98.2	99.5	94.8	99.8	89.3
weather-whether	12234	98.9	98.6	99.4	95.8	99.7	91.7
you're-your	14071	98.5	98.1	99.2	93.8	99.6	87.4
Set Average	376250	98.1	97.3	99.0	92.6	99.5	85.9
All Sets Average	6117483	97.3	94.6	99.0	86.2	99.6	77.0

Table 3: Confidence Results for Specific Confusion Sets: Here we see results for three specific prediction thresholds. For each prediction threshold, Perf refers to the overall accuracy for predictions, and Will gives the Willingness of the system to make a prediction. Set Average refers to the average for the 19 sets shown here, and All Sets Average refers to the average across all 265 sets. All experiments were run using 5-fold cross-validation and a 10% eligibility ratio.

to label its training examples. And, as we show, it yields significantly better performance if the system is previously trained on the diverse corpus.

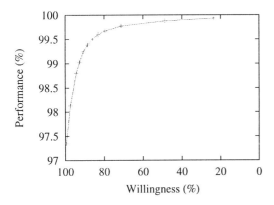

Figure 1: Performance vs. Willingness for 19 Confusion Sets

Prediction Confidence

We have seen that we can perform context-sensitive text correction with an accuracy of greater than 90%, and maintain that accuracy while scaling up to hundreds of confusion sets, and while pruning our networks to compact representations. However, performing at the 90–95% level is not sufficient

for a practical system with wide coverage (that is, where many of the words in each sentence are in one of the confusion sets). In this case, if we make only 5 predictions per sentence, then our sentence level performance is only 50–75%. Even the most tolerant user would object to a system that makes a mistake every couple of sentences. Until we develop methods with basic performance in the range of 98–99%, our solution is to assign a confidence to predictions and make a prediction only when our confidence in that prediction is high. This approach requires that the learning approach assign a robust measure of confidence to its predictions so that this can be done reliably. Given that, our hope is that we can improve performance if we sacrifice some coverage; but, this will only be in cases in which we are not confident enough to voice our prediction. This will not annoy users but rather serve to increase their confidence in the system. An orthogonal benefit of this is that it also provides a mechanism for the user to adjust the confidence threshold at prediction-time. Users can adjust the behavior of the system to suit their personal preferences and abilities. Also, in most practical applications the user's word choice will be correct more often than not, and so abstaining from uncertain predictions will slightly favor the correct choice.

In order to explore this notion of confidence, we note that the activation of a target node is computed using a sigmoid function over the linear sum of *active* weights. Specifically, the activation of the target t is given by

$$a_t = \frac{1}{1 + \exp\left\{\sum_{i \in \mathcal{A}_t} w_i^t - \theta\right\}},\qquad (1)$$

where $\mathcal{A}_t = \{i_1, \ldots, i_m\}$ is the set of features that are active in an example and are linked to the target node t, w_i^t is the weight on the edge connecting the ith feature to the target node t, and θ_t is the threshold for the target node t. With this, one can verify that the output behaves as a distribution function. A prediction is made only when

$$|a_1 - a_2| > C,$$

where a_1 and a_2 are the two highest activations in the confusion set, and C is the confidence threshold. If the confidence function does not exceed the threshold then no prediction is made. In a practical system, this is the equivalent of leaving the text as is – if we are not certain of our prediction, we leave the user's original word choice there.

For the experiment we used the same subset of 19 confusion sets presented in the previous experiments. The results are shown in figure 1. The *performance* axis is the percentage of predictions the system actually makes that are correct and the *willingness* is defined as the percentage of queries (occurrences of confusion set members) on which the system makes a prediction. So for example, a willingness of 80% means that the system is passive on 20% of the queries. The actual threshold used (C) is held fixed for all confusion sets. The experiment use five-fold cross validation as before and a 10% eligibility ratio.

We see that for the subset of 19 confusion sets, the performance rises above 99% when the willingness is around 92% (that is, by abstaining in only 8% of predictions).

Table 3 gives the results for both the 19 confusion sets and the average for all 265 sets. Each column represents a different value for the prediction threshold. Some sets which tend to do well in general (for example, $\{I, me\}$), have high accuracy and tend to have higher willingness than other sets for a given prediction threshold. In general, though, we see each set gaining substantially in accuracy as its willingness decreases. The averages for all 265 confusion sets show that we reach accuracy of 99% with willingness above 85%. These confidence experiments were all performed using a 10% eligibility ratio, demonstrating that we can effectively boost performance while cutting down on our resource requirements at the same time.

Conclusions

Intelligent human-machine interaction relies heavily on the ability to perform context-sensitive inferences. These are knowledge intensive tasks that are hard to perform without a significant learning component. The main challenge in an effort to build a realistic system with context-sensitive inference capabilities, beyond accuracy, is scalability.

In this work we study a learning approach to context sensitive text correction and directly address the crucial issue of scalability. While we have chosen to use a proven learning approach tailored towards large scale processes, significant enhancements in terms of both data and computation are still required before this can support a practical approach.

This paper has explored several issues relating to the scaling up of this task to provide wide word coverage while limiting resource requirements to reasonable levels and increasing the performance levels to those that are acceptable to users. The most significant finding is that a robust prediction confidence can be used to trade coverage for performance and a moderate reduction in willingness can increase the overall performance to over 99% – a level usable in a real-world system.

Acknowledgments
This research is supported by NSF grants IIS-9801638 and IIS-9984168 and a gift from IBM Research.

References

Carlson, A.; Cumby, C.; Rosen, J.; and Roth, D. 1999. The SNoW learning architecture. Technical Report UIUCDCS-R-99-2101, UIUC Computer Science Department.

Even-Zohar, Y., and Roth, D. 2000. A classification approach to word prediction. In *NAACL-2000, The 1st North American Conference on Computational Linguistics*, 124–131.

Golding, A. R., and Roth, D. 1996. Applying Winnow to context-sensitive spelling correction. In *Proc. of the International Conference on Machine Learning*, 182–190.

Golding, A. R., and Roth, D. 1999. A Winnow based approach to context-sensitive spelling correction. *Machine Learning* 34(1-3):107–130. Special Issue on Machine Learning and Natural Language.

Herbster, M., and Warmuth, M. K. 1998. Tracking the best regressor. In *Proc. 11th Annu. Conf. on Comput. Learning Theory*, 24–31. ACM Press, New York, NY.

Kukich, K. 1992. Techniques for automatically correcting words in text. *ACM Computing Surveys* 24(4):377–439.

Littlestone, N. 1988. Learning quickly when irrelevant attributes abound: A new linear-threshold algorithm. *Machine Learning* 2:285–318.

Mangu, L., and Brill, E. 1997. Automatic rule acquisition for spelling correction. In *Proc. 14th International Conference on Machine Learning*. Morgan Kaufmann.

Marcus, M. P.; Santorini, B.; and Marcinkiewicz, M. 1993. Building a large annotated corpus of English: The Penn Treebank. *Computational Linguistics* 19(2):313–330.

Punyakanok, V., and Roth, D. 2001. The use of classifiers in sequential inference. In *NIPS-13; The 2000 Conference on Advances in Neural Information Processing Systems*. MIT Press.

Roth, D., and Zelenko, D. 1998. Part of speech tagging using a network of linear separators. In *COLING-ACL 98, The 17th International Conference on Computational Linguistics*, 1136–1142.

Roth, D.; Yang, M.-H.; and Ahuja, N. 2000. Learning to recognize objects. In *CVPR'00, The IEEE Conference on Computer Vision and Pattern Recognition*, 724–731.

Roth, D. 1998. Learning to resolve natural language ambiguities: A unified approach. In *Proc. National Conference on Artificial Intelligence*, 806–813.

Electric Elves: Applying Agent Technology to Support Human Organizations

Hans Chalupsky, Yolanda Gil, Craig A. Knoblock, Kristina Lerman,
Jean Oh, David V. Pynadath, Thomas A. Russ, Milind Tambe
Information Sciences Institute and Computer Science Department
University of Southern California
4676 Admiralty Way, Marina del Rey, CA 90292

Abstract

The operation of a human organization requires dozens of everyday tasks to ensure coherence in organizational activities, to monitor the status of such activities, to gather information relevant to the organization, to keep everyone in the organization informed, etc. Teams of software agents can aid humans in accomplishing these tasks, facilitating the organization's coherent functioning and rapid response to crises, while reducing the burden on humans. Based on this vision, this paper reports on *Electric Elves*, a system that has been operational, 24/7, at our research institute since June 1, 2000.

Tied to individual user workstations, fax machines, voice, mobile devices such as cell phones and palm pilots, Electric Elves has assisted us in routine tasks, such as rescheduling meetings, selecting presenters for research meetings, tracking people's locations, organizing lunch meetings, etc. We discuss the underlying AI technologies that led to the success of Electric Elves, including technologies devoted to agent-human interactions, agent coordination, accessing multiple heterogeneous information sources, dynamic assignment of organizational tasks, and deriving information about organization members. We also report the results of deploying Electric Elves in our own research organization.

Introduction

Many activities of a human organization are well-suited for software agents, which can devote significant resources to perform these tasks, thus reducing the burden on humans. Indeed, teams of such software agents could assist all organizations, including disaster response organizations, corporations, the military, universities and research institutions.

Based on the above vision, we have developed a system called *Electric Elves* that applies agent technology in service of the day-to-day activities of the Intelligent Systems Division of USC/ISI. Electric Elves is a system of about 15 agents, including nine proxies for nine people, plus two different matchmakers, one flight tracker and one scheduler running continuously for past several months. This paper discusses the tasks performed by the system, the research challenges it faced and its use of AI technology in overcoming those challenges.

One key contribution of this paper is understanding the challenges faced in deploying agents to support organizations. In particular, the complexity inherent in human organizations complicates all of the tasks agents must perform. First, since agents must interact with humans, issues of *adjustable autonomy* become critical. In particular, agents acting as proxies for people must automatically adjust their own autonomy, e.g., avoiding critical errors, possibly by letting people make important decisions while autonomously making the more routine decisions. Second, to accomplish their goals, agents must be provided reliable access to information. Third, people have a wide variety of capabilities, interests, preferences and engage in many different tasks. To enable teaming among such people for crisis response or other organizational tasks, agents acting as their proxies must represent and reason with such capabilities and interests. We thus require powerful matchmaking capabilities to match both interests and capabilities. Fourth, coordination of all of these different agents, including proxies, is itself a significant research challenge. Finally, the entire agent system must scale-up: (i) it must scale-up in the sense of running continually 24 hours a day 7 days a week (24/7) for months at a time; (ii) it must scale-up in the number of agents to support large-scale human organizations.

The Electric Elves

In the Electric Elves project we have developed technology and tools for deploying agents into human organizations to help with organizational tasks. We describe the application of the Electric Elves to two classes of tasks. First, we describe the problem of coordinating activities within an individual research project. These tasks must be tightly coordinated and a significant amount of information is known in advance about the participants and their goals and capabilities. Second, in order to demonstrate the capabilities of the system in a more open environment, we applied the system to the problem of meeting planning with participants outside the organization where some of the necessary information about participants is not known in advance.

Coordinating Project Activities

Our agents help coordinate the everyday activities of a research project: they keep the project running smoothly, rescheduling meetings when someone is delayed, ordering food for meetings or if someone has to work late, and identifying speakers for research meetings. Each person in the project is assigned their own personal proxy agent, which represents that person to the agent system.

A proxy agent keeps track of a project member's current location using several different information sources, including their calendar, Global Position System (GPS) device when outside of the building (Fig. 1), infrared communications within the building, and computer activity. When a proxy agent notices that someone is not attending a scheduled meeting or that they are too far away to make it to a scheduled meeting in time, then their agent sends them a request using a wireless device (i.e., a cell phone or Palm Pilot) asking if they want to cancel the meeting, delay the meeting, or have the meeting proceed without them. If a user responds, their decision is communicated to the other participants of the scheduled meeting. If they are unable to respond, the agent must make a decision autonomously.

Figure 1: A Palm VII PDA with GPS receiver

For weekly project meetings, the agents coordinate the selection of the presenter and arrange food for the meetings. Once a week an auction is held where all of the meeting participants are asked about their capability and willingness to present at the next meeting. Then the system compiles the bids, selects a presenter, and notifies all of the attendees who will be presenting at the next project meeting. The agents also arrange food for lunch meetings. They order from a set of nearby restaurants, select meals that were highly rated by others, and fax the orders directly to the restaurant with instructions for delivery. We have begun relying on our agents so heavily to order lunch that one local "Subway" restaurant owner even remarked: *"...more and more computers are getting to order food...so we might have to think about marketing [to them]."*

Some of the technical challenges in building this application are in determining how much autonomy the agents should assume on behalf of the user, dynamically building agent teams, determining how to assign the organizational tasks (e.g., presentations), and providing access to online data such as calendars and restaurants.

Organizing External Meetings

To demonstrate how the technology supports less structured environments, we also applied the Electric Elves to the task of planning and coordinating ad hoc meetings at conferences and workshops involving individuals across different organizations. The system identifies people that have similar research interests, coordinates scheduling a meeting with those people, locates a suitable restaurant for a meeting that takes into account dietary constraints, and makes a reservation using an online reservation service.

To identify individuals with related interests, the agents use an online bibliography service that provides a list of the papers written by an individual. When a person is going to a meeting, their agent can check an online source to locate in-

dividuals going to the same meeting and then build a model of the research interests of the different participants based on their publications. Using this information, the user selects the participants for the meeting and the agent sends out an invitation to each of the potential attendees.

Once the agent has finalized the set of participants for a meeting, it selects an appropriate place to have the meeting. It does this by checking for any known dietary restrictions and uses that information to identify suitable cuisine types. Next, the agent goes out to an online restaurant reservation site to find the set of restaurants closest to the given location and matches up these restaurants with a restaurant review site to select the high-quality restaurants. The user selects from a small set of close, highly-recommended restaurants and the agent then makes a reservation for the meeting using the online reservation system.

This application highlights two additional technical challenges: gathering information about people from other organizations and ensuring the robustness of the interaction with online sources that change frequently.

Underlying Technologies

In this section we describe how we addressed some of the technical challenges, namely the issues of interacting with human users within an organization, providing reliable access to organization-related data, dynamic assignment of organizational tasks, deriving knowledge about the participants in an organization, and coordination of agent teams.

Agent Interactions with Human Users

Electric Elves agents must often take actions on behalf of the human users. Specifically, a user's agent proxy (named "Friday" after Robinson Crusoe's servant and companion) can take autonomous actions to coordinate collaborative activities (e.g., meetings). Friday's decision making on behalf of a person naturally leads to the issue of *adjustable autonomy*. An agent has the option of acting with full autonomy (e.g., delaying a meeting, volunteering the user to give a presentation, ordering a meal). On the other hand, it may act without autonomy, instead asking its user what to do. Clearly, the more decisions that Friday makes autonomously, the more time and effort it saves its user. Yet, given the high uncertainty in Friday's knowledge of its user's state and preferences, it could potentially make very costly mistakes while acting autonomously. For example, it may order an expensive dinner when the user is not hungry, or volunteer a busy user to give a presentation. Thus, each Friday must make intelligent decisions about when to consult its user and when to act autonomously.

Our initial attempt at adjustable autonomy was inspired by CAP (Mitchell *et al.* 1994), an agent system for advising a user on scheduling meetings. As with CAP, each Friday tried to learn its user preferences using decision trees under C4.5 (Quinlan 1993). One problem became apparent when applying this technique in Electric Elves: a user would not grant autonomy to Friday in making certain decisions, but s/he would sometimes be unavailable to provide any input at decision time. Thus, a Friday could end up waiting indefinitely for user input and miscoordinate with its teammates.

We therefore modified the system so that if a user did not respond within a fixed time limit, Friday acted autonomously based on its learned decision tree. Unfortunately, when we deployed the system in our research group, it led to some dramatic failures. For instance, one user's proxy erroneously volunteered him to give a presentation. C4.5 had overgeneralized from a few examples to create an incorrect rule. Although Friday tried asking the user at first, because of the timeout, it had to eventually follow the incorrect rule and take the undesirable autonomous action.

It was clear, based on this experience, that the team context in Electric Elves would cause difficulties for existing adjustable-autonomy techniques (Dorais *et al.* 1998; Ferguson, Allen, & Miller 1996; Mitchell *et al.* 1994) that focused on solely individual human-agent interactions. Therefore, we developed a novel, decision-theoretic planning approach that used Markov Decision Processes (MDPs) (Puterman 1994) to support explicit reasoning about team coordination. The MDPs used in our framework (Scerri, Pynadath, & Tambe 2001) provide Friday with a novel three-step approach to adjustable autonomy: (i) Before transferring decision-making control, an agent explicitly weighs the cost of waiting for user input and any potential team miscoordination against the likelihood and cost of erroneous autonomous action; (ii) When transferring control, an agent does not rigidly commit to this decision, but it instead flexibly reevaluates when its user does not respond, sometimes reversing its decision and taking back autonomy; (iii) Rather than force a risky decision in situations requiring autonomous action, an agent changes its coordination arrangements by postponing or reordering activities to potentially buy time to lower decision cost/uncertainty. Since these coordination decisions and actions incur varying costs and benefits over time, agents look ahead over the different sequences of possible actions and plan a policy that maximizes team welfare.

We have implemented MDPs that model Friday's decisions on meeting rescheduling, volunteering its user to give a presentation, and selecting *which* user should give a presentation. For instance, consider one possible policy, generated from an MDP for the rescheduling of meetings. If the user has not arrived at the meeting five minutes prior to its scheduled start, this policy specifies "ask the user what to do". If the user does not arrive by the time of the meeting, the policy specifies "wait", so the agent continues acting without autonomy. However, if the user *still* has not arrived five minutes after the meeting is scheduled to start, then the policy chooses "delay by 15 minutes", which the agent then executes autonomously.

Flexible Assignment of Tasks

The human agents and software agents in our organization perform a wide variety of tasks that are often interrelated. Agents often need to delegate a subtask to another agent capable of performing it (e.g., reserve a meeting room), invoke another agent to gather and report back necessary information (e.g., find the location of a person), or rely on another agent to execute some task in the real world (e.g., attend a lunch meeting). Simple agent matchmaking is sufficient in many multi-agent systems where agents perform one (or at most a few) kind of task, and their capabilities are designed by the system developers to fit the interactions anticipated among the agents. In contrast, our agents are complex and heterogeneous, and the agents that issue a request cannot be expected to be aware of what other agents are available and how they are invoked.

We have developed an agent matchmaker called PHOSPHORUS (Gil & Ramachandran 2001), which builds on previous research on matching problem solving goals and methods in EXPECT (Swartout & Gil 1995; Gil & Gonzalez 1996). The main features of this approach are: 1) a declarative language to express task descriptions that includes rich parameter type expressions to qualify task types; 2) task descriptions are fully translated into description logic to determine subsumption relations among tasks; 3) task descriptions are expressed in terms of domain ontologies, which provide a basis for relating and reasoning about different tasks and enables reformulation of tasks into subtasks.

Agent capabilities and requests are represented as verb clauses with typed arguments (as in a case grammar), where each argument has a name (usually a preposition) and a parameter. The type of a parameter may be a specific instance, an abstract concept (marked with spec-of), an instance type (marked with inst-of), and extensional or intensional sets of those three types. Here are some examples of capabilities of some researchers and project assistants:

```
"agents that can discuss Phosphorus"
    ((capability (discuss (obj Phosphorus-project)))
     (agents (gil surya chalupsky russ)))

"agents that can setup an LCD projector in a meeting room"
    ((capability (setup (obj (?v is (inst-of lcd-projector)))
                        (in (?r is (inst-of meeting-room)))))
     (agents (itice)))
```

Requests are formulated in the same language, and can ask about general types of instances (e.g., what agents can setup any kind of equipment for giving research presentations in a meeting room).

Description logic and subsumption reasoning are used to relate different task descriptions. Both requests and agent capabilities are translated into Loom (MacGregor 1991). Loom's classifier recognizes that the capability to "setup equipment" will subsume one to "setup LCD projector", because according to the domain ontologies equipment subsumes LCD projector.

PHOSPHORUS performs *task reformulations* when there are no agents with capabilities that subsume a request. In that case, it may be possible to fulfill the request by decomposing it into subtasks. This allows a more flexible matching than if one required a single agent to match all capabilities in the request. PHOSPHORUS supports set reformulations (breaking down a task on a set into its individual elements) and covering reformulations (decomposing a task into the disjoint subclasses of its arguments). For example, no single agent can discuss the entire Electric Elves project, since no single researcher is involved in all the aspects of the project. But PHOSPHORUS can return a set of people who can collectively cover the topic based on the subprojects:

```
(COVERING -name ARIADNE-PROJECT
              -matches KNOBLOCK MINTON LERMAN
          -name PHOSPHORUS-PROJECT
              -matches GIL SURYA CHALUPSKY RUSS
          -name TEAMCORE-PROJECT
              -matches
                  (COVERING
                  -name ADJUSTABLE-AUTONOMY-PROJECT
                      -matches TAMBE SCERRI PYNADATH
                  -name TEAMWORK-PROJECT
                      -matches TAMBE PYNADATH MODI)
          -name ROSETTA-PROJECT
              -matches GIL CHALUPSKY)
```

Many additional challenges lay ahead regarding capability representations for people within the organization. For example, although anyone has the capability to call a taxi for a visitor (and will do so if necessary), project assistants are the preferred option. Extensions to the language are needed to express additional properties of agents, such as reliability, efficiency, and invocation guidelines.

Reliable Access to Information

Timely access to up-to-date information is crucial to the successful planning and execution of tasks in the Electric Elves organization. Agents making decisions on behalf of human users need to extract information from multiple heterogeneous information sources, including organizational databases (personal schedules, staff lists) and external Web sites, such as airline schedules, restaurant information, traffic and weather updates, etc. In order to pick a restaurant for a scheduled lunch meeting, the agents access the Restaurant Row site to get the locations of restaurants that meet the specified criteria, e.g., dietary restrictions. Wrappers enable Web sources to be queried as if they were databases by other applications, such as the Electric Elves agents. A critical part of a wrapper is a set of extraction rules that enable the wrapper to quickly locate the beginning and end of the data to be extracted from a Web page in response to some query.

The Ariadne component (Knoblock *et al.* 2000; 2001) of Electric Elves learns wrappers from pages in which relevant data has been labeled by the user. Previous research has focused on applying machine learning techniques to rapidly generate wrappers (Muslea, Minton, & Knoblock 2000; Kushmerick 2000), but few attempts have been made to validate data, detect failures (Kushmerick 1999) or repair wrappers when the source pages change in a way that breaks the wrapper. Automatically monitoring external information sources and repairing wrappers when errors are detected is a critical part of a robust dynamic organization.

We address the problem of wrapper verification by applying machine learning techniques to learn a set of patterns that describe the content of the extracted data. Since the information for a single data field can vary considerably, the system learns a statistical distribution of patterns. Wrappers can be verified by comparing newly extracted data to the learned patterns. When a significant difference is found, we can launch the wrapper repair process.

The learned patterns represent the structure of data as a sequence of words and wildcards. Wildcards represent syntactic categories to which words belong—alphabetic, numeric, capitalized, *etc.*. For example, a set of street addresses all start with a pattern "_Number_ Capitalized_": a number followed by a capitalized word. The algorithm we developed (Lerman & Minton 2000) finds all statistically significant starting and ending patterns in a set of positive examples of the data field. A pattern is significant if it occurs more frequently than would be expected by chance if the tokens were generated randomly and independently of one another. Our approach is similar to work on grammar induction (Carrasco & Oncina 1994), but our pattern language is better suited for capturing the regularities in small data fields (as opposed to languages). For verification, we learn the patterns from training examples (data extracted by the wrapper that is known to be correct). Next, the wrapper generates a set of test examples from pages retrieved using the same or similar set of queries. If the patterns describe statistically the same proportion of the test examples as the training examples, the wrapper is deemed correct; otherwise, it has failed.

The most common causes of wrapper failure are changes in Web site layout. Even minor changes can break the wrapper's data extraction rules. However, since the content tends to remain the same, it is often possible to automatically repair the wrapper by learning new extraction rules. We exploit the learned patterns to find correct examples of data on the new pages. The Restaurant Row wrapper allows us to retrieve several examples of restaurant addresses, and the verification algorithm learned that some of the examples start with the pattern "_Number_ Capitalized_" and end with the pattern "Avenue". If Restaurant Row changes to look more like the Zagat Web site, the wrapper will no longer extract addresses correctly. In the verification phase we will detect the failure because the extracted data is not described by the patterns. However, since restaurant addresses still start with "_Number_ Capitalized_" and end with "Avenue", we should be able to find addresses on the changed pages. Once the desired information has been found, these examples and the new pages are sent to the wrapper generation system to learn new data extraction rules. We use prior knowledge about the content of data, as captured by the learned patterns, along with *a priori* expectations about the data to identify correct examples on the changed pages. We can expect the same data field to appear in roughly the same position and in a similar context on each page; moreover, we expect at least some of the data to remain unchanged.

Our approach can be extended to automatically create wrappers for new information sources using data extracted from a known source. Thus, once we learn what restaurant addresses look like, we can use this information to extract addresses from any yellow pages-type source, and use it to create a wrapper for this source.

Knowledge from Unstructured Sources

As mentioned above, an agent-assisted organization crucially depends on access to accurate and up-to-date information about the humans it supports as well as the environment in which they operate. Some of this information can be provided directly from existing databases and online sources, but other information—people's expertise, capabilities, interests, etc.—will often not be available explicitly and might need to be modeled by hand. In a dynamic environment such as Electric Elves, however, manual modeling is only feasible for relatively static information. For example, if at some conference we want to select potential candidates for a lunch meeting with Yolanda Gil based on mutual research interests, it is not feasible to manually model relevant knowledge about each person on the conference roster before such a selection can be made.

To support team-building tasks such as inviting people for a lunch meeting, finding people potentially interested in a presentation or research meeting, finding candidates to meet with a visitor, etc., we developed a matchmaking service called the Interest Matcher. It can match people based on their research interests but also take other information into account such as involvement in research projects, present and past affiliation, universities attended, etc. To minimize the need for manual modeling in a dynamic environment, we combined statistical match techniques from the area of information retrieval (IR) with logic-based matching performed by the PowerLoom knowledge representation (KR) system. The IR techniques work well with unstructured text sources available online on the Web, which is the form in which information is typically available to outside organizations. PowerLoom facilitates declarative modeling of the decision process, modeling of missing information, logical inference, explanation and also customization.

The matchmaker's knowledge base contains an ontology of research topic areas and associated relations; rules formalizing the matchmaking process; and manually modeled, relatively static information about staff members, research projects, etc. To perform a particular matchmaking task, a requesting agent sends a message containing an appropriate PowerLoom query to the Interest Matcher. For example, the following query finds candidates for lunch with Yolanda Gil:

```
(retrieve all ?x (should-meet ?x Gil))
```

The should-meet relation and one of its supporting relations are defined as follows in PowerLoom:

```
(defrelation should-meet ((?p1 Person) (?p2 Person))
  :⇐ (or (interests-overlap ?p1 ?p2)
         (institution-in-common ?p1 ?p2)
         (school-in-common ?p1 ?p2)))

(defrelation interests-overlap ((?p1 Person) (?p2 Person))
  :⇐ (exists (?interest1 ?interest2)
         (and (research-interest ?p1 ?interest1)
              (research-interest ?p2 ?interest2)
              (or (subset-of ?interest1 ?interest2)
                  (subset-of ?interest2 ?interest1)))))
```

For more specific purposes, any of the more basic relations comprising should-meet such as interests-overlap could be queried directly by a client. Using a general purpose KR system as the matching engine provides us with this flexibility. Note, that for interests-overlap we only require a subsumption relationship, e.g., interest in planning would subsume (or overlap with) interest in hierarchical planning.

To deal with incompleteness of the KB, we allow a requesting agent to introduce new individuals and then

the Interest Matcher automatically infers limited structured knowledge—their research interests—by analyzing relevant unstructured text sources on the Web.

The key idea is that people's research interests are implicitly documented in their publication record. We make these interests explicit by associating each research topic in the PowerLoom topic ontology with a statistical representation of a set of abstracts of research papers representative of the topic. These topic sets are determined automatically by querying a bibliography search engine such as Cora or the NEC ResearchIndex with seed phrases representative of the topic (access to such Web sources is facilitated by Ariadne wrappers). We then query the same search engine for publication abstracts of a particular researcher and then classify them by computing statistical similarity measures between the researcher's publications and the topic sets determined before. We use a standard IR vector space model to represent document abstracts and compute similarity by a cosine measure and by weighting terms based on how well they signify particular topic classes (Salton & McGill 1983).

Coordination of Component Agents

The diverse agents in Electric Elves must work together to accomplish the complex tasks of the whole system. For instance, to plan a lunch meeting, the interest matcher finds a list of potential attendees, the Friday of each potential attendee decides whether s/he will attend, the capability matcher identifies dietary restrictions of the confirmed attendees, and the reservation site wrapper identifies possible restaurants and makes the final reservation. In addition to low-level communication issues, there is the complicated problem of getting all these agents to work together as a team. Each of these agents must execute its part in coordination with the others, so that it performs its tasks at the correct time and sends the results to the agents who need them.

However, constructing teams of such agents remains a difficult challenge. Current approaches to designing agent teams lack the general-purpose teamwork models that would enable agents to autonomously reason about the communication and coordination required. The absence of such teamwork models makes team construction highly labor-intensive. Human developers must provide the agents with a large number of problem-specific coordination and communication plans that are not reusable. Furthermore, the resulting teams often suffer from a lack of robustness and flexibility. In a real-world domain like Electric Elves, teams face a variety of uncertainties, such as a member agent's unanticipated failure in fulfilling responsibilities (e.g., a presenter is delayed), members' divergent beliefs, and unexpectedly noisy communication. It is difficult to anticipate and pre-plan for all possible coordination failures.

In Electric Elves, the agents coordinate using Teamcore, a domain-independent, decentralized, teamwork-based integration architecture (Pynadath et al. 1999). Teamcore uses STEAM, a general-purpose teamwork model (Tambe 1997) and provides core teamwork capabilities to agents by wrapping them with Teamcore proxies (separate from the Friday agents that are *user* proxies). By interfacing with Teamcore proxies, existing agents can rapidly assemble themselves into a team to solve a given problem. The Teamcore proxies form a distributed *team-readiness* layer that provides the following social capabilities: (i) coherent commitment and termination of joint goals, (ii) team reorganization in response to member failure, (iii) selective communication, (iv) incorporation of heterogeneous agents, and (v) automatic generation of tasking and monitoring requests. Although other agent-integration architectures such as OAA (Martin, Cheyer, & Moran 1999) and RETSINA (Sycara *et al.* 1996) provide capability (iv), Teamcore's use of an explicit, domain-independent teamwork model allows it to support all five required social capabilities.

Each and every agent in the Electric Elves organization (Fridays, matchers, wrappers) has an associated Teamcore proxy that records its membership in various teams and active commitments made to these teams. Given an abstract specification of the organization and its plans, the Teamcore proxies *automatically* execute the necessary coordination tasks. They form joint commitments to team plans such as holding meetings, hosting and meeting with visitors, arranging lunch, etc. Teamcore proxies also communicate amongst themselves to ensure coherent and robust plan execution. The Teamcore proxies automatically substitute for missing roles (e.g., if the presenter is absent from the meeting) and inform each other of critical factors affecting a team plan. Finally, they communicate with their corresponding agents to monitor the agents' ability to fulfill commitments (e.g., asking Friday to monitor its user's attendance of a meeting) and to inform the agents of changes to those commitments (e.g., notifying Friday of a meeting rescheduling).

Electric Elves Architecture

Electric Elves is a complex and heterogeneous system spanning a wide variety of component technologies and languages, communication protocols as well as operating system platforms. Figure 2 shows the components of the current version of Electric Elves. Teamcore agents are written in Python and Soar (which is written in C), Ariadne wrappers are written in C++, the PHOSPHORUS capability matcher is written in Common-Lisp and the PowerLoom interest matcher is written in STELLA (Chalupsky & MacGregor 1999) which translates into Java. The agents are distributed across SunOS 5.7, Windows NT, Windows 2000 and Linux platforms, and use TCP/IP, HTTP and the Lockheed KQML API to handle specialized communication needs.

Tying all these different pieces together in a robust and coherent manner constitutes a significant engineering challenge. Initially we looked for an implementation of KQML, but there was none available that supported all the languages and platforms we required. To solve this integration problem, we are using the DARPA supported CoABS Grid technology developed by Global InfoTek, Inc. and ISX Corporation[1]. The CoABS Grid is a Java-based communication infrastructure built on top of Sun's Jini networking technology. It provides message and service-based communication mechanisms, agent registration, lookup and discovery services, as well as message logging, security and visualization facilities. Since it is is written in Java, it runs on a wide variety of OS platforms, and it is also relatively easy to connect with non-Java technology. Grid proxy components connect non-Java technology to the Grid.

We primarily use the CoABS Grid as a uniform transport mechanism. The content of Grid messages are in KQML format and could potentially be communicated via alternative means. Not all Electric Elves message traffic goes across the Grid. For example, the Teamcore agents communicate via their own protocol (the Lockheed KQML API) and only use the Grid to communicate with non-Teamcore agents such as the capability and interest matchers. Similarly, the information retrieval engine communicates with Ariadne wrappers directly via HTTP instead of going through the Grid.

Related Work

Several agent-based systems have been developed that support specific tasks within an organization, such as meeting scheduling (Dent *et al.* 1992) and visitor hosting (Kautz *et al.* 1994; Sycara & Zeng 1994). In contrast to these systems, we believe that our approach integrates a range of technologies that can support a variety of tasks within the organization. Agent architectures have been applied to organizational tasks (Sycara *et al.* 1996; Martin, Cheyer, & Moran 1999; Lesser *et al.* 1999), but none of them include technology for team work, adjustable autonomy, and dynamic collection of information from external sources.

To our knowledge, Electric Elves represents the first agent-based system that is used for routine tasks within a human organization. Several other areas of research have looked at complementary aspects of the problems that we aim to address. Research on architectures and systems for Computer-Supported Cooperative Work include a variety of information management and communication technologies that facilitate collaboration within human organizations (Greenberg 1991; Malone *et al.* 1997). In contrast with our work, they do not have agents associated with people that have some degree of autonomy and can make decisions on a human's behalf. Our work is also complementary and can be extended with ongoing research on ubiquitous computing and intelligent buildings (Lesser *et al.* 1999). These projects are embedding sensor networks and agents to control and improve our everyday physical environments. This kind of infrastructure would make it easier for Electric Elves to locate and contact people as well as to direct the environmental control agents in support of organizational tasks.

Current Status

The Electric Elves system has been in use within our research group at ISI since June 1, 2000; and operating continuously 24 hours a day, 7 days a week (with interruptions for bug fixes and enhancements). Usually, nine agent proxies are working for nine users, with one proxy each for a capability matcher and an interest matcher. The proxies communicate with their users using a variety of devices: workstation display, voice, mobile phones, and palm pilots. They

---

[1]http://coabs.globalinfotek.com/coabs_public/coabs_pdf/gridvision.pdf

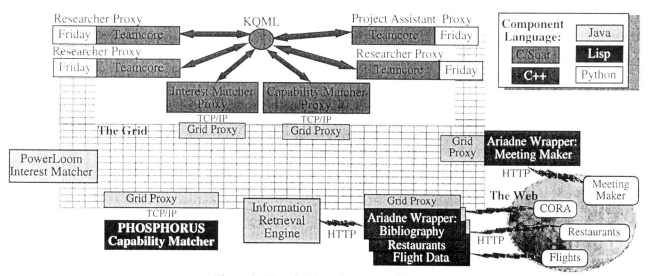

Figure 2: Electric Elves System Architecture

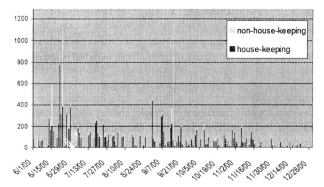

Figure 3: Number of daily coordination messages exchanged by proxies over a seven-month period.

also communicate with restaurants by sending faxes.

Figure 3 plots the number of daily messages exchanged by the proxies for seven months (June 1, 2000 to December 31, 2000). The size of the daily counts demonstrates the large amount of coordination actions necessary in managing all of the activities such as meeting rescheduling. The high variability is due to the variance in the number of daily activities, e.g., weekends and long breaks such as the Christmas break, usually have very little activity. Furthermore, with continually increasing system stability, the amount of housekeeping activity necessary has reduced automatically.

Several observations show the effectiveness of Electric Elves. First, over the past several months, few emails have been exchanged among our group members indicating to each other that they may get delayed to meetings. Instead, Friday agents automatically address such delays. Also the overhead of waiting for delayed members in meeting rooms has been reduced. Overall, 1128 meetings have been monitored, out of which 285 have been rescheduled, 230 automatically and 55 by hand. Both autonomous rescheduling and human intervention were useful in Elves.

Furthermore, whereas in the past, one of our group members would need to circulate emails trying to recruit a presenter for research meetings and making announcements, this overhead has almost completely vanished—weekly auctions automatically select the presenters at our research meetings. These auctions are automatically opened when the system receives notification of any meeting requiring a presentation. Auction decisions may be made without requiring a full set of bids; in fact, in one case, only 4 out of 9 possible bids were received. The rest of the group simply did not bid before the winner was announced. Most of the time, the winner was automatically selected. However, on two occasions (July 6 and Sept 19) exceptional circumstances (e.g., a visitor) required human intervention, which our proxy team easily accommodates.

Discussion

As described in this paper we have successfully deployed the Electric Elves in our own real-world organization. These agents interact directly with humans both within the organization and outside the organization communicating by email, wireless messaging, and faxes. Our agents go beyond simply automating tasks that were previously performed by humans. Because hardware and processing power is cheap, our agents can perform a level of monitoring that would be impractical for human assistants, ensuring that activities within an organization run smoothly and that events are planned and coordinated to maximize the productivity of the individuals of an organization.

In the process of building the applications described in this paper we addressed an number of key technology problems that arise in any agent-based system applied to human organizations. In particular we described how to use Markov Decision Processes to determine the appropriate degree of autonomy for the agents, how to use knowledged-based matchmaking to assign tasks within an organization, how to apply machine learning techniques to ensure robust access to the data sources, how to combine knowledge-based and statistical matchmaking techniques to derive knowledge about the participants both within and outside an organization, and how to apply multi-agent teamwork coordination to dynamically assemble teams.

Acknowledgements

The research reported here was supported in part by the Rome Laboratory of the Air Force Systems Command and the Defense Advanced Research Projects Agency (DARPA) under contract numbers F30602-97-C-0068, F30602-98-2-0109 and F30602-98-2-0108; and in part by the Air Force Office of Scientific Research under Grant Number F49620-01-1-0053. The views and conclusions contained herein are those of the authors and should not be interpreted as necessarily representing the official policies or endorsements, either expressed or implied, of any of the above organizations or any person connected with them.

Surya Ramachandran also contributed to the success of this project.

References

Carrasco, R., and Oncina, J. 1994. Learning stochastic regular grammars by means of a state merging method. In *Lecture Notes In Computer Science*, 862.

Chalupsky, H., and MacGregor, R. 1999. STELLA – a Lisp-like language for symbolic programming with delivery in Common Lisp, C++ and Java. In *Proc. of the 1999 Lisp User Group Meeting*. Berkeley, CA: Franz Inc.

Dent, L.; Boticario, J.; McDermott, J.; Mitchell, T.; and Zabowski, D. 1992. A personal learning apprentice. In *Proc. of AAAI-1992*, 96–103.

Dorais, G. A.; Bonasso, R. P.; Kortenkamp, D.; Pell, B.; and Schreckenghost, D. 1998. Adjustable autonomy for human-centered autonomous systems on Mars. In *Proc. of the First International Conference of the Mars Society*.

Ferguson, G.; Allen, J.; and Miller, B. 1996. TRAINS-95: Towards a mixed initiative planning assistant. In *Proc. of the 3rd Conf. on Artificial Intelligence Planning Systems*, 70–77.

Gil, Y., and Gonzalez, P. 1996. Subsumption-based matching: Bringing semantics to goals. In *International Workshop on Description Logics*.

Gil, Y., and Ramachandran, S. 2001. PHOSPHORUS: A task-based agent matchmaker. In *Proc. of the Fifth International Conference on Autonomous Agents*.

Greenberg, S., ed. 1991. *Computer Supported Cooperative Work and Groupware*. London: Academic Press.

Kautz, H.; Selman, B.; Coen, M.; and Ketchpel, S. 1994. An experiment in the design of software agents. In *Proc. of AAAI-1994*.

Knoblock, C. A.; Lerman, K.; Minton, S.; and Muslea, I. 2000. Accurately and reliably extracting data from the web: A machine learning approach. *Data Engineering Bulletin* 23(4).

Knoblock, C. A.; Minton, S.; Ambite, J. L.; Ashish, N.; Muslea, I.; Philpot, A. G.; and Tejada, S. 2001. The ARIADNE approach to web-based information integration. *International Journal of Cooperative Information Systems* 10(1/2).

Kushmerick, N. 1999. Regression testing for wrapper maintenance. In *Proc. of AAAI-1999*, 74–79.

Kushmerick, N. 2000. Wrapper induction: efficiency and expressiveness. *Artificial Intelligence* 118(1-2):15–68.

Lerman, K., and Minton, S. 2000. Learning the common structure of data. In *Proc. of AAAI-2000*, 609–614.

Lesser, V.; Atighetchi, M.; Benyo, B.; Horling, B.; Raja, A.; Vincent, R.; Wagner, T.; Xuan, P.; and Zhang, S. X. 1999. The UMASS intelligent home project. In *Proc. of the 3rd Annual Conf. on Autonomous Agents*, 291–298.

MacGregor, R. 1991. Inside the LOOM description classifier. *ACM SIGART Bulletin* 2(3):88–92.

Malone, T. W.; Crowston, K.; Lee, J.; Pentland, B.; Dellarocas, C.; Wyner, G.; Quimby, J.; Osborne, C.; and Bernstein, A. 1997. *Tools for inventing organizations: Toward a handbook of organizational processes*. Center for Coordination Science Working Paper No. 198.

Martin, D. L.; Cheyer, A. J.; and Moran, D. B. 1999. The open agent architecture: A framework for building distributed software systems. *Applied Artificial Intelligence* 13(1-2):92–128.

Mitchell, T.; Caruana, R.; Freitag, D.; McDermott, J.; and Zabowski, D. 1994. Experience with a learning personal assistant. *Communications of the ACM* 37(7):81–91.

Muslea, I.; Minton, S.; and Knoblock, C. 2000. Hierarchical wrapper induction for semistructured information sources. *Journal of Autonomous Agents and Multi-Agent Systems* 4(1/2).

Puterman, M. L. 1994. *Markov Decision Processes*. John Wiley & Sons.

Pynadath, D. V.; Tambe, M.; Chauvat, N.; and Cavedon, L. 1999. Toward team-oriented programming. In Jennings, N. R., and Lespérance, Y., eds., *Intelligent Agents VI: Agent Theories, Architectures and Languages*. Springer-Verlag. 233–247.

Quinlan, J. R. 1993. *C4.5: Programs for machine learning*. San Mateo, CA: Morgan Kaufmann.

Salton, G., and McGill, M. 1983. *Introduction to Modern Information Retrieval*. Tokio: McGraw-Hill.

Scerri, P.; Pynadath, D. V.; and Tambe, M. 2001. Adjustable autonomy in real-world multi-agent environments. In *Proc. of the Conference on Autonomous Agents*.

Swartout, W. R., and Gil, Y. 1995. Expect: Explicit representations for flexible acquisition. In *Proc. Ninth Knowledge Acquisition for Knowledge-Based Systems Workshop*.

Sycara, K., and Zeng, D. 1994. Towards an intelligent electronic secretary. In *CIKM-94 (International Conference on Information and Knowledge Management), Intelligent Information Agents Workshop*.

Sycara, K.; Decker, K.; Pannu, A.; Williamson, M.; and Zeng, D. 1996. Distributed intelligent agents. *IEEE Expert*.

Tambe, M. 1997. Towards flexible teamwork. *Journal of Artificial Intelligence Research* 7:83–124.

Token allocation strategy for free-flight conflict solving

Track: Emerging Applications, Technology and Issues

Géraud Granger and Nicolas Durand and Jean-Marc Alliot

CENA*/LOG[†]

7, av Ed Belin

31055 Toulouse Cedex France

tel: (33) 5 62 17 40 54 - fax: (33) 5 62 17 41 43

email: granger@recherche.enac.fr - durand@tls.cena.fr - alliot@dgac.fr

Abstract

For the last 10 years, airlines have widely supported research on the development of airspaces where aircraft would be free to decide their trajectory: these areas where called Free-flight airspaces. However, as soon as two aircraft are in the same area, their separation must be guaranteed. FACES[1] is an autonomous and coordinated embarked (on board) conflict solver for Free Flight airspace. It solves conflict by computing simple manoeuvres that guarantees conflict free trajectories for the next 5 minutes (min). Coordination is ensured by giving sequential manoeuvres to aircraft with a token allocation strategy. FACES can be implemented with the current positioning, broadcasting and flight management technology. Moreover, it is robust to communication or system failure for time up to one or two minutes. FACES was tested with a traffic simulator on busy traffic days over France. Airspace over flight level[2] 320 was considered as Free Flight.

Introduction

We have all experienced at least once a long wait in an overcrowded air terminal. Reading magazines distributed by airlines during these long hours, we often found that they consider air traffic control as one of the major cause for delays. And it is true that the air traffic control system is becoming saturated. But, if delays due to overloaded airports are easy to understand, it is much harder to comprehend delays due to the En Route control system. In fact, if we ask a mathematician to analyze the system in cold blood, it can be proved that the collision probability over flight level 320 is very low for aircraft flying direct routes, especially if some elementary precautions are taken regarding face to face or overtaking conflicts. So, En Route control could be considered as expensive (En route charges), inefficient (delays induced) and statistically of very little use. However, if the Free Route and Free Flight concepts are attractive, especially to airlines, we still must consider safety as the first priority, and design new algorithms and systems for these new airspaces (airspace above flight level 320).

The most well known reactive collision avoidance concept is certainly the ACAS/TCAS system. It is a very short term collision avoidance system (less than 60 seconds) and should only be looked upon as the last safety filter of an ATC system. Experiments with TCAS to control aircraft on simulated traffic have shown that poor coordination could leads to disastrous situations (Bosc 1997). Other simple techniques using repulsive forces (Zeghal 1998b; 1998a) have also been investigated but drawbacks remain (Bosc 1997).

This paper presents an algorithm for autonomous embarked (on board) conflict resolution with a coordination mechanism, called FACES (Free-flight Autonomous Coordinated Embarked Solver). Moreover, it is robust to communication or system failure for time up to one or two minutes. This algorithm could be implemented with current technology (GPS, FMS, ADS-B) at low cost.

Section deals with the hypothesis we made and the modelling chosen. Section presents the ordering strategy. In section , the A^* algorithm used to optimize a conflict free trajectory for one aircraft is detailed. In section , the basic algorithm is tested with the air traffic simulator CATS (Alliot *et al.* 1997) on a heavily loaded traffic day in the French airspace over flight level[1] 320. Experimental results led us to introduce slight improvements to the basic algorithm also presented in section ; then we finally discuss results of simulations on the enhanced algorithm.

Modelling

Hypothesis

The idea is to build an embarked - that is, an on-board - solver able to compute a manoeuvre each time a conflict is detected with another aircraft in a defined detection area around the aircraft. This solver should continuously (every minute[1]) guarantee a 5^3 minutes conflict free trajectory to each aircraft. This 5 minutes conflict free period guarantees that a transient failure of communications would not have a disastrous effect: the system could still restart later on; resolutions would be less optimal, more vertical manoeuvres could be necessary to solve all conflicts, as anticipation would be shorter, but the risk of collision would remain close to zero.

---

*Centre d'Etudes de la Navigation Aérienne

[†]Laboratoire d'Optimisation Globale

[1]Free flight Autonomous and Coordinated Embarked Solver

[2]flight level X or FL X stands for $X \times 100$ feet of altitude

---

[3]These parameters can be modified. This first study does not discuss the opportunity of increasing or decreasing these values.

Manoeuvres suggested have to be simple to understand and to execute. No manoeuvre can be given during the first minute (called the quiescent period) in order to give enough time to the solver to compute a solution and inform the pilot (or directly program the FMS). Moreover, only one manoeuvre can be given to one aircraft during a 5 minutes time window, and no manoeuvre can start as long as the previous one is not finished.

The algorithm enforces a global resolution order between conflicting aircraft. The general principle is as follows: the aircraft which is first chooses its trajectory without considering other aircraft. Then, the next aircraft in the priority queue takes this trajectory into account, and computes its own, and so on (see section).

Airspace over flight level[1] 320 is considered as a Free Flight airspace. This area is not a so low density area, especially in France. So it is an excellent test zone for a Free Flight solver. All aircraft entering this airspace are supposed to be separated for 5 minutes when entering the Free Flight zone, and are sent back separated for the next 5 minutes when leaving it. All aircraft entering this airspace have to be Free Flight compliant, i.e:

- they all have synchronous clock;

- they are able to receive all broadcast information from other aircraft which are within a 90 nmi zone around them (see part);

- they are all equipped with the FACES solver.

- they are able each minute at the same time to compute, and store their current position, their Free Flight airspace exit point and their predicted trajectory for the next 5 minutes.

- they are able to reliably broadcast the latter information as soon as it has been computed.

This information consists of 20 3D-points, one every 15 seconds (in fact, only 16 are needed, those beginning at $t = 1$ min). Extra information is added to the predicted position that indicates its accuracy (the uncertainty model is detailed in part). Of course, the more accurate the information, the more efficient detection and resolution. This prediction has to be *contractual*, i.e. as soon as an aircraft has broadcast these informations, it has to keep to this trajectory for the next 5 minutes as long as the solver does not give a manoeuvre. It must be noticed that on exceptional occasions, one aircraft can modify this trajectory, or aircraft not equipped for Free Flight can be accepted in the Free Flight zone. This can also take into account exceptional events such as the failure of one aircraft conflict solver. Theses aircraft will be given the highest priority number (see part) and all other aircraft will build their trajectory in order to avoid them. This should be a last resort as the algorithm might fail if two such aircraft are present at the same time in the same zone.

Manoeuvre modelling

As stated above, time is discretized into 15 seconds[4] time steps. As manoeuvres must remain simple to understand and execute, the turning point modelling is chosen in the horizontal plane (see figure 1). In this article, no manoeuvre is given in the vertical plane[5]. As shown on figure 1, a ma-

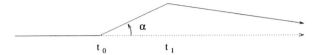

Figure 1: Turning point modelling.

noeuvre is a heading change of 10, 20 and 30 degrees right or left, it starts at time t_0, and ends at time t_1. As stated above, t_0 (and t_1) are always larger than 1 minute.

Uncertainty modelling and 1-to-1 conflict detection

A very simple filter is first applied: only aircraft within a 90 nmi zone are considered as being potential threats. This radius is such that 2 aircraft facing each other at 500 kn cannot be in conflict[6] during the next 5 minutes if they are not in the detection zone of the facing aircraft.

We then assume that there is an error about the aircraft's future location because of ground speed prediction uncertainties[7]. Uncertainties on climbing and descending rates are even more important[8]. Uncertainties on the future positions of aircraft are all the more important because the prediction is faraway.

In the vertical plane, we use a cylindrical modelling (figure 2). Each aircraft has a maximal altitude and a minimal altitude. To check if two aircraft are in conflict, the minimal altitude of the higher aircraft is compared to the maximal altitude of the lower aircraft.

In the horizontal plane, an aircraft is represented by a point at the initial time. The point becomes a line segment in the uncertainty direction (the speed direction here, see figure 2). The first point of the line "flies" at the maximum possible speed, and the last point at the minimum possible speed. When changing direction ($t = 4$), the segment becomes a parallelogram that increases in the speed direction. When changing a second time direction ($t = 7$), the parallelogram

---

[4]This value is not chosen at random. With 15 s time steps, detection can be made only on these points (and not on the segments between these points) with the guaranty that two aircraft can not cross each other without noticing a serious conflict.

[5]Vertical manoeuvres were put aside on purpose. They are more difficult to execute, and less comfortable for both pilots and passengers. Results of part show that they should only be used as a last resort, on the very rare occasions where the solver fails.

[6]In this article the separation standards are 6 nmi in the horizontal plane and 1000 ft in the vertical plane.

[7]Uncertainties on ground track will not be considered, as they do not increase with time and will be included in the separation standard.

[8]The error percentages on vertical and horizontal speed are specific to each aircraft. For example, aircraft with very accurate FMS will have very low percentages.

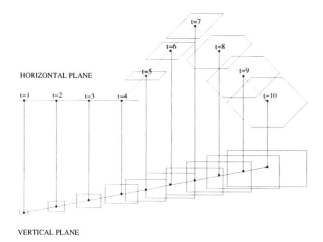

HORIZONTAL PLANE

VERTICAL PLANE

Figure 2: Modelling of speed uncertainties.

becomes a hexagon that increases in the new speed direction. To check the separation standard at time t, we compute the distance between the two polygons modelling the aircraft positions and compare it to the separation standard at each time step of the simulation. It must be noticed that, as only one manoeuvre can be given in a 5 minutes time window, and as no manoeuvre can start as long as the previous one is not finished, the convex can only be a line, a parallelogram or an hexagon.

A classical problem in 1 to 1 conflict detection is symmetry. If aircraft A considers it is in conflict with aircraft B, then B must consider A as a conflicting aircraft. In FACES, broadcasting of positions guarantees that two aircraft that can detect each other share exactly the same information regarding their positions. As detection algorithms are identical, 1 to 1 detection will always be symmetrical.

Ordering strategy

The coordination problem

Centralized automatic solvers as described by N. Durand(Durand 1996) find a global solution to clusters involving many aircraft. Manoeuvres are then given to aircraft simultaneously. An on board solver cannot be based on the same principle: aircraft do not share the same information, as they do not have the same detection zone (limited to 90nmi). A coordination problem appears and must be solved.

The Free-R (VU N. Duong 1997) project uses extended flight rules to solve this problem. The TCAS system uses the transponder code to decide which aircraft has to manoeuvre; giving resolution priorities to aircraft is a way often adopted for solving the coordination problem.

A resolution priority order[9] has to be total if we want each aircraft to solve all conflicts when there is more than 2 aircraft. For example, the Visual Flight Rule that gives priority to the aircraft coming from the right does not define a global

---

[9]An order relation must be anti-symmetrical and transitive. An order relation is total if every pair of individuals can be compared.

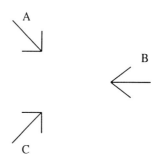

Figure 3: 3 aircraft conflict.

order if there are more than 2 aircraft simultaneously in conflict. Figure 3 gives an example of conflict involving 3 aircraft for which this priority resolution rule does not define an order because transitivity is not ensured.

Moreover, as aircraft do not share the same information, defining which aircraft will be the first to choose its trajectory is not obvious, even if we have a total priority order.

Building a global resolution order

A token allocation strategy We have to define a global resolution order such as each aircraft can know when it can start to build a conflict free trajectory and which aircraft it has to avoid.

We first suppose that a total priority order relation exists on the aircraft population. We can use the simple order based on transponder numbers discussed above (but more elaborated orders will be discussed in part). At each resolution step, we build a global resolution order from this priority order with the following strategy:

1. First, every aircraft sends its predicted trajectory to its neighbours. Each aircraft is then able to know wether it is conflicting with another aircraft or not for the next five minutes.

2. Each aircraft receives a token from every conflicting aircraft which has a higher priority in its detection zone. Aircraft that are not in conflict never receive any token.

3. Then, each conflicting aircraft with no token solves conflicts with every aircraft in its detection zone that has no token (at the first iteration step, they will just go straight). It does not take into account aircraft that have one or more tokens.

4. When this trajectory has been computed, the aircraft broadcasts its new trajectory; all aircraft which have received a token from this aircraft take this new trajectory into account, and cancel the token received from this aircraft.

5. Steps 3 and 4 are repeated until no token remains.

Detailed example The following example has been observed in the simulations presented in part . 8 aircraft belong to the same cluster (figure 4). The detection area of each aircraft is given on the figure.

Aircraft $A7$ detects every other aircraft. $A8$ detects $A5$, $A6$ and $A7$. $A4$ detects $A1$, $A2$ and $A7$. $A6$ detects $A2$, $A3$,

Step	1	2	3	4	5	6
A7	6	4	3	1	0	
A8	4	3	3	2	1	0
A4	2	1	0			
A6	2	2	1	0		
A2	1	0				
A3	1	1	0			
A1	0					
A5	0					

Table 1: Token allocation at the different steps of resolution

$A7$ and $A8$. $A2$ detects $A1$, $A3$, $A4$, $A6$ and $A7$. $A3$ detects $A2$, $A6$ and $A7$. $A1$ detects $A2$, $A4$ and $A7$. $A5$ detects $A7$ and $A8$. Conflicting aircraft are $A1-A2$, $A1-A4$, $A2-A3$, $A2-A7$, $A3-A6$, $A5-A7$ and $A5-A8$. Aircraft that has the highest priority is $A1$ and the lowest priority order is $A8$ ($A1 > A2 > A3 > A4 > A5 > A6 > A7 > A8$).

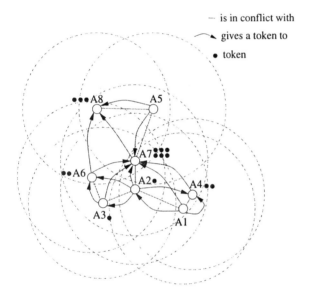

— is in conflict with

⌐ gives a token to

• token

Figure 4: Cluster of aircraft in conflict

Tokens are allocated as presented on figure 4.

Table 1 gives the token allocation at the different steps of the resolution.

During step 1, $A1$ and $A5$ (0 token) choose their trajectories without considering other aircraft in their detection area (which have at least 1 token). Then, they broadcast their unmodified trajectories and all aircraft that have received a token from them cancel it. $A2$, $A4$ and $A7$ cancel the tokens sent by $A1$, $A7$ and $A8$ cancel the tokens sent by $A5$. During step 2, $A2$ (0 token) has no token and modifies its trajectory to solve conflict with $A1$ (0 token). $A3$, $A4$, $A6$, and $A7$ cancel the tokens sent by $A2$. During step 3, $A3$ (0 token) modifies its trajectory to solve conflict with $A2$ (0 token), $A4$ (0 token) modifies its trajectory to solve conflict with $A1$ (0 token) ;the new trajectory must not interfere with $A2$ (0 token). $A6$ cancels one token sent by $A3$ and $A7$ cancels

two tokens sent by $A3$ and $A4$. During step 4, $A6$ (0 token) modifies its trajectory to solve conflict with $A3$ (0 token), the new trajectory must not interfere with $A2$ (0 token). $A7$ and $A8$ cancel one token sent by $A6$. During step 5, $A7$ (0 token) modifies its trajectory to solve conflict with $A2$ (0 token) and $A5$ (0 token); the new trajectory must not interfere with $A1$ (0 token), $A3$ (0 token), $A4$ (0 token) and $A6$ (0 token). $A8$ cancels the token sent by $A7$. 1. During step 6, $A8$ (0 token) modifies its trajectory to solve conflict with $A5$ (0 token); the new trajectory must not interfere with $A6$ (0 token) and $A7$ (0 token).

Provability

The allocation-resolution method described above cannot lead to situations where all aircraft would have at least one token or situations where two aircraft detecting each other without any token would have to solve simultaneously. This is guaranteed by the use of a total priority order on aircraft. At each step, an aircraft with no token cannot have any other conflicting aircraft (that has not already solved) with no token in its detection area. In such a case, one of these two aircraft would have given a token to the other. At each step, among the conflicting aircraft that have not already solved, there is one that has the highest priority. This aircraft cannot have any token. It can solve and get back its tokens. The algorithm can be mathematically proved.

The A^* algorithm

As soon as the resolution order is chosen, the problem is to solve a 1 to n conflict problem: we have to find the minimum length trajectory for an aircraft avoiding n already fixed aircraft trajectories, that can be considered as obstacles. This is a classical robotics problem, therefore a classical A^* algorithm (see (Pearl 1984)) is used.

In the present application, the initial state is the state of the solving aircraft at $t = 1$ minute. The terminal states are the possible states of the solving aircraft after 5 minutes of flight or when they have reached their destination.

Each branch of the tree represents a possible trajectory of the solving aircraft. Fortunately, the heuristic function is used to only develop a small part of the tree.

The cost of a path is the trajectory length described by this path. Before starting a manoeuvre, an aircraft is in S_0 state. At each time step, each S_0 state generates 6 S_1 states corresponding to the 6 possible deviations of the trajectory (10, 20, 30 degrees right or left), and 1 S_0 state (the aircraft is not manoeuvred). At each time step, each S_1 state generates one S_1 state (the manoeuvre is extended) and one S_2 state (the aircraft is sent back to its Free Flight zone exit point). Every state generates a terminal S_3 state after 5 minutes or if the aircraft has reached its destination.

The cost function $k(u, v)$ measures the distance between the position of the aircraft at node u (time step t_{t_u}, state S_{s_u}) and the position of the aircraft at node v (time step t_{l_v}, state S_{s_v}). If a conflict occurs between node u and node v, the value $k(u, v)$ is widely increased so that the corresponding branch is no longer developed.

The heuristic function $h(u)$ is here the direct distance between node u and the Free Flight exit point (destination) of the solving aircraft. This heuristic is clearly an underestimating one, which guarantees that the optimal solution will always be found.

Generally, many different paths are developed and the depth of the tree is 16 (4 minutes). In this applications, the solution is given in less than 5 seconds on a Pentium II 300, even for the biggest 1-to-35 conflict.

Experimental results and improvements

The CATS simulator

The algorithm described in part and was tested on the CATS (Alliot *et al.* 1997) simulator. The core of the CATS system is an En-route traffic simulation engine. It is based on a discrete, fixed time slice execution model: the position and speed of aircraft are computed at fixed time steps, usually every 5, 10 or 15 seconds.

Aircraft performances are in tabulated form describing ground speed, vertical speed, and fuel burn as a function of altitude, aircraft type and flight segment (cruise, climb or descent.)

In the further applications, aircraft use direct routes to their destination. The separation standard used is 6 nautical miles in the horizontal plane and 1000 ft vertically [10]. Conflicts were not solved under flight level 320, and a delay t_e was added when necessary for aircraft entering the Free Flight zone in order to separate them on entry points. Uncertainties on speed (either vertical or horizontal) were set to minimal values.

Results

Results presented in this part are obtained with the 6381 flight plans of the 21st of June 1996 with no regulation. The Free Flight zone defined is the airspace above flight level 320. The allocation-resolution strategy described in part is repeated every minute and the trajectory prediction is done on the next 5 minutes.

It was found that 2763 aircraft enter the Free Flight zone. 641 conflicts are detected in this zone during the day.

As described in section , the algorithm requires the definition of a total order among aircraft.

The following order is used: an aircraft that is manoeuvre free has a lower priority order than an aircraft that has already started a manoeuvre. The CAUTRA number is used to compare two manoeuvre free aircraft or two manoeuvred aircraft. A maneuver efficiency criteria is also added to the cost criteria in order to prevent aircraft from postponing a crossing maneuver when necessary. Therefore, when two aircraft must cross, the manoeuvre that enforces crossing must have a lower cost than the manoeuvre that postpones the crossing. This new criteria is included in the A^* algorithm.

With this new priority order, the A^* algorithm is called 2654 times. At the end of the simulation, 3 conflicts remain

[10]The 6 nmi value is certainly quite high for an on-board solver. We do think that it could seriously be reduced, regarding GPS and FMS precision. This would even improve airspace capacity and resolution efficiency.

unsolved, but they can easily be solved by a very simple vertical manoeuvre.

Delays

There were 897 manoeuvres given during the day to 367 aircraft (2.44 manoeuvre per aircraft). 13.28% of the aircraft flying in the Free Flight zone are manoeuvred.

73 aircraft are delayed when entering the Free Flight zone, because they are not conflict-free at that moment (that is 2.64% of the traffic in the Free Flight zone).

Delays are given in table 2.

Delay	Mean per aircraft	Mean per delayed acft	Max
while entering	$2s$	$1mn14s$	$3mn$
inside (man)	$3,6s$	$27,4s$	$40s$

Table 2: Delays

The maximum manoeuvre lasts 2 : 30 minutes.

Table 3 gives the number of steps aircraft have to wait because they have been given tokens. In the most complex conflict, one aircraft has to wait for 7 resolutions before it can choose its trajectory.

Number of steps	Waiting aircraft	percentage / Total
1	1516	$76,6\%$
2	253	$12,78\%$
3	162	$8,19\%$
4	27	$1,36\%$
5	17	$0,86\%$
6	3	$0,16\%$
7	1	$0,05\%$

Table 3: Number of waiting aircraft.

So, regarding delays, the performance of the algorithm is very good.

Unsolved conflicts and priority order

There are 3 aircraft in each remaining unsolved conflicts. These conflicts appear because the order between aircraft is not well chosen.

Moreover, it looks extremely difficult to devise an algorithm that would find the best possible order without seriously increasing the complexity of the global algorithm and the necessary capacity of the communication medium. On-board conflict solvers which have only a partial information on the global situation will almost certainly remain suboptimal, while centralized conflict solvers are able to find the global optimal solutions. However, this may not be a too serious concern in the upper airspace: the simulation above shows that this algorithm is almost always able to solve conflicts, even with situations as complex as the one presented on on figure 5 where 35 aircraft are involved, while delays remain small.

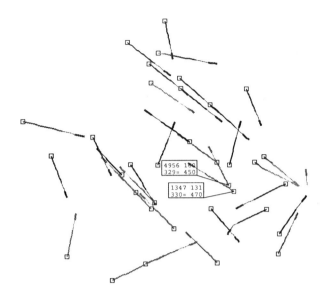

Figure 5: 35 aircraft in the detection zone.

Conclusion

We have demonstrated in this article that an efficient on board algorithm for Free Flight conflict resolution can be designed and implemented. This algorithm has the following advantages:

- Compared to a centralized automated system, the development of such a system could be relatively low cost. Most hypothesis are quite weak: synchronous clocks are already available with GPS, FMS are now elaborate enough to provide the information needed for trajectory prediction in the next 5 minutes, provides sufficient capacity for communications; the 1 to n resolution algorithm is simple to implement and has already been widely used for similar problems in robotics; computing power needed fits in a standard PC computer.

- Compared to rule based system, the algorithm is mathematically provable, and the simulation above shows that it would be efficient in upper airspace, even when density is quite high

- Compared to purely reactive systems (Zeghal 1998b), which usually requires permanent changes in headings, the manoeuvre model is classical and easy to implement. Further, and this is the main point to stress, as trajectories are guaranteed conflict free for at least 5 minutes, a transient failure of communications would not have a disastrous effect: the system could still restart later on; resolutions would be less optimal, more vertical manoeuvres could be necessary to solve all conflicts, as anticipation would be shorter, but the risk of collision would remain insignificant.

- The system could be progressively put into service by first defining Free Flight airspace over oceanic areas, and gradually extending them. This would help solving the classical transition problem from the current system to a partially automated one.

We are aware that the whole system depends on the fiability and availability of transmissions. Requirements on the bandwidth are low enough to enable multiple emissions of messages. But error correlations would have to be considered. We miss informations and results on these issues. However, we believe that an airborne implementation of this algorithm can be seriously considered.

References

Alliot, J.; Durand, N.; Bosc, J.; and Maugis, L. 1997. Cats: a complete air traffic simulator. *16th AIAA/IEEE Digital Avionics Systems Conference, IRVINE.*

Bosc, J.-F. 1997. *Techniques d'évitement réactif et simulation du trafic aérien.* Ph.D. Dissertation, Ecole Nationale de L'aviation civile.

Durand, N. 1996. *Optimisation de Trajectoires pour la Résolution de Conflits en Route.* Ph.D. Dissertation, ENSEEIHT, Institut National Polytechnique de Toulouse.

Granger, G.; Durand, N.; and Alliot, J. 1998. FACES: a Free flight Autonomous and Coordinated Embarked Solver. In *2 ST U.S.A/EUROPE ATM R & D Seminar.*

Pearl, J. 1984. *Heuristics.* Addison-Wesley.

VU N. Duong, Eric Hoffman, J.-P. N. 1997. Autonomous aircraft. *1st U.S.A. / EUROPE Air Traffic Management R&D Seminar, SACLAY.*

Zeghal, K. 1998a. A comparison of different approaches based on force fields for coordination among multiple mobiles. In *IEEE International Conference on Intelligent Robotic System (IROS).*

Zeghal, K. 1998b. A review of different approaches based on force fields for airborne conflict resolution. *AIAA Guidance, Navigation and Control Conference.*

Collaborative Kodama Agents with Automated Learning and Adapting for Personalized Web Searching

Tarek Helmy   Satoshi Amamiya   Makoto Amamiya

Department of Intelligent Systems

Graduate School of Information Science and Electrical Engineering

Kyushu University

6-1 Kasugakoen, Kasuga-shi

Fukuoka 816-8580, Japan

E-mail: [helmy,roger,amamiya]@al.is.kyushu-u.ac.jp   & Fax: 81-92-583-1338

Abstract

The primary application domain of Kodama[1] is the World Wide Web and its purpose in this application is to assist users to find desired information. Three different categories of Kodama's agents are introduced here, Web Page Agents (WPA), Server Agents (SA), and User Interface Agents (UIA). Kodama agents learn and adapt to the User's Preferences (UP), which may change over time. At the same time, they explore these preferences to get any relevancy with the future queries. The main trust of Kodama research project is an investigation into novel ways of agentifying the Web based on the pre-existing hyper-link structure. These communities of Kodama agents automatically achieve and update their Interpretation Policies (IP) & UP and cooperate with other agents to retrieve distributed relevant information on the Web. We focus in this paper on the implementation and the evaluation on the adaptability of Kodama agents with the UP. This paper proposes a new method for learning the UP directly from user's interaction with the system and adapting the preferences with user's responses over the time. The user's feedback is used by the Kodama to support a credit adaptation mechanism to the IP of the WPA that is responsible for this URL and to adapt the weight and the query fields in user's query history and bookmark files. In terms of adaptation speed, the proposed methods make Kodama system acts as a PinPoint information retrieval system, converges to the user's interests and adapts to the sudden change of user's interests over time.

Introduction

The number of information sources available to the Internet user has become extremely large. This information is loosely held together by annotated connections, called hyperlinks [Kleinberg, 1999], [Chakrabarti et al., 1998]. This information abundance makes increasing the complexity of locating relevant information. The model behind Traditional Search Engines (TSE) analyzes collected documents once to produce indices, and then amortizes the cost of such processing over a large number of queries, which access the same index. This model assumes that the environment is static. The Web is however highly dynamic, with new documents being added, deleted, changed, and moved all the time [Menczer and Monge, 1999]. At any given time an index of the TSE will be somewhat inaccurate (e.g., containing stale information about recently deleted or moved documents) and somewhat incomplete (e.g., missing information about recently added or changed documents). Also users normally face with very large hit lists with low precision. Moreover, the information gathering and retrieving processes in TSE are independent of user's preference, and therefore feedback from the later process is hardly adaptive to improve the quality of the former process. These factors make it necessary to investigate new techniques to address such problems. Intelligent agents may be the way to improve search and retrieval process as active personal assistants. The combination of the search engine, the agent, the UP algorithm, and the Information Retrieval (IR) algorithm addresses the trust and competence issues of agents.

Researchers in Artificial Intelligence (AI) and IR fields have already succeeded in developing agent-based techniques to automate tedious tasks and to facilitate the management of information flooding [Pann and Sycara, 1996], [Chen and Sycara, 1998], [Edmund et al., 2000]. A way to partially address the scalability problems posted by the size and dynamic nature of the Web is to decentralize the index-building process. Dividing the task into localized SAs that agentify specific domains by a set of WPAs developed in this project. The success of this project has been achieved by the cooperation among the WPAs [Helmy et al., 2000a], [Helmy et al., 1999b], [Helmy et al., 1999c]. The approach is based on a distributed, adaptive and on-line agent population negotiating and making local decisions for retrieving the most relevant information to the user's query.

In this paper we will start by describing the architecture and the communication of Kodama agents. Next, we describe the mechanism of agentifying a Web site. We then discuss our new methodologies of calculating the relevancy of retrieved Web page contents to the UP, which is used in UIA and WPA. We focus on the

---

[1] Kyushu university Open Distributed Autonomous Multi-Agent

implementation and evaluation on the adaptability of Kodama agents with the UP. We also describe the learning techniques used in WPA and UIA. Finally we present the experimental results and future work of Kodama system.

Kodama Architecture and Communication

Figure 1 illustrates the architecture of Kodama agent. Each agent draws upon a sophisticated reasoning architecture that consists of different reusable modules. We divided an agent into a kernel unit and an application oriented unit. The former unit contains standard modules, data structures, and methods for communications, message interpretations, coordination and learning provided by Kodama, and the latter is defined by a designer and contains inter-agent specific communications, interpretations and processes. Kodama framework is being used to develop distributed collections of intelligent agents that cooperate asynchronously to perform goal-directed information retrieval and integration. Kodama system allows agents to find each other by providing a mechanism for registering each agent's capabilities. Each agent must be able to interpret the input message sent to it from other agents if the performative field of the message requests the agent to do it. If an agent is unable to interpret some input, it consults its down-chain agents. The software designer has been responsible for providing each agent with its IP so far [Hodjat and Amamiya, 2000]. In Kodama this is done automatically by the WPA itself. Kodama agent actuates other modules based on the messages received from other agents. Each message is comprised of a message content, and a performative that specifies what should be done with that content.

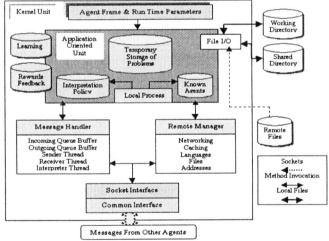

Figure 1. KODAMA Agent Architecture

Communication

From the viewpoints of Kodama system, the communication cost is one of the most important performance factors. Agents will register themselves and their abilities to one another at the beginning of or during

the execution. Therefore, one of the major features of Kodama is that, agents can be added to or removed from the application at runtime. Each agent, upon receiving input with an "Is-This-Yours?" performative, attempts to interpret the input by itself. If the interpretation is successfully done, the agent will report success using the "It-Is-Mine" performative with a confidence factor that reflects the similarity between the input query and its Web page contents. On the other hand, if the agent can not interpret the query as its own, before reporting failure, the agent checks with its down-chain agents. If all down-chain agents report "Not-Mine," this agent will also report "Not-Mine" to its requesting agent. If at least one down-chain agent is able to interpret the input successfully and reports back with "It-Is-Mine," this agent will also report success. Agents receiving a "This-Is-Yours" request may reinterpret the delegated input query, or they may use pre-stored interpretation of it.

Register	Agents make each other aware of their existence.
This-Is-Yours	An agent announces another agent as responsible for handling certain input.
Is-This-Yours?	An agent that can not interpret a particular input requests interpretation from down-chain agents.
Not-Mine	Down-chain agent has failed to interpret input sent down with an *Is-This-Yours?* Performative, "confidence zero".
It-Is-Mine	Down-chain agent has been successful in interpreting input sent down with an Is-This-Yours? Performative.
Learn	A new interpretation policy is suggested to an agent or an agent is asked to modify the weight of an existing one.

Table 1. Kodama Inter-Agent Performative Messages

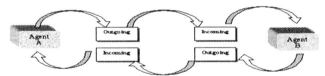

Figure 2. Message Passing and Queuing in Kodama

Kodama is a concurrent system in the architecture level and in the implementation level. Each agent has a message queue and looks it while communicating with its down-chain agents (Figure 2). Kodama agents communicate through message passing using predefined general performatives (Table 1). Agents distributed over a collection of hosts must send problem parameters and results to other agents. Among distributed agents on a network, the information is typically communicated with explicit message-passing calls. Kodama agent passes a communication message with its down-chain agents using the best-first technique.

Web Site Agentification

Cooperating intelligent Kodama agents are employed to agentify the Web where the hyper structure is preexisting in the form of Web links (Figure 3) [William et. al., 2000]. Our system uses three types of Kodama agents in the agentification mechanism (Figure 4) for searching the Web. A Server Agent (SA) assigned to each Web server, a Web Page Agent (WPA) assigned to each Web page, and a User Interface Agent (UIA) assigned to each user [Helmy et al., 2000a]. There is a clear mapping between the problem of searching the Web in Kodama system and the classic AI search paradigm. Each WPA of the agentified Web pages is a node, and the hypertext links to the other down chain WPAs are the edges of the graph to be searched. In typical AI domains a good heuristic will rate nodes higher as we progress towards some goal node [Youngblood, 1999]. In the Kodama system domain, the heuristic models how a page is relevant to the given query.

Figure 3. A Schematic view of Linked Web Pages

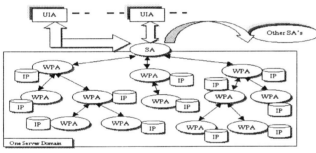

Figure 4. The Hierarchical of an Agentified Domain

A best-first search algorithm is used by the SA and the WPAs while interacting with the down chain agents. It has been slightly modified so that it will finish after reaching a predefined depth value, and return the best WPAs, which have a good relevancy to the given query.

Server Agent

A SA is assigned to one Web server to be responsible. The SA starts from the portal address of the Web server and creates the hyper structure of WPAs based on the hyper link structure in the Web server. The SA knows all WPAs in the server and works as a gateway when a WPA communicates with each other or with one in another server. The SA initiates all WPAs in its server when it starts searching relevant information to the user's query.

Web Page Agent

At the initialization phase, each WPA analyzes the content of its Web page. Each WPA starts with the base address when the WPA has got it from the SA with a serial ID number. Each WPA has its own parser, to which the WPA passes a URL, and a private Interpretation Policy (IP), in which the WPA keeps all the policy keywords, found in its URL. All URLs found in its page are passed to the shared static data member, from it all other down-chain WPAs take their next URLs. Every time a WPA finishes, it registers itself to the SA and writes all the words into an IP. The WPA takes essential properties and principles by the SA to create the IP as an ontology that represents the context of the Web page as follows. The WPA sets the URL of that Web page as its name, loads the HTML document of that Web page, parses the HTML document, and extracts links, images, text, headers, applets, and title. Then the WPA eliminates the noisy words (non-informative words), stemming a plural noun to its single form and inflexed verb to its infinitive form. After that, the WPA creates its IP using an additional heuristics, in which additional weights are given to words in the title and headings of the Web page. Then, the created WPAs are registered to SA. WPA uses its IP in order to calculate the similarity between the user's query and its page. At the retrieval phase, WPAs, when received a user's query from SA initiate search by interpreting the query and/or either asking 'Is this yours?' or announcing 'This is yours,' to its down-chain WPAs. The selected WPAs and/or their down-chain WPAs of each Web server, in turn, interpret the query according to their IPs and reply the answer 'This is mine' with some confidence or 'Not mine' (0 confidence).

User Interface Agent

An UIA is implemented as a browser independent Java application. Monitoring the user-browsing behavior is accomplished via a proxy server that allows the UIA to inspect HTTP requests from its browser. Each UIA resides in the user's machine and communicates with WPAs via an SA to retrieve information relevant to the user's query, and shows the results returned by the WPAs to the user after filtering and re-ranking them. It receives user's responses of his/her interest (or not interest) to the results and regards them as rewards to the results. The UIAs in Kodama system look over the shoulders of the users, record every action into the query history file. After enough data has been accumulated, the system uses this data to predict a user's action based on the similarity of the current query to already encountered data.

Relevancy Algorithm with User's Query History and Bookmark Files (UP) by UIA

Recording and analyzing user's accessing history and bookmark by the UIA are quite important to catch his/her preferences. The query history file, contains information about previously visited pages for specific queries, and the bookmark file, contains a user's hot-list of Web links, will be scanned by the UIA at first to find relevant answers to the given query. A query history file (Figure 5) records the URL that a user selected, the number of occurrences that this URL is visited, both time of visiting and leaving, and the query. The bookmark file (Figure 6) records the URL, the number of occurrences that this URL is visited, bookmaking time of the URL, and its title. The query and the title fields in query history and bookmark files are represented as a vector of keywords sorted in alphabetical order, a weight value is assigned to each keyword to reflect the correlation between the keyword and the URL and is modified according to the User's Responses ($\Re$).

URL	No. of Visiting	Time of Visiting	Time of Leaving	Query		
URL$_1$	N$_1$	T$_{I1}$	T$_{O1}$	k$_{11}$,w$_{11}$	...	k$_{1m}$,w$_{1m}$
...	...	...	...	...	...	
URL$_x$	N$_x$	T$_{Ix}$	T$_{Ox}$	k$_{x1}$,w$_{x1}$	...	k$_{xm}$,w$_{xm}$
URL$_n$	N$_n$	T$_{In}$	T$_{On}$	k$_{n1}$,w$_{n1}$	...	k$_{nm}$,w$_{nm}$

Figure 5. User's Query History File Representation

URL	No. of Visiting	Time of Bookmaking	Title		
URL$_1$	N$_1$	T$_1$	k$_{11}$,w$_{11}$	...	k$_{1m}$,w$_{1m}$
...		...	...	...	
URL$_x$	N$_x$	T$_x$	k$_{x1}$,w$_{x1}$	...	k$_{xm}$,w$_{xm}$
URL$_n$	N$_n$	T$_n$	k$_{n1}$,w$_{n1}$	...	k$_{nm}$,w$_{nm}$

Figure 6. User's Bookmark File Representation

User's Responses ($\Re$) are *Useless, Not very useful, Mildly interesting, Neutral, Interesting and Bookmark*. Each of these responses has a value between 0 and 1. When looking up relevant URL from the UP, the UIA calculates similarities as follows:

First: We define equations to calculate the similarity between a user's query and his/her query history file. Assume we have a query history file or a bookmark file of n URL lines gathered. $Q_{in} = <k_1, k_2, \cdots, k_n>$ stands for a vector of keywords sorted in alphabetical order, of the query given by the user. $Q_j = <K_{j,1}^h, K_{j,2}^h, ..., K_{j,m}^h>$, ($1 \le j \le n$) stands for the vector, sorted in alphabetical order, of the query of j th line in the user's query history file, where $K_{j,i}^h = k_{j,i}^h \cdot w_{j,i}^h$, $k_{j,i}^h$ is the i th keyword in the j line and $0 \le w_{j,i}^h \le 1$ is its weight.

Similarly, $T_j = <K_{j,1}^b, K_{j,2}^b, ..., K_{j,l}^b>$ and $K_{j,i}^b = k_{j,i}^b \cdot w_{j,i}^b$ are defined for the title of j th line in the user's bookmark file. The weight $w_{j,i}^h$ and $w_{j,i}^b$ are incrementally computed with the number t_j of visiting to URL_j.

$$w_{j,i}(t_j + 1) = \rho \cdot w_{j,i}(t_j) + (1 - \rho) \cdot \Re \quad (1)$$

Where $w_{j,i}$ means $w_{j,i}^h$ or $w_{j,i}^b$, and $0 \le \Re \le 1$ is a user's response described above. Initial value $w_{j,i}(1)$ is set by the user's first response. $0 < \rho \le 1$ is a weight of how much the user's response history should be accumulated. Notice that $w_{j,i}$ means the accumulated user's preference of keyword in the j th line. ρ is a function of t_j, i.e.,

$\rho(t_j)$, and $\rho(t_j)$ depends on how long user's response history upon the keyword will be involved in calculating and adapting the next weight $w_{j,i}(t_j + 1)$.

For instances $\rho(t_j) = 1/2$ has the effect of weighting $(1/2)^t$ to the t times past response. $\rho = \frac{t_j}{t_j + 1}$ means to keep track of all the user's history, and $\rho = 0$ means to discard the user's history while calculating the weight value. The value of ρ reflects how much the system trusts the user's current response. One way to automate this heuristic is to calculate for instance the variance of user's past responses ($\Re$) and predicts the value of ρ.

Now, we calculate the similarity s_j^h between Q_{in} and the query field of j th line of the user's query history file, and similarity s_j^b between Q_{in} and the title field of j th line of the user's bookmark file.

$$S_j^h = \sum_i w_{j,i} \cdot g(k_i) \quad (2)$$

$$S_j^b = \sum_i w_{j,i} \cdot g'(k_i) \quad (3)$$

Where, $g(k_i) = 1$ if $k_i \in Q_{in} \cap Q_j$, otherwise $g(k_i) = 0$, and $g'(k_i) = 1$ if $k_i \in Q_{in} \cap T_j$, otherwise $g'(k_i) = 0$. Also, we calculate the similarity S_j^{url} between Q_{in} and the URL of j th line.

$$S_j^{url} = \frac{s_{url}}{c_{in} + d_j - s_{url}} \quad (4).$$

Where, $c_{in} = |Q_{in}|$, $s_{url} = |Q_{in} \cap URL_j|$, $d_j = |URL_j|$, and URL_j stands for the set of words in the URL of j th line. Then, the total similarity between user's query and his/her query history file is calculated by using equation (5), with a heuristic-weighting factor $0 \le \alpha \le 1$.

$$\arg \max_j \left(\alpha \cdot S_j^{url} + (1 - \alpha) \cdot S_j^h \right) \quad (5)$$

Second: By the same way as the *first* step, we calculate the total similarity between the user's query and his/her bookmark file, using a heuristic-weighting factor $0 \le \beta \le 1$:

$$\arg \max_j \left(\beta \cdot S_j^{url} + (1 - \beta) \cdot S_j^b \right) \quad (6)$$

IP Representation and Relevancy by WPA

An IP is used by the WPA to decide whether or not the keywords in the query belong to the WPA. The IP is a vector of important terms, which is extracted and weighted by analyzing the contents of the Web page. Since the terms are not all equally important for content representation of IP vector of each WPA, an importance factor (λ) is assigned to each term and decided by the kind of HTML tag, in which the term is included in the Web page. This means that WPA will emphasize/de-emphasize some keywords based on the value of λ. The WPA calculates the weight of the term and constructs its IP vector from the number of appearance (*tf*) and the kind of tag, which includes the term within the Web page (e.g., in title, in header, in link, is bold, underline, italic, keyword or normal), using equation (7).

$$w_{ik} = \lambda_k \cdot tf_{ik} \qquad (7)$$

Where w_{ik} stands for the weight of term i in position k, and tf_{ik} stands for the number of occurrences that term i appears in position k specified by HTML tags. λ_k stands for the weight decided by the kind of HTML tag_k that includes the term i in the Web page. The total weight of a term i in the IP is the sum of all the weights in the HTML document of the Web page and is calculated by:

$$w_i = \sum_{k=1}^{n} w_{ik} \qquad (8)$$

Where n is the number of HTML tags within the Web page. The WPA_i calculates the confidence factor that reflects the relevancy between the input query vector Q_{in} and its IP vector using equation (9).

$$Sim(Q_{in}, IP) = \frac{\sum_{i=1}^{n} h(k_i) \cdot w_i}{\sqrt{\sum_{i=1}^{n} h(k_i)^2} \cdot \sqrt{\sum_{i=1}^{n} w_i^2}} \qquad (9)$$

Where, $h(k_i) = 1$ if $k_i \in Q_{in} \wedge k_i \in IP$, otherwise $h(k_i) = 0$.

Query and URL Similarity

The WPAs calculate the similarity between the user's query and their documents based on the terms they have in both of the IPs and the hyperlink structures of the WPAs. This similarity function is based on both query-IP and query-URL similarities. It is a hybrid similarity function that includes two components. The S_{ij}^{Q-link} component measures the similarity between the user's query i and the URL of a Web page j and is calculated using equation (4). The S_{ij}^{Q-IP} component measures the similarity between the user's query i and the IP of a WPA of Web page j and is calculated using equation (9). The whole similarity is calculated using equation (10) and $0 \le \partial \le 1$.

$$S_{ij}^{Total} = (\partial \cdot S_{ij}^{Q-Link} + (1-\partial)S_{ij}^{Q-IP}). \qquad (10)$$

Exploiting User's Preferences by UIA

The UIA takes care of the user's interests and preferences to assist of finding relevant Web pages his/her query. The user can provide positive or negative feedback to the retrieved document. In contrast to other systems that learn a UP and use it to determine relevant documents [Pann and Sycara, 1996], [Chen and Sycara, 1998], Kodama's UPs are continuously evolving according to the dynamically changing user's preferences. The followings are the UIA's job stream (Figure 7):

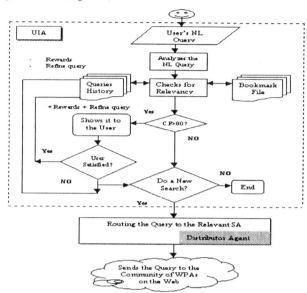

Figure 7. A Schematic Diagram of UIA's Behaviors

(1) The user starts by sending a Natural Language (NL) query to the UIA.

(2) UIA analyzes the NL query using a simple NL algorithm, and transforms it to Q_{in}.

(3) UIA calculates the similarity with the method described above and looks for relevant URLs in UP by using equations (5) and (6).

(4) If UIA finds relevant URLs then shows them and asks the user whether the user is satisfied or wants to search the Web.

(5) If UIA could not find in its UP files any URLs relevant to Q_{in} then UIA routes Q_{in} to a relevant SA, which in turn forwards it to its community of WPAs.

(6) The UIA receives the search results returned by the WPAs via the SA. The results consist of a set of contents of Web pages.

(7) The UIA takes a set of queries, whose similarity to Q_{in} is over the predefined threshold value, from the UP to expand Q_{in}. Then, the UIA makes a vector from them and Q_{in} to be used in the filtration process.

(8) The user explicitly marks the relevant documents using UIA's feedback. This response is stored in the response field of the UP.

The most relevant SA to the user's query selected either by having the user explicitly define the SA as a specific portal or by having the system determines by itself by examining the user's bookmark, query history and SA's attributes.

Learning and Adaptation in KODAMA

Because we are automatically creating the IP of each WPA based on the contents of its corresponding Web page and creating the UP based on the user's preferences, it is necessary to improve the IP and UP dynamically. There are several approaches that can be used to learn a UP [Budzik and Hammond, 1999], [Joachims *et al.*, 1997]. In Kodama a WPA interacts with the UIA as following (Figure 8). The UIA sends the Q_{in} to WPAs through the SA. The WPAs choose an action to perform based on Q_{in} and send the results back to the SA, which in turn forwards the results to the UIA. The UIA presents the results to the user. The user can click on those URLs and the UIA opens its browser to that specific URL. The user can check and evaluate this URL's contents and sends feedback through UIA's menu.

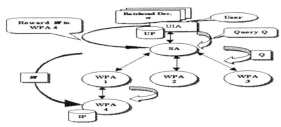

Figure 8. Interaction between WPA & UIA

Adaptation in WPA

The WPA allows only relatively small change of the term's weight based on the user's response, because adding/removing some terms into/from the IP may change the context of the Web page. When the user says the page is interesting, WPA changes the weight of the terms in its IP, if and only if these terms appear in Q_{in}, in order to make better match with the query to be entered next time. This means that, WPA will emphasize/de-emphasize some terms, frequently, reflecting the user's responses. If the user's query is $Q_{in}=\{q_1, q_2,.., q_n\}$, then the WPA checks if $q_i \in IP$ then changes its weight w_i by adding a reward's value $\Re_i$ to be $w_i + \Re_i$, else ignores it.

Adaptation in UIA

The UIA picks a number of keywords from the title and the headers of the selected document K_s in addition to the keywords of Q_{in} and creates a new list of keywords for the feedback K_f. Where, $K_f = Q_{in} \cap K_s$. According to $\Re$, the UIA will do the followings on the UP files:

♦ Modify the weight of the keyword using equation (1).

♦ Modify the number of visiting.

♦ If one of the keywords does not exist in the query field then adds it with an initial weight reflecting the user's response.

♦ Refine the contents of the UP files by deleting the keywords that have weights less than a predefined threshold value.

♦ If the selected URL does not exist in the UP then adds a new record and initializes its query field.

This process iterates until the user's is satisfied with the retrieved information. By this way, the UP will evolve over time to reflect the user's interests. Also, the keywords of the query and title fields continually moved closer to or away from their URLs.

Experimental Results

We have performed several experiments to make a consistent evaluation of Kodama system performance. The results we have obtained for users, who used the system from 10_{th} of October until 25_{th} of December, verify the facts that Kodama can learn and adapt to the UP over time. Also, the idea of Web page agentification promises to achieve more relevant information to the user.

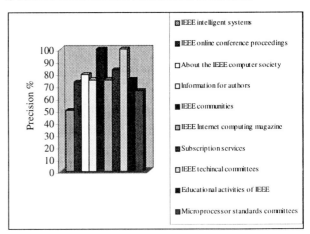

Figure 9 Precision of the Retrieved URLs to the User's Queries to the IEEE Agentified domain

In the first experiments, we attempted to verify that the mechanism of agentifying the Web is useful for retrieving relevant information. We agentified several Web servers by giving the portal address of the Web servers to the system, the system creates the hyper structure of the WPA communities based on the hyperlink structure of each Web server. Then, we calculated the Precision of the retrieved URLs to user's queries. Figure 9 shows the Precision for user's queries to the IEEE agentified domain http://computer.org/. The number of agentified Web pages in this Web server is about 2000. Also, we agentified the AAAI domain, http://www.aaai.org/. The number of agentified Web pages in this Web server is 2736. Figure

10 shows the Precision for user's queries to the AAAI's agentified domain. The results depicted in Figures 9 and 10 show that the idea of Web page agentification promises to achieve relevant information to the users and also, promoted using Kodama as a PinPoint IR system.

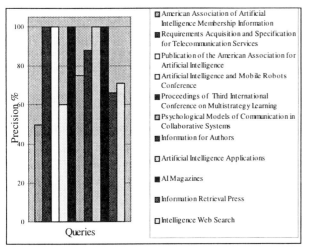

Figure 10 Precision of the Retrieved URLs to the User's Queries to the AAAI Agentified domain

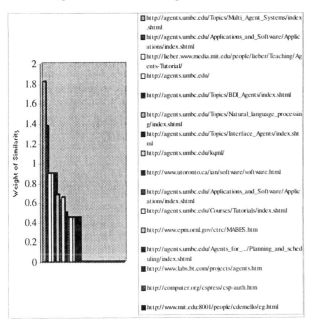

Figure 11. URL's Correlation with the Relevant Keywords

In the second experiments, we measured how well Kodama can get correlation between the contents of the URLs and the queries over time to predict the UP. The user starts by giving the following five queries three times, *"Conferences and workshops of agents," "Natural language processing agent," "Electronic commerce agent systems," "KQML agent communication language,"* and *"Collaborative intelligent interface agents."* At this point, the system has already been

customized to user's current interest and the URLs get correlated with the queries by inserting new keywords, deleting non-relevant keywords and modifying the weights of the existing keywords. After that, the user gives more general and ambiguous query, *"intelligent agent systems."* The highest-weighted URLs, which were retrieved and satisfied the user, are the most relevant URLs to the given query in the UP. Figure 11 shows the URLs in descending order of similarity within the UP.

In the third experiments, we measured how well Kodama is being able to adapt to the UP over time and to get a good correlation between each URL and its relevant keywords. In order to understand the experiment, we define a Fitness value, which will show the correlation between the weights of keywords calculated by UIA and user's actual interest to each keyword, as follows.

(1) User's actual interest: $S_j = \sum_{k=1}^{m} b_k \cdot W_k$, where W_k is the weight of keyword$_k$, and $b_k = 1$ if the user judges keyword$_k$ in the URL$_j$ as relevant for his/her query, else $b_k = 0$.

(2) Interest calculated by UIA: $T_j = \sum_{k=1}^{m} W_k$.

We define the Fitness value $F_j = S_j / T_j$, which reflects the correlation between the two interests for URL j.

In the experiment, a user gave fifteen different queries, each of which consists of 1 to 5 keywords, then, after frequent interactions of retrieval, the user checked the relevancy of each keyword in the retrieved URL, then Fitness value was calculated for each URL in the UP. The Fitness values calculated after five and ten times retrieval interactions are shown in Figure 12. Figure 12 shows that the values of S and T are converging over time to each other, and this means that UIA is being able to predict and adapt to its actual user's interests.

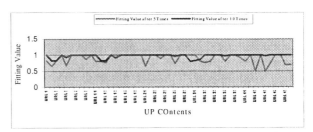

Figure 12 Converging to the User's Interest over Time

In the fourth experiments, we measured how well the feedback mechanism of UIA enables users to access to more relevant information with high relevancy. We define the Feasibleness of the feedback mechanism by *M/N*. Where **N** means the number of queries given by a user, and **M** means the number of the retrieved results at highest rank with which the user get satisfied. In the experiment, a user initially starts by giving a set of ambiguous and non-sense queries. At this point, URLs are retrieved and held in UP. Then, the system repeats the interaction process, in which the user gives a query, gives back the evaluation to the retrieved URLs, and the rank of URLs in UP is changed according to the user's responses. In the experiment, the interactions were repeated ten times. The Result of the experiment is shown in Figure 13. Figure 13 shows that the Feasibleness gradually goes up with time, and this means that UIA is helpful for users to retrieve relevant URLs.

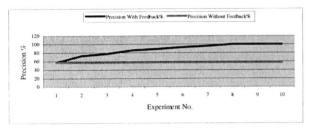

Figure 13 Feasibleness while Catching the User's Behavior

Conclusion and Future Work

This paper discussed a multi-agent-based approach to build scalable information searching techniques to let users retrieve information in highly distributed and decentralized databases, such as the Web. In this sense, the multi-agent system is not composed of a few agents, but rather composed of possibly large number of agents, which collectively try to satisfy the user's request. We reported methods to agentify the Web, and to exploit UP & IP adaptively on the Kodama system. We carried out several experiments to investigate the performance of the Kodama system. Through these experiments, we ensure that the idea of Web page agentification promises to achieve relevant information to the user. So, Kodama can be used as a PinPoint IR system that learns and adapts to the user's preferences over time. The system is able to change the weights of some keywords and classifies URLs in query history and bookmark files in a way that reflects user's interest in these keywords of the related URLs. Future step in Kodama is extending our experiments in multiple SA domains and developing a smart query routing mechanism in the UIA for routing the user's query. Routing refers to the process of selecting the SA to be queried and forwarding queries to it. UIA will route the query to an appropriate SA, instead of sending the query to all SAs and gathering a large amount of noisy Web pages. In such a situation, the UIA and SA need an intelligent query routing mechanism that suggests the most relevant SA based on user's query history and some attributes of the SAs. By sending the queries to the relevant SAs, the traffic of the network will be minimized, and also users will receive only a relevant information.

References

[Budzik and Hammond, 1999] Budzik J. and Hammond K. "Watson: Anticipating and Contextualizing Information Needs", in Proceedings of Sixty-second annual Meeting of the American Society for Information Science.

[Chakrabarti et al., 1998] S. Chakrabarti, B. Dom, D. Gibson, J. Kleinberg, P. Raghavan, and S. Rajagopalan, "Automatic Resource Compilation by analyzing Hyperlink Structure and Associated Text", Proceedings of the 7th WWW Conference.

[Chen and Sycara, 1998] Liren Chen and Katia Sycara, WebMate: A Personal Agent for Browsing and Searching", Proceedings of the Second International Conference of Autonomous Agents, Minneapolis/ST, MN USA, May 9-13, 1998, pp.132-138.

[Edmund et al., 2000] Edmund S. Yu, Ping C. Koo, and Elizabth D. Liddy: Evolving Intelligent Text-based Agents, Proceedings of the 4th International Conference of Autonomous Agents, June 3-7- 2000, Barcelona, Spain, pp.388-395.

[William et. al., 2000] G. William, S. Lawrence and C. Giles, "Efficient Identification of Web Communities", ACM Proceedings of KDD 2000, Boston, MA, USA.

[Helmy et al., 1999a] T. Helmy, B. Hodjat and M. Amamiya, " Multi-Agent Based Approach for Information Retrieval in the WWW", Proceedings of the First Asia-Pacific International Conference on Intelligent Agent Technology (IAT'99), Hong Kong, 15-17/12, 1999, pp. 306-316.

[Helmy et al., 2000b] T. Helmy, T. Mine, G. Zhong, M. Amamiya, "A Novel Multi-Agent KODAMA Coordination for On-line Searching and Browsing the Web", Proceedings of The Fifth International Conference and Exhibition on The Practical Application of Intelligent Agents and Multi-Agents, 10-12/4, 2000, Manchester, UK, pp. 335-338.

[Helmy et al., 2000c] T. Helmy, T. Mine, G. Zhong and M. Amamiya, " Open Distributed Autonomous Multi-Agent Coordination on the Web", Proceedings of The Seventh International Conference on Parallel and Distributed Systems Workshops, pp. 461-466: July 4-7, 2000, Iwate, Japan.

[Helmy et al., 2000d] T. Helmy, T. Mine and M. Amamiya, "Adaptive exploiting User Profile and Interpretation Policy for Searching and Browsing the Web on KODAMA System", Proceedings of the 2nd International Workshop on Natural Language and Information Systems NLIS, London, Greenwich, United Kingdom, September 4-8, 2000, pp. 120-124.

[Hodjat and Amamiya, 2000] B. Hodjat and M. Amamiya, "Applying the Adaptive Agent Oriented Software Architecture to the Parsing of Context Sensitive Grammars", IEICE TRANS. INF. & SYST., VOL. E83-D, No.5 May 2000.

[Kleinberg, 1999] J. Kleinberg "Authoritative sources in a hyperlinked environment", ACM Journal, 46(s), PP. 604-632.

[Menczer and Monge, 1999] F. Menczer, A.E. Monge:" Scalable Web Search by Adaptive Online Agents: An InfoSpiders Case Study". Intelligent Information Agents.

[Pann and Sycara, 1996] K. Pann, A. And Sycara, K. " A Personal Text Filtering Agent", Proceedings of the AAAI Stanford Spring Symposium on Machine Learning and Information Access, Stanford, CA, March 25-27, 1996.

[Youngblood, 1999], G. Michael Youngblood, "Web Hunting: Design of a Simple Intelligent Web Search Agent", ACM Crossroads Student Magazine.

Image-Feature Extraction for Protein Crystallization: Integrating Image Analysis and Case-Based Reasoning

I. Jurisica and **P. Rogers**
Ontario Cancer Institute
610 University Avenue
Toronto, ON M5G 2M9
{ij,rogers}@uhnres.utoronto.ca

J. Glasgow and **S. Fortier**
Queen's University
Kingston, ON K7L 3N6
janice@cs.queensu.ca

J. Luft, M. Bianca,
R. Collins, G. DeTitta
Haumptman-Woodward MRI
Buffalo, NY 14203
detitta@hwi.buffalo.edu

Abstract

This paper describes issues related to integrating image analysis techniques into case-based reasoning. Although the approach is generic, a high-throughput protein crystallization problem is used as an example. Our solution to the crystallization problem is to store outcomes of experiments as images, extract important image features, and use them to automatically recognize different crystallization outcomes. Subsequently, we use the outcomes of image classification to perform case-based planning of crystallization experiments for new proteins. Knowledge-discovery techniques are used to extract general principles for crystallization. Such principles are applicable to the adaptation phase of case-based reasoning. The motivation for automated image-feature extraction is twofold: (1) the human interpretation/analysis of image content is subjective, and (2) many problem domains require reasoning with large databases of uninterpreted images. In this paper we present the design and implementation of our integrated system, as well as some preliminary experimental results.

Introduction

This paper describes an application of image analysis techniques to protein crystallization experiment classification. We also describe how this is integrated into our case-based reasoning (CBR) system for protein crystallization experiment design. Image analysis is applicable in many domains that require reasoning about cases (e.g., X-ray interpretation, understanding of NMR images, geographic information systems, satellite image understanding, etc.). Image information plays a crucial role in the domain of molecular biology, where the understanding of the 3D geometry of a molecular structure is often essential to problem solving (Leherte *et al.* 1997). Of particular concern are domains that require image processing without human intervention due to the high throughput (HTP) approaches used for data acquisition.

Case-Based Reasoning With Images A standard technique for human problem solving is to recall past experiences that are in some way similar to the current situation. These experiences, called cases, are then adapted and used to construct a solution for a given problem. CBR systems are computer programs that incorporate such past experiences

as a guide to problem solving. CBR may involve adapting old solutions to meet new demands, or using old cases to explain new situations or to critique new solutions.

Cases capture problem-solving processes by storing "important" features of problems and their solutions. Unfortunately, there is no one "right" scheme for representing images as cases; how we choose to represent an image depends on the type of questions we seek to answer. By making particular features of the image explicit, we can provide for efficient pattern matching, retrieval and adaptation in our CBR system. For example, consider the multiple representations of a molecular structure illustrated in Figure 1. If we wish to determine how many atoms of carbon are contained in a molecule, then the formula in Figure 1 a) is sufficient. However, if we need to derive connectivity, angle, distance or shape information, then more complex diagrammatic representations, such as those in Figure 1 b) or c) are more appropriate.

We propose that image information may be stored explicitly (e.g., using a bit map representation) or implicitly (e.g., using shape descriptors that capture some of the shape features of the image). An image may be stored in a way that preserves all relevant visual information, or a simplified model (such as a graph or an array representation) might be the most appropriate form to extract and compare image features. Some form of indexing is required for sizeable image databases where manual indexing is not an option. Following we discuss several issues related to integrating image representations and CBR, including image analysis, automatic image feature extraction, and combining of symbolic and visual information during case retrieval.

CBR with images may involve determining the similarity of images as well as adapting image representations. Psychological studies have provided evidence that suggests the existence of an isomorphism between physical and imagined image transformations (Shepard & Metzler 1971). Similarly, we can propose a set of primitive computational transformation operations that can form the basis for image adaptation. For example, Ohkawa *et al.* (1996) describe a protein classification method using structural transformations, such as deletion, creation, magnification, rotation, movement, exchange or change of kind. In their work, authors compute similarity between proteins on the basis of the cost of individual transformations and their number. Thus, if many

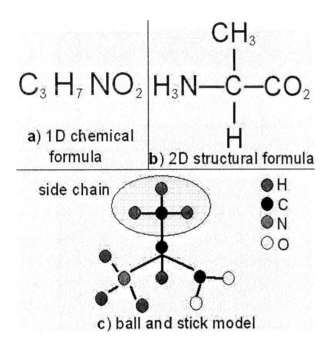

a) 1D chemical formula

b) 2D structural formula

c) ball and stick model

Figure 1: Alternative representations for molecule.

transformations are needed or expensive transformations are required then protein structures are marked dissimilar.

A similar approach has been applied in spatial analogy to the problem of comparing and classifying molecular structures (Conklin et al. 1996). The similarity between two images can be measured in terms of the transformations necessary to bring them into equivalence. Considered transformations may include replacing, deleting or moving a part, or rotation of the entire image.

Image Retrieval, Analysis and Use   Human interpretation of image content is subjective, and in many domains it may not be feasible due to the complexity of the image or the size of the image database. For such situations, we propose an image-feature extraction system which provides *image segmentation* tools to identify objects within the image, and *image analysis* tools to analyze objects within the image.

Image segmentation has been used to locate objects within an image (Xu, Olman, & Uberbacher 1996) and separate objects during classification (Agam & Dinstein 1997). Popular approaches are based on region-oriented or edge-oriented segmentation. Region-oriented segmentation is based on searching for connected regions with similar gray level values, while edge-oriented segmentation searches for abrupt changes in gray levels that are likely to indicate edges between neighboring objects. An integration of knowledge-based techniques for segmentation is presented in (Tresp et al. 1996). Here, a knowledge base is used to determine what objects should be recognized when they have fuzzy boundaries. One can also specify a bias, i.e., domain knowledge about the object.

Image analysis can be used to automatically extract features from images that can subsequently be used for more

efficient image retrieval or for decision support. Several approaches have been proposed for the problem of identifying image features: (1) polynomial fitting of flexible curves (McInerney & Terzopoulos 1996; 2000) or planes (Leclerc 1997); (2) attributed relational graphs (ARG) (Petrakis & Faloutsos 1997); (3) similarity invariant coordinate systems (SICS) (Li 1997); and (4) transformational approaches (Basri & Weinshall 1992; Conklin & Glasgow 1992; Ohkawa et al. 1996).

Next we introduce a CBR system for protein crystallization. We focus on describing the automated image interpretation and analysis module.

MAX: Protein Crystallization Experience Management System

Proteins are macromolecules which are involved in every biochemical process that maintains life in a living organism. Most disease processes and disease treatments are manifested at the protein level. Through an increased understanding of protein structure we can gain insight into the functions of these important molecules. However, elucidation and understanding of the laws by which proteins adopt their 3D structure is one of the most fundamental challenges in modern molecular biology. Currently, the most powerful method for protein structure determination is single crystal X-ray diffraction. A crystallography experiment begins with a well-formed crystal that ideally diffracts X-rays to high resolution. For proteins this process is often limited by the difficulty of growing crystals suitable for diffraction. This is partially due to the large number of parameters affecting the crystallization outcome (e.g., purity of proteins, intrinsic physico-chemical, biochemical, biophysical and biological parameters) and the unknown correlations between the variation of a parameter and the propensity for a given macromolecule to crystallize.

An ongoing problem in crystal growth is a historically non-systematic approach to knowledge acquisition: *"the history of experiments is not well known, because crystal growers do not monitor parameters"* (Ducruix & Giege 1992, page 14). The Biological Macromolecular Crystallization Database (BMCD) stores data from published crystallization papers, including information about the macromolecule itself, the crystallization methods used, and the crystal data (Gilliland et al. 1994). There have been several attempts to analyze the BMCD in order to discover underlying principles of the crystal growth process. These efforts include approaches that use cluster analysis (Farr, Perryman, & Samuzdi 1998; Samuzdi, Fivash, & Rosenberg 1992), inductive learning techniques (Hennessy, Gopalakrishnan, & Buchanan 1994), and statistical analysis (Hennessy et al. 2000) to extract knowledge from this existing database of crystallization experiments. Previous studies were limited because negative results are not reported in the database and because many crystallization experiments are not reproducible due to an incomplete method description, missing details, or erroneous data. Consequently, the BMCD is not currently being used in a strongly predictive fashion.

To address these challenges, we are developing MAX, a

case-based reasoning system for the design and evaluation of macromolecular crystal growing experiments. Our objective is that MAX will act as a decision-support system that will incorporate a case base of prior crystal growing experiments to assist an expert crystallographer in the planning of experiments for a novel protein. We extend basic case-based reasoning functionality by providing:

1. image-based processing to extend expressibility of case representation, provide protein similarity measure, and to assure an objective classification of crystallization experiment outcomes with appropriate image-feature extraction;

2. database techniques for case retrieval to support scalability;

3. knowledge-discovery techniques to support domain-knowledge evolution and system optimization.

The repository of crystal growth experiments being developed for our project addresses both of the shortcomings of the BMCD, since it comprises a comprehensive case base of crystallographic experiments that contains both positive and negative experiment outcomes. To build this repository systematically, we combine a HTP crystallization setup and evaluation in the wet lab with computational analysis of the outcomes. We have implemented a scalable, conversational CBR system that uses prior crystal growing experiments to assist an expert crystallographer in the planning of experiments for a novel protein. To support scalability we use an incremental similarity-based retrieval algorithm and the IBM DB2 database system as a back-end storage manager. The information repository contains data and knowledge. Data comprises existing databases (verified information from the Protein Data Bank (PDB) (Bhat *et al.* 2001), the Biological Macromolecule Crystallization Database (BMCD) (Gilliland *et al.* 1994), and GenBank (Database of DNA sequences) (Benson *et al.* 2000)), as well as specialized information about proteins (amino acid sequence, protein properties, etc.), chemicals, and agents.

Knowledge in the system is represented as *cases* – experiments with diverse crystallization outcomes, recorded as a function of time, and *rules* – general principles acquired from crystallographers, or principles derived using knowledge-mining tools. Rules are used to adapt a previous plan to derive a crystallization recipe for a new protein. A mature case base will be used to retrospectively search the cases for interesting and unanticipated relationships. Using data visualization tools and formal knowledge-discovery algorithms for numeric and conceptual cluster analysis, we hope to uncover interesting trends in the outcomes that can be exploited as we face new crystallization challenges.

Essential to building the repository systematically is the automated analysis of experiment outcome. The wet lab uses a robotic HTP crystallization setup with the capacity to prepare and evaluate the results of over sixty thousand (61.4K) crystallization experiments in a work week. This creates a need for an automatic image analysis system. Individual experiments are done in high density microassay plates. Each protein is subjected to 1536 crystallization cocktails, covering a wide range of crystallizing agents.

Experiments are evaluated automatically on a computer-controlled XY table with micron positioning accuracy by photographing each well with a 2Mpixels digital camera. The XY stand can accommodate 28 plates of experiments, allowing us to photograph 43,008 experiments in about 9 hours. Each photograph is saved as a JPG image (320 x 320 pixels in RBG). Photographs are taken at several time steps: immediately following setup, one day later, two days later, one week later and two weeks later. Each photograph is analyzed and classified according to the outcome, which can be clear drop, amorphous precipitate, phase separation, microcrystals, crystals, and uncertain outcome. Next we describe the processes of image analysis in more detail.

Image Processing

In addition to the issue of scalability, automated image processing is necessary in the crystallization domain because there is no general solution for quantitatively evaluating reaction outcomes under a microscope. The major weakness of existing scoring methods is the tendency to confuse micro crystalline and amorphous precipitates. To increase objectivity, we have implemented a system to extract image features, and to use them to classify crystallization outcomes. The system runs under Matlab on an IBM RS/6000 SP machine.

Figure 2: Different crystallization experiment outcomes.

An example of the problem is shown in Figure 2. Image processing is done in four main steps: (1) drop recognition, (2) drop analysis, (3) image-feature extraction, and (4) image classification. Based on image processing, experiment outcomes are classified into appropriate classes to form a precipitation index, which is used to measure similarity between cases during CBR. A precipitation index is a vector with 1536 positions representing crystallization outcomes for one protein and 1536 different crystallizing agents. Its binary representation has 0 for "clear drop" and 1 for "any precipitate" (we also distinguish unknown). A precipitate result can be further broken down into one of amorphous precipitate, phase separation, microcrystals or crystal. During case retrieval, we use both versions of the precipitation index. The binary precipitation index ensures scalability and high recall, while a more detailed precipitation index improves precision in case retrieval.

Drop recognition Drop recognition is performed by locating the well in the image, finding the droplet within the well, and selecting the largest square region contained within the properly illuminated portion of the droplet. The region of interest is then passed on to the drop analysis routine.

The tricky part is identifying the boundaries of the droplet. Our approach generates several feasible outlines of the drop and then uses a weighting mechanism to remove unlikely candidates. The drop is expected to be of a certain shape, a certain size, and in a certain position (although variations do exist and must be recognized). Figure 3 shows several alternative droplet outlines and Figure 4 presents two examples of processed images, with the oval and square representing the recognized droplets and largest areas of interest respectively. Each image is processed in about 8 seconds, which matches the rate of the HTP capture of crystallization experiment results. Experimental results suggest that the average error rate of the recognition process is ≤0.4%.

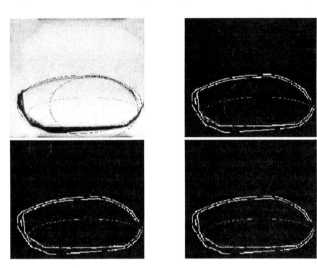

Figure 3: Drop identification process.

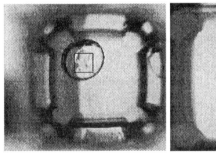

Figure 4: Selecting the area of interest for further image processing.

Drop analysis The goal of analyzing the region of interest is to process the image in a way that enables us to later extract image features that discriminate among different possible crystallization experiment outcomes.

At the moment, we use Fourier transformations to analyze the content of the drop, as seen in Figure 5. In the future, we plan to experiment with alternative techniques, such as wavelet analysis, neural networks, CBR, and combinations of the above approaches.

Image-feature extraction The third step in image processing involves extracting image properties for statistical

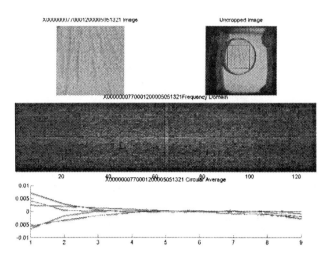

Figure 5: Analysis of the drop content: the recognized drop; the largest square; the spectrum of the Fourier analysis; analysis of the spectrum.

analysis and classification. Currently, we use two types of features: (1) spatial domain features extracted from the 2D intensity map of the image, and (2) frequency domain features extracted from the 2D frequency spectrum of the image.

The spatial domain features correspond to the quadtree decomposition of the image using three different threshold levels. The quadtree decomposition involves splitting the image into four squares and examining the difference between the minimum and maximum values of the pixels in each square. If the difference is greater than a given threshold then the square is further subdivided into four squares, and the quadtree function is called on each square. This process repeats until the minimum and maximum value in each square differs by less than the threshold. We store the number of squares examined.

Other features that are extracted from the spatial domain include the length of edges, the number of bends found in edges, the ratio of the length of edges to their minimum length, and the intensity of edges. We are also experimenting with including the length of edges in a contour plot of the image, and features extracted from the wavelet decomposition of the image.

Frequency domain features are calculated by using a Fourier transformation to find the 2D frequency spectrum of the image, which is then normalized to yield a 2D map of intensity values ranging from 0 to 1. The map is converted to a boolean mask by comparing each value to a threshold constant (currently the value is 0.00007). which is selected empirically so that the shape of the spectrum is well characterized by the boolean mask.

After thresholding, isolated values are filtered out of the mask to simplify the measurements. Measurements are made to parameterize the features of this shape. The height of the horizontal bar of the cross is measured at five different locations chosen to capture the variations in the height of the bar. The width of the vertical bar of the cross is measured at five different locations, chosen to capture the variations in the width of the bar. The ratio of the height of the horizontal bar to the width of the vertical bar and the ratio of the length of the horizontal bar to the length of the vertical bar are computed. Radial measurements made from the center of the mask to the edge of the cross at varying degrees, along with their variance, are computed and stored as parameters. Finally the number of pixels in the mask is stored in the area parameter.

Features are also extracted from the frequency domain by calculating the circular average. The 2D frequency domain is reduced to a 1D vector by taking the average intensity of all values at different radial distances from the center of the image. The resulting vector is then sampled at three different locations. A fifth-degree polynomial is then fit to the curve and its third derivative and roots are calculated. Currently, about 70 features are extracted to classify experimental outcomes.

Classification of experiment outcomes Extracted features comprise an image description of a case (see Figure 6). Since none of the extracted features is a sole predictor of experiment outcome, the weighted contribution of extracted features is used to automatically classify the outcome of the experiment. We have used CBR to identify the appropriate combination of features and their relative contribution to experiment classification. The example presented in Figure 7 shows the classification of three outcomes. Currently, the accuracy of the experiment outcome classification is 85%.

Classification of crystallization experiment outcomes is used to compute the precipitation index (see Figure 8), which in turn is used to measure similarity between proteins. MAX constructs a solution for the current crystallization problem by using appropriate descriptors from relevant experiments, i.e., both successful and failed crystallization experiments of proteins that have similar precipitation indices. The solution is a recipe for crystallization (i.e, crystal growth method, temperature and pH ranges, concentration of protein, and crystallization agent). Once a novel set of experiments for a protein has been planned, executed and the results recorded, a new case, which reflects this new experience, is added to the case base. Cases with both positive and negative outcomes are equally valuable for future decision-making processes and for the application of machine-learning techniques to the case base.

Case-Based Reasoning for Crystallization Experiment Planning

We address the hurdle of protein crystal growth by combining a HTP wet lab work and computational approaches to systematically create and use a comprehensive repository of protein crystallization experiments (Jurisica *et al.* 2000). We apply CBR to plan new crystallization experiments. Our approach is based on a generic system called $TA3$ (Jurisica & Glasgow 1997; Jurisica, Glasgow, & Mylopoulos 2000).

Crystallization experiments contain experiential information, such as initial input information about the protein at the beginning of the experiment, the process of carrying out the experiment, the outcome of the experiment, which we rep-

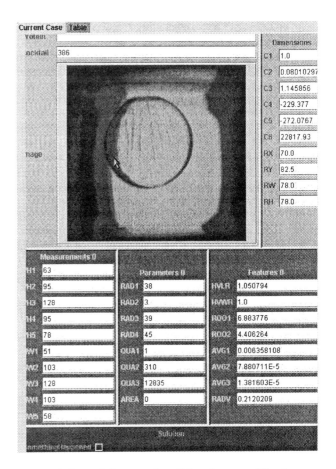

Figure 6: Part of the case describing the crystallization experiment, which is created using features extracted from the drop.

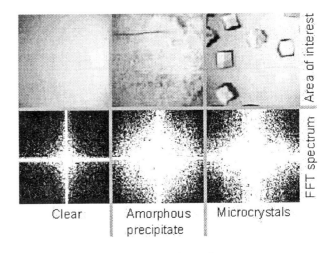

Figure 7: Classification of experiment outcome.

Figure 8: Precipitation index, white represents crystals, light grey (green) is clear drop, black is precipitate, dark grey (red) is unknown.

resent as cases. Thus, we need to address issues of how to represent crystallization experiments flexibly, how to measure similarity among experiments, and how to adapt relevant crystallization recipes to better fit current problem (Jurisica *et al.* 2001).

In general, a *case* represents knowledge of how a specific task was carried out and the outcome for that specific situation. For our domain, an individual case captures the problem-solving process of a crystal growth experiment by representing an episode of such a process: input parameters, results of the initial precipitation experiments, and the final results. Cases are represented as a set of descriptors – attribute-value pairs, organized into attribute categories. Category membership is determined using information about the usefulness of individual attributes and their properties. This information is obtained either from domain knowledge or with help of a knowledge-mining algorithm. Categories bring additional structure to a case representation. This reduces the impact of irrelevant attributes on system competence by selectively using individual categories during matching. A context explicitly defines attributes that are used during similarity assessment and any constraints that may be applicable to attribute values. Thus, context defines how similarity is measured.

As discussed earlier, we use still images to describe individual crystallization experiments. Since our goal is to provide a high-quality information repository cases are linked to external information sources, such as articles describing crystallization methods used, databases of protein information, and chemical properties of agents.

Case retrieval is a primary process for partial pattern matching of an input case to cases in the case base. A similarity function is used to determine which cases are most relevant to the given problem. In MAX case retrieval function is used to locate successful and unsuccessful crystallization experiments that have similar precipitation indexes. The process has two stages. In the first stage, only a binary classification of crystallization outcomes is used (i.e, nothing happened, something happened). In the second stage, a more detailed classification of the result is used to partially order retrieved experiments based on their relevance. Retrieved cases are presented to the user, at which time the user can modify the selection criteria dynamically and thus alter the set of retrieved cases. The retrieval process is interactive and iterative. The retrieval function used in MAX is flexible, effective, and scalable (Jurisica, Glasgow, & Mylopoulos 2000).

The *adaptation* process in CBR manipulates the solution from a set of source cases to solve the target case. MAX constructs a solution for the current crystallization problem by using appropriate descriptors from relevant experiments. The solution is a recipe for crystallization (i.e, crystal growth method, temperature and pH ranges, concentration of protein, and crystallization agent). We propose two functions: *1)* to suggest almost-right solutions to problems, which can be modified automatically (or by the expert user) to suit the new protein situation, and *2)* to warn of potential errors or failures in a proposed experimental plan.

Adaptation is guided by domain knowledge (i.e., adaptation rules, concept hierarchies, or extensive number of examples) that is stored in the MAX information repository or by information provided by the user (in the later scenario, MAX will store the new information for later reuse).

Conclusions

The idea of combining image-based reasoning and CBR is novel, and there are many avenues that need to be explored. Above we have presented just a brief overview of some of the issues involved in integrating these two approaches to reasoning and problem solving. In particular, we have focused on how CBR could be applied in image domains. In some such domains, the combination brings objectivity, in other domains, it is needed to cope with scalability of HTP applications.

We are currently considering the use of CBR in several domains involving image data. In particular, we have considered CBR for the problem of *molecular scene analysis* (Glasgow, Conklin, & Fortier 1993). This work focuses on determining how structural protein data can be organized to permit efficient and rapid retrieval from a case base of molecular scenes. CBR is used to anticipate 3D substructures that might occur within a novel protein image (constructed from an X-ray diffraction experiment).

Medicine is another area with potential for integrating CBR and image-based reasoning. Earlier it was shown that CBR can be successfully applied for prediction and diagnosis in *in vitro* fertilization (Jurisica *et al.* 1998). This system initially worked only with symbolic patient data. Later, more detailed information was collected, including oocyte and embryo images. These images were analyzed by embryologists and the extracted information is used by doctors to potentially provide an explanation of multiple failed implantations. Computer-based image analysis has been used to evaluate morphology and developmental features of oocytes and embryos (including cell number, fragmentation, cellular appearance, zona thickness, etc.) objectively (Jurisica & Glasgow 2000). Although humans can analyze images more flexibly, computer vision techniques help to make the process more objective and precise.

We have implemented MAX using a generic CBR shell called $\mathcal{T}\mathcal{A}3$ in Java 2, with both memory and JDBC drivers. Cases can be stored in a hierarchical manner to support more efficient storage (as one protein may be part of multiple crystallization experiments), improved case retrieval performance, and knowledge discovery through exploiting meaningful structure of case base. A web-based interface and relational schema to store the information about crystallization experiments has been implemented. We are working on improving its performance and extending its knowledge-discovery capabilities. Currently, knowledge discovery supports only case similarity explanation, and $\mathcal{T}A3$ optimization by case schema refinement and domain knowledge analysis. Once the repository contains more experiments, we can use knowledge-discovery algorithms to support the extraction of general principles of experimental crystal growing plans. In order to extract principles from the crystallization repository, we apply two steps: searching for patterns and describing their properties. We will use conceptual proximity techniques to organize protein crystallization information into groups that reflect reoccurring patterns. Conceptual clustering methods determine clusters not only by attribute similarity but also by conceptual cohesiveness, as defined by background information. We will use an interactive, context-based, nearest-neighbor clustering that supports explicit background knowledge and works with symbolic attributes. Interactive clustering algorithms prove to be useful especially in evolving domains, such as crystallization. Following group analysis we will apply summarization techniques to describe characteristic properties of the identified clusters. These sets of properties can be used to differentiate individual clusters, to identify associations among the clusters, and to identify relationships between properties and individual items (i.e., associations). In addition, we will explore relationships between the outcomes observed in crystallization experiments and other characteristics of the proteins, such as their sequences, observed biophysical properties, which could also be useful in predicting probable crystallization recipes.

Future work in the crystal growth domain involves the implementation of a distributed storage management system using a robotic tape library attached to the IBM RS/6000 SP, Tivoli storage management system and IBM DB2 EEE database. This is essential to keep up with the increasing volume of image data and to support archiving of important information (we already have over 200GB of compressed images containing crystallization experiment outcomes). By improving the quality of the image capture process, we also hope to improve the current error rate of drop recognition (0.4%) and classification accuracy (85%). Our approach has the potential to significantly reduce the time spent looking for initial conditions. The results of our research may thus eliminate a primary bottleneck in modern structural biology.

Acknowledgments

The computing part of this research is supported in part by the Natural Sciences and Engineering Research Council of Canada, Communications and Information Technology Ontario, and IBM Canada; the wet lab is supported in part by the John R. Oishei Foundation and NASA Grant NAG8-1152. Both labs are supported in part by the NIH grant – Northeastern Structural Genomics Consortium (http://www.nesgc.org).

References

Agam, G., and Dinstein, I. 1997. Geometric separation of partially overlapping nonrigid objects applied to automatic chromosome classification. *IEEE Transactions on Pattern Analysis and Machine Intelligence* 19(11):1212–1222.

Basri, R., and Weinshall, D. 1992. Distance metric between 3D models and 2D images for recogntion and classification. Technical Report AIM-1373, MIT, AI Lab.

Benson, D.; Karsch-Mizrachi, I.; Lipman, D.; Ostell, J.; Rapp, B.; and Wheeler, D. 2000. Genbank. *Nucleic Acids Res* 28(1):15–18.

Bhat, T. N.; Bourne, P.; Feng, Z.; Gilliland, G.; Jain, S.; Ravichandran, V.; Schneider, B.; Schneider, K.; Thanki, N.; Weissig, H.; Westbrook, J.; and Berman, H. M. 2001. The PDB data uniformity project. *Nucleic Acids Res* 29(1):214–218.

Conklin, D., and Glasgow, J. 1992. Spatial analogy and subsumption. In Sleeman, and Edwards., eds., *Machine Learning: Proceedings of the Ninth International Conference ML(92)*, 111–116. Morgan Kaufmann.

Conklin, D.; Fortier, S.; Glasgow, J.; and Allen, F. 1996. Conformational analysis from crystallographic data using conceptual clustering. *Acta Crystallographica* B52:535–549.

Ducruix, A., and Giege, R. 1992. *Crystallization of Nucleid Acids and Proteins. A Practical Approach.* New York: Oxford University Press.

Farr, R.; Perryman, A.; and Samuzdi, C. 1998. Re-clustering the database for crystallization of macromolecules. *Journal of Crystal Growth* 183(4):653–668.

Gilliland, G.; Tung, M.; Blakeslee, D.; and Ladner, J. 1994. The biological macromolecule crystallization database, version 3.0: New features, data, and the NASA archive for protein crystal growth data. *Acta Crystallogr* D50:408–413.

Glasgow, J.; Conklin, D.; and Fortier, S. 1993. Case-based reasoning for molecular scene analysis. In *Working Notes of the AAAI Spring Symposium on Case-Based Reasoning and Information Retrieval*, 53–62.

Hennessy, D.; Buchanan, B.; Subramanian, D.; Wilkosz, P. A.; and Rosenberg, J. M. 2000. Statistical methods for the objective design of screening procedures for macromolecular crystallization. *Acta Crystallogr D Biol Crystallogr* 56(Pt 7):817–827.

Hennessy, D.; Gopalakrishnan, V.; and Buchanan, B. G. 1994. Induction of rules for biological macromolecule crystallization. In *ISMB'94*, 179–187.

Jurisica, I., and Glasgow, J. 1997. Improving performance of case-based classification using context-based relevance. *International Journal of Artificial Intelligence Tools. Special Issue of IEEE ITCAI-96 Best Papers* 6(4):511–536.

Jurisica, I., and Glasgow, J. 2000. Extending case-based reasoning by discovering and using image features in IVF. In *ACM Symposium on Applied Computing (SAC 2000)*.

Jurisica, I.; Mylopoulos, J.; Glasgow, J.; Shapiro, H.; and Casper, R. F. 1998. Case-based reasoning in IVF: Prediction and knowledge mining. *Artificial Intelligence in Medicine* 12(1):1–24.

Jurisica, I.; Rogers, P.; Glasgow, J.; Fortier, S.; Luft, J.; Wolfley, J.; Bianca, M.; Weeks, D.; and DeTitta, G. 2000. High throughput macromolecular crystallization: An application of case-based reasoning and data mining. In *Methods in Macromolecular Crystallography*. Kluwer Academic Press. in press.

Jurisica, I.; Rogers, P.; Glasgow, J.; Fortier, S.; Luft, J.; Wolfley, J.; Bianca, M.; Weeks, D.; and DeTitta, G. 2001. Intelligent decision support for protein crystal growth. *IBM Systems Journal* 40(2). To appear.

Jurisica, I.; Glasgow, J.; and Mylopoulos, J. 2000. Incremental iterative retrieval and browsing for efficient conversational CBR systems. *International Journal of Applied Intelligence* 12(3):251–268.

Leclerc, Y. G. 1997. Continuous terrain modeling from image sequences with applications to change detection. In *Workshop on Image Understanding*.

Leherte, L.; Glasgow, J.; Baxter, K.; Steeg, E.; and Fortier, S. 1997. Analysis of three-dimensional protein images. *Journal of Artificial Intelligence Research (JAIR)* 125–159.

Li, S. Z. 1997. Invariant representation, matching and pose estimation of 3D space curves under similarity transformation. *Pattern Recognition* 30(3):447–458.

McInerney, T., and Terzopoulos, D. 1996. Deformable models in medical image analysis: A survey. *Medical Image Analysis* 1(2):91–108.

McInerney, T., and Terzopoulos, D. 2000. T-snakes: topology adaptive snakes. *Med Image Anal* 4(2):73–91.

Ohkawa, T.; Namihira, D.; Komoda, N.; Kidera, A.; and Nakamura, H. 1996. Protein structure classification by structural transformations. In *Proc. of the IEEE International Joint Symposia on Intelligence and Systems*, 23–29.

Petrakis, E. G. M., and Faloutsos, C. 1997. Similarity searching in medical image databases. *IEEE Transactions on Knowledge and Data Engineering* 9(3):435–447.

Samuzdi, C. L.; Fivash, M.; and Rosenberg, J. 1992. Cluster analysis of the biological macromolecule crystallization database. *Journal of Crystal Growth* 123:47–58.

Shepard, R., and Metzler, J. 1971. Mental rotation of three-dimensional objects. *Science* 171:701 – 703.

Tresp, C.; Jager, M.; Moser, M.; Hiltner, J.; and Fathi, M. 1996. A new method for image segmentation based on fuzzy knowledge. In *Proc. of the IEEE International Joint Symposia on Intelligence and Systems*, 227–233.

Xu, Y.; Olman, V.; and Uberbacher, E. C. 1996. A segmentation algorithm for noisy images. In *IEEE Int. Joint Symposium on Intelligence and Systems*, 220–226.

An Open Architecture for Multi-domain Information Extraction

Thierry Poibeau

Thales Research and Technology
Domaine de Corbeville, F-91404 Orsay France

Laboratoire d'Informatique de Paris-Nord
avenue J.-B. Clément, F-93430 Villetaneuse France

Thierry.Poibeau@thalesgroup.com

Abstract

This paper presents a multi-domain information extraction system. The overall architecture of the system is detailed. A set of machine learning tools helps the expert to explore the corpus and automatically derive knowledge from this corpus. Thus, the system allows the end-user to rapidly develop a local ontology giving an accurate image of the content of the text, so that the expert can elaborate new extraction templates. The system is finally evaluated using classical indicators.

Introduction

Information Extraction (IE) is a technology dedicated to the extraction of structured information from texts. This technique is used to highlight relevant sequences in the original text or to fill pre-defined templates (Pazienza 1997). A well-known problem of such systems is the fact that moving from one domain to another means re-developing some resources, which is a boring and time-consuming task (for example Riloff (1995) mentions a 1500 hours development).

Moreover, when information is often changing (think of the analysis of a newswire for example), one might want to elaborate new extraction templates. This task is rarely addressed by the research studies in IE system adaptation, but we noticed that it is not an obvious problem. People are not aware of what they can expect from an IE system, and most of the time they have no idea of how deriving a template from a collection of texts can be. On the other hand, if they defined a template, the task cannot be performed because they are waiting for information that is not contained in the texts.

In order to decrease the time spent on the elaboration of resources for the IE system and guide the end-user in a new domain, we suggest to use a machine learning system that helps defining new templates and associated resources. This knowledge is automatically derived from the text collection, in interaction with the end-user to rapidly develop a local ontology giving an accurate image of the content of the text. The experiment also aims at reaching a

better coverage thanks to the generalization process provided by the machine learning system.

We will firstly present the overall system architecture and principles. The learning system is then what allows the learning of semantic knowledge to help define templates for new domains. We will show to what extent it is possible to speed up the elaboration of resources without any decrease in the quality of the system. We will finish with some comments on this experiment and we will show how domain-specific knowledge acquired by the learning system such as the subcategorization frame of verbs could be used to extract more precise information from texts.

Application Description

The architecture consists in a multi-agent platform. Each agent performs a precise subtask of the information extraction process. A supervisor controls the overall process and the information flow. The overall architecture is presented below.

Information Extraction System

The system can be divided into five parts: information extraction from the structure of the text, the module for named entity recognition (location, dates, etc), semantic filters, modules for the extraction of specific domain-dependent information and modules for the filling of a result template.

• Some information is extracted from the structure of the text. Given that the AFP newswire is formatted, some wrappers automatically extract information about the location and the date of the event. This non-linguistic extraction increases the quality of the result by providing 100% good results. It is also accurate when one thinks of the current development of structured text (HTML, XML) via the web and other corporate networks.

• The second stage is concerned with the recognition of relevant information by means of a linguistic analysis. This stage allows a recognition of various named entities (person names, organizations, locations and dates) of the text. New kinds of named entities can be defined according to a new domain (for examples, gene names to analyze a genome database). We use the finite-state

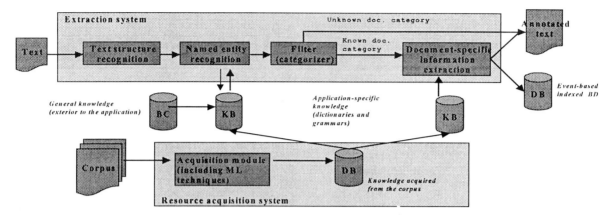

Figure 1: The information extraction system architecture

toolbox Intex to design dictionaries and automata (Silberztein 1993).

Figure 2: The named entity recognizer

• The third stage performs text categorization from the seek of "semantic signatures" automatically produced from a rough semantic analysis of the text. We use an external industrial system implementing a vector space model to categorize texts (the Intuition™ system from the French company Sinequa, cf. Salton (1988)).

• The fourth stage extracts specific information (most of time, specific relationships between named entities). It can be for example the number of victims of a terrorist event. This step is achieved in applying a grammar of transducers (extraction patterns) over the text.

• The next stage links all these information together to produce one or several result template(s) that present(s) a synthetic view of the information extracted from the text. The template corresponding to the text is chosen among the set of all templates, according to the identified category of the text (registered by the system at the third analysis step). A specific template is produced only if some main slots are filled (the system distinguished among obligatory and optional slots). Partial templates produced by different

sentences are merged to produce only one template per text. This merging is done under constraints on what can be unified or not. The results are then stored in a database, which exhibit knowledge extracted from the corpus.

The architecture exhibits, outside from the information extraction system in itself, a machine learning module that can help the end-user produce resources for information extraction. The end-user who wants to define a new extraction template has to process a representative set of documents in the learning module to obtain an ontology and some rough resources for the domain he wants to cover. The acquisition module is presented in the next section.

Template Creation Module

The system can be divided into three main parts:

1. A machine learning engine used to produce semantic clusters from the corpus. These clusters are weighted and are intended to give to the expert a rough idea of the topic addressed in the text;

2. A system to help the creation of extraction template once the relevant topic of the corpus have been identified;

3. The information extraction system in itself, that will use the resources defined at the previous stage to fill the templates.

Figure 3 gives an overview of the overall architecture. The corpus is processed by the machine learning system (1), in order to produce semantic clusters organized in a superficial ontology. The template creation module (2) helps the expert define his own extraction template from the ontology. The lower part of the schema describes the information extraction system in itself (3), processing a text to fill the extraction template.

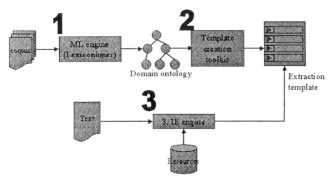

Figure 3: Architecture of the system

Apart from the information extraction system, the machine learning module is intended to help the end-user produce the extraction template. A representative set of documents has to be processed by the learning module to obtain an ontology and some rough resources for the domain he wants to cover. The resources have to be manually completed to obtain a good coverage of the domain.

Uses of AI Technology: Extraction of Semantic Clusters from Lexical Resources

A mainly automatic method has been elaborated to combine knowledge contained in on-line resources and statistical data obtained from the training corpus of the chosen domain. This method is implemented through the LexiconTuner, which was initially developed for French but can be used for any language if correct resources are provided.

Semantic clusters – that is to say clusters of semantically related words – can be acquired from on-line resources including dictionaries, thesauri and taxonomies (Véronis and Ide 1990) (Wilks *et al*, 1995), (Aguirre and Rigau 1996). Dictionaries model the meanings of lexical items using textual definitions. Textual definitions are written in natural language and the full information encoded in these definitions can't be extracted easily. However, partial information, which can be used as semantic clusters, can be extracted from the definitions relatively easily. The method is inspired from (Luk 1995) and described in details in (Ecran 1996), (Poibeau 1999) and (Poibeau 2001).

The idea of building networks from definitions was first proposed by Véronis and Ide (1990), along with a propagation technique for computing clusters of related words. Many authors have proposed techniques for deriving some kind of clusters or associations of concepts from graphs of concepts, among others transitive closures and computation of graph "cliques", simulated annealing, etc. In our approach, the content words in the definitions of a word sense are used as component concepts of the word sense (Luk 1995), that is to say that a concept is a lexical item considered as a member of a semantic cluster.

In the LexiconTuner, the generation of the clusters is carried out in two steps. Firstly, the list of all the concepts occurring in the corpus is generated. For each word in the corpus, the program looks for its textual definition(s) in the lexicon. The words in the definitions are treated as concepts and are recorded. This step allows us to go from a French word (e.g. *opéra*) to some concepts labeled with English words (`dramatic`, `performance`, `composition`, `music`), by means of a bilingual dictionary (*opera* being defined as a "dramatic performance or composition of which music is an essential part").

Secondly, semantic clusters are generated by clustering related concepts in the list. The program uses a semantic net as its semantic knowledge source to determine the semantic relatedness between the concepts. The net is

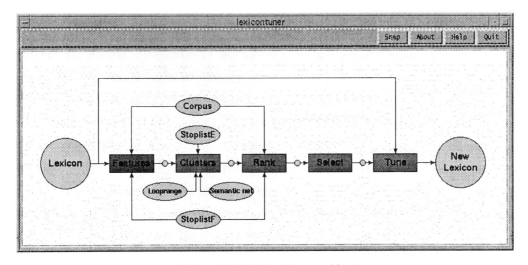

Figure 4: The LexiconTuner architecture

derived from the *Oxford Advanced Learner's Dictionary* (OALD). Each node represents a word, and for any two words $w1$ and $w2$, $w1$ is linked to $w2$ if $w2$ appears in the definitions of $w1$ in OALD (`music` will be linked to `composition` if `music` appears in the definition of `composition`). The link from $w1$ to $w2$ is weighted inversely proportionally to the product of the number of senses of $w1$ as defined in OALD and the number of words in the definition of $w1$ that contains $w2$. The clusters are formed in 3 steps:

- Circles that share one or more nodes are merged. Thus, (`opera`, `performance`, `dramatic`) and (`dramatic`, `composition`, `music`) are merged into a single set (`opera`, `performance`, `dramatic`, `composition`, `music`). This is called a "core cluster".

- Lastly, peripheral words (words which are part of a circle which length is inferior to the user-defined number) are related to the core cluster. If two words like `dramatic` and `comic` are related, then `comic` will be added to the cluster, being related to `dramatic`.

- Every circle in the semantic net which length is equal to a user-defined number is identified. For example, if the number is 3, the system will generate all the sets consisting of three related words according to the dictionary definition. For `opera`, the following associations will be considered: (`opera`, `performance`, `dramatic`) and (`dramatic`, `composition`, `music`).

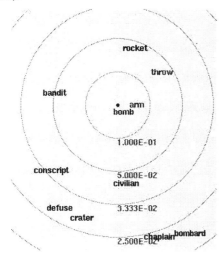

Figure 5: A cluster generated by the LexiconTuner

Lastly, the membership of a cluster is "weighed". The weight of a core member is considered as the inverse of the number of senses of the word as defined in OALD. The weight of a non-core member is considered as the mean of the weights of the core members of the cluster to which it is related. Then, semantic clusters can capture notions appearing in texts independently from the lexical items expressing these notions.

Template Design

Semantic classes produced by the LexiconTuner are proposed to the end-user, who chooses which clusters are of interest to him. Once he has chosen one cluster, the system automatically proposes him an interface to refine the cluster, aggregate a part of the closest clusters and develop a hierarchy. This hierarchy can be assimilated to a local ontology, describing a part of the world knowledge related to the event of interest for the end-user.

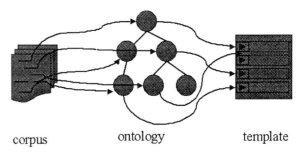

corpus   ontology   template

Figure 6: From corpus to template, through the ontology…

The semantic clusters produced by the LexiconTuner give to the expert a rough idea of the topics addressed in the corpus. The expert has to navigate among these clusters to select relevant topics and establish a candidate template. The chosen topics has to be named and to be associated with a slot in the template. The system automatically generates the corresponding information into the database: the creation of a new template leads to the creation of a new table and each new slot in the template corresponds to a new column in the table. This technical part of the template creation process can be compared to the Tabula Rasa toolkit developed at New Mexico State University to help end-users define their own templates (Ogden and Bernick 1997).

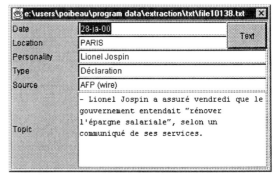

Figure 7: A specific template

The evaluation of the template creation task is not obvious since it necessitates domain knowledge and text manipulation from the experts. No clear reference can be established. The only way to evaluate the contribution of the semantic clusters is to ask the expert firstly to manually elaborate templates from a corpus and secondly to do it with the help of the Lexicontuner.

The expert we worked with made the following comments:

- The semantic clusters produced by the Lexicon-Tuner give an appropriate idea of the overall topic addressed by the texts.

- These clusters help the elaboration of templates and allows to focus on some part of information without reading large part of texts.

- However, the elaboration of the template itself remains largely dependant of the domain knowledge of the expert because (a) he knows what kind of information he wants to find in relation with a given topic and (b) the clusters are too coarse-grain to directly correspond to slots.

When the template corresponds to an event, the information to be found generally refers to classical *wh-questions*: who, what, where and when. Some additional slots can be added but most of the time they correspond to classical associations of ideas. For example, if one wants to extract information about football matches, he will immediately create a slot corresponding to the score of the match. However, this comment is due to the fact that the system is analyzing news stories, for which one can associate stereotypic reduced templates (sometimes called *templettes* in the IE community).

We observed that the template creation task is frequently a problem in more technical domains for which no clear *a priori* schema exists. In this experiment, the LexiconTuner can be seen as a tool to explore the corpus and give a rough idea of tentative templates rather than a tool designed to help the creation of the content of the templates themselves. However, the LexiconTuner results is also useful for the creation of the resources of the system (next section).

Experiment Description and Evaluation

We asked an expert to define a new template and the associated resources, using the tools we presented above. We chose the terrorist event domain from the AFP newswire, because it is a well-established task since the MUC-4 and MUC-5 conferences. Moreover, similar experiments has been previously done that give a good point of reference (see Poibeau (1999) and Faure and Poibeau (2000)).

Homogeneous semantic clusters learned by the LexiconTuner are refined: a manual work of the expert is necessary to exploit semantic classes (merging of scattered classes, deletion of irrelevant elements, addition of new elements, etc.). About five hours have been dedicated, after the acquisition process, to the refinement of data furnished by LexiconTuner. Merging and structuring

classes incrementally develop a local ontology, which nodes are related to slots in the extraction template. This knowledge is also considered as a resource for the finite-state system and is exploited either as dictionaries or as transducers, according to the nature of the information. If it is a general information that is not domain specific, the development guidelines advise the user to use dictionaries that can be reused, otherwise, he designs a transducer.

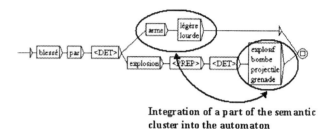

Integration of a part of the semantic cluster into the automaton

Figure 8: a part of the "weapon" automaton

The elaboration of linguistic knowledge, from clusters produced by the LexiconTuner, to the design of the Intex resources, spent about 15 hours. This duration has to be compared with the two weeks (about 80 hours) needed for the manual resources development for a previous experiment on the same subject.

A hundred texts have been used as "training corpus" and a hundred different texts have been used as "test corpus". Texts are first parsed with our system, and then some heuristics allow to fill the extraction template: the first occurrence of a number of victims or injured persons is stored. If a text deals with more than one terrorist event, we assume that only the first one is relevant. Thanks to the nature of the channel, very few texts deal with more than one event.

Our results have been evaluated by two human experts who did not follow our experiment. Let Pos be the total number of good answers and Act the number of solutions proposed by the system. Our performance indicators are defined as:

- (Ok) if extracted information is correct;

- (False) if extracted information is incorrect or not filled;

- (None) if there were no extracted information and no information has to be extracted.

Using these indicators, we compute two different values for each slot:

- Precision (Prec) is defined as Ok/Pos.

- Recall (Rec) is defined as Ok/(Act).

Slot name	Precision	Recall	P&R
Event date	.95	.96	.95
Event location	.88	.92	.90
Nb of killed people	.83	.73	.77
Nb of injured people	.80	.69	.74
Weapon	.85	.82	.83
Total	.86	.82	.83

The performances are good according to the state-of-the-art and to the time spent on resource development. However, we can analyze the remaining errors as follows:

The date of the story is nearly fully correct because the wrapper uses the formatted structure of the article to extract it. The errors for the location slot are due to two "contradictory" locations found by the system. A more complete linguistic analysis or a database providing lists of cities in different countries would reduce this kind of errors. The errors in the number of dead or injured persons slot are frequently due to silence: for example the system fails against too complex syntactic forms. The silence for the weapon slot is frequently due to incompleteness of semantic dictionaries.

Conclusion and Future Work

The experiment that has been described is based on an external knowledge base derived from a dictionary. It is thus different from (Faure and Poibeau 2000) which tries to acquire knowledge directly from the text. The use of an external database allows to work on middle-size corpora that are not as redundant as technical texts. We also think that using a general dictionary is interesting when dealing with general texts like a newswire. Clusters contain words that were not contained in the training part of the corpus, allowing a better coverage of the final result.

The multi-domain extraction system is currently running in real time, on the AFP newswire. About 15 templates have been defined that cover about 30% of the stories. From the remaining 70%, the system only extract surface information, especially thanks to the wrappers. The performances are between .55 and .85 P&R, if we do not take into account the date and location slots that are filled by means of wrappers. New extraction templates are defined to prove system scalability (about one new template per week). We hope to reach the number 50 templates towards summer 2001.

Acknowledgement

A part of this study re-used some pieces of software developed in the framework of the ECRAN project (1996-1999). I would like to thank Alpha Luk and other people having participated to the development of the Lexicon Tuner. I am also indebted to David Faure, Tristelle Kervel, Adeline Nazarenko and Claire Nedellec for useful comments and discussions on this subject.

References

Aguirre E. and Rigau G. 1996. Word Sense Disambiguation using conceptual density. In *Proceedings of the 16th International Conference on Computational Linguistics (COLING)*, Copenhagen.

Ecran. 1996. D-2.5.1 - Methods for Lexical Items Modification/Creation and D-2.6.1 - Heuristics for Automatic Tuning. ECRAN Project Deliverable.

Faure D. and Poibeau T. 2000. First experiments of using semantic knowledge learned by Asium for Information Extraction task using Intex. In *Proceedings of the workshop on learning ontologies*, during *ECAI'2000*, Berlin.

Luk A. K. 1995. Statistical Sense Disambiguation with Relatively Small Corpora using Dictionary Definitions. In *Proceedings of the 33rd Annual Meeting of the Association for Computational Linguistics*.

Ogden W. and Bernick P. 1997. "Tabula Rasa Meta-Tool: Text Extraction Toolbuilder Toolkit". Technical Report MCCS-97-305. Las Cruces: Computing Research Laboratory.

Pazienza M. T. ed. 1997. *Information extraction (a multidisciplinary approach to an emerging information technology)*, Springer Verlag (Lecture Notes in Computer Science), Heidelberg, Germany.

Poibeau T. 1999. "A statistical clustering method to provide a semantic indexing of texts". In *Workshop on machine learning for information filtering*, during *IJCAI'1999*, Stockholm.

Poibeau T. 2001. "Deriving a multi-domain information extraction system from a rough ontology". In *Proceeding of the 17th International Conference on Artificial Intelligence*, Seattle, USA.

Riloff E. 1995. "Little Words Can Make a Big Difference for Text Classification". In *Proceedings of the 18th Annual International Conference on research and Development in Information Retrieval (SIGIR_95)*.

Salton G. 1988. *Automatic Text Processing*. Addison-Wesley, Reading, MA.

Silberztein M. 1993. *Dictionnaires électroniques et analyse automatique des textes*. Masson, Paris.

Véronis J. and Ide N. M. 1990. "Word Sense Disambiguation with Very Large Neural Networks Extracted from Machine Readable Dictionaries". In *Proceedings of the 13th International Conference on Computational Linguistics (COLING'90)*, Helsinki, Finland.

Wilks Y., Slator B. and & Guthrie L. 1995. *Electric words: dictionaries, computers and meanings*, MIT Press, Cambridge, MA.

Constraint-Based Modeling of InterOperability Problems Using an Object-Oriented Approach

Mohammed H. Sqalli and Eugene C. Freuder

Department of Computer Science
University of New Hampshire
Durham, NH 03824 USA
msqalli,ecf@cs.unh.edu

Abstract

ADIOP is an application for Automated Diagnosis of InterOperability Problems. Interoperability testing involves checking the degree of compatibility between two networking devices that implement the same protocol. In ADIOP, each interoperability test case is first modeled as a Constraint Satisfaction Problem. Object-Oriented Programming is used to implement ADIOP. In this paper, we present the modeling language we use in ADIOP and how it allows the user to easily and efficiently create test cases and use them for diagnosis. The specific domain of application is interoperability testing of protocols in ATM (Asynchronous Transfer Mode) networks.

Introduction

We present a simple modeling language that allows the user to build models of interoperability test cases. Interoperability testing involves checking the degree of compatibility between two networking devices that implement the same protocol. The Constraint Satisfaction Problem (CSP) paradigm provides a uniform framework for an accurate representation of the model.

We discuss the use of Object-Oriented Programming (OOP) in conjunction with CSP. The notion of *Metavariable* is introduced and allows much better flexibility of representation of variables encapsulated in an object. Values also are represented as objects namely *Metavalues*.

Each test case is modeled as a CSP using a many-models architecture and represented as an object with metavariables and constraints as its parameters and methods respectively. These objects inherit all the information on how to construct metavariables from a class hierarchy.

ADIOP (Automated Diagnosis of InterOperability Problems) is the implementation of a system which includes CSP modeling using OOP. A modeling interface based on a Graphical User Interface (GUI) is used by the ADIOP system and provides a user-friendly interaction with the tester. The diagnosing part of ADIOP is not addressed in details in this paper.

CSP Modeling of InterOperability Testing

A Constraint Satisfaction Problem (CSP) consists of a set of variables, a set of constraints relating these variables and a set of domains of values for the variables. A solution to the CSP is an assignment of domains' values to variables such that all constraints are satisfied.

In our domain of application, CSP is used as a modeling tool and as a problem solving mechanism. One of the main contributions of this paper is in modeling interoperability tests. CSP is useful in modeling because it is declarative and powerful in expressing and describing many application domains. (Wallace 1996) states that "One major contribution of constraints is to problem modelling. It has been claimed that 'constraints are the normal language of discourse for many applications.' Whilst this advantage pays off in all applications, it is central to the design and verification of VLSI circuits and to the specification, development and verification of control software for electro-mechanical systems."

A protocol specification is usually written by an organization such as standardization bodies (e.g., ISO) and others (e.g., ATM Forum (ATMF)). Most specifications used to implement ATM protocols are taken from the ATMF. From this protocol specification a test suite is written by one of these organizations. In the protocol we are using in this paper that is PNNI (Private Network-Network Interface), ATMF provides both the protocol specification and the interoperability test suite documents.

The interoperability test suite is a set of test cases organized into sections. Each section allows for the testing of a part of the protocol. Each section contains a set of interoperability test cases. Each test case tests for a specific issue in the protocol. Each test case is described in details as to what configuration should be used, what are the steps to follow in testing and what is the verdict criteria to use in deciding whether this test case passes or fails. Each test case's result provides a very specific and limited information about the devices being tested. When all the test cases are combined, the result is a detailed interoperability testing of each aspect of the protocol.

One Model Architecture

In interoperability testing, we want to test whether two devices when connected behave correctly according to the statements in the protocol specification. One way of doing this is by modeling the entire protocol specification as one CSP (Sqalli & Freuder 1996) (Riese 1993a) (Riese 1993b).

This CSP model can then be used to test the interoperability of two devices by checking the observations against the CSP model. The observations represent a set of packets captured. Each packet has many fields as defined in the corresponding protocol specification. The data contained in these fields represent the values that are assigned to the corresponding variables in the model. Then the constraints defined in the CSP model are checked for consistency. If all the constraints are satisfied for an assignment, then the interoperability test passes.

Many Models Architecture

In this design, the CSP models are derived from the test cases in the test suite written from the protocol specification (Figure 1). In this paper, we use this form of modeling where each test is represented as a CSP. If the observations form a solution to this CSP then the corresponding test case passes. This is then repeated for each test case in the test suite.

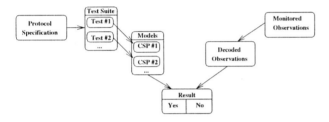

Figure 1: Many Models Architecture

The advantages of this form of modeling are that:

- It is easy to come up with models for specific test cases

- Models are easy to work with (i.e., use, debug, etc) because they are small

- It is easier to generate reports for interoperability testing

- This is closer to how interoperability testing is done

- It is easier to give explanations using small models

There are disadvantages to this form of modeling:

- We need to write as many models as there are test cases. This is alleviated in our system ADIOP by providing a tool that makes it easy to create models

- More inconsistencies might be added to the model, since there are errors that might originate from the protocol specification or from the interoperability testing document. In ADIOP, the debugger, which is not discussed in this paper, addresses inconsistencies independently of their origin

- Some parts of testing might be included in more than one test case causing redundant testing. This is not a major concern since we can copy parts of one model into another one.

Object-Oriented Programming

Object-Oriented Programming (OOP) has become a very widely used paradigm in software development. Its success can be attributed to its natural way of modeling real-world objects. Many languages are OO such as C++ and Java. Java has combined the benefits of many of its predecessor programming languages. Java also provides conveniently the development tools for GUI-based and web-based software. Our system ADIOP is implemented using Java.

In the OO terminology, a particular object is called an instance of a class. In the same way we use the term instance variables and instance methods. A class is a set of objects that share a common structure and behavior.

In this paper, we refer to class as the implementation of a class of objects, and to object as one instance of this class. For example, when we refer to the **Hello** class, we mean the implemented **Hello** class, and when we refer to a **Hello** object, we mean a particular object defined to be from the **Hello** class which may have a name such as **OneWayInA**. We also use the name **"parameter"** to refer to an object's variable so that there is no confusion between CSP variables and object's variables.

There are many properties in OOP that make modeling more efficient. Two of which we are interested in here are: Encapsulation and Inheritance.

Encapsulating related variables and methods into a neat software bundle is a simple yet powerful idea that provides two primary benefits to software developers: modularity and information hiding (Campione & Walrath 1998). Modularity means that objects can be created and maintained independently of other objects. This makes it easy to use the same object by different components of the system. Information hiding means that an object can have private information that other objects can not access but they can still use its functionality.

Inheritance is the ability to define classes in terms of other classes. A subclass inherits variables and methods from a superclass. Subclasses can add variables and methods of their own to the ones they inherit, and they can override inherited methods. This is called specialization. Superclasses can be of abstract nature. An abstract class defines the behavior that subclasses can inherit. Inheritance can be of many levels to constitute a class hierarchy.

Description of the CSP Modeling Process Using OOP

In terms of modeling, we propose to model each test case from the test suite as a CSP. This guarantees that the CSPs obtained are small and can be solved efficiently. This is also closer to how interoperability testing is done in the real world since the companies testing their devices prefer to get a report of specific tests and failures. The breakdown of the interoperability testing into small test cases allows us to do incremental testing and to easily detect problems at each level of this testing.

We also propose to use the Object-Oriented methodology to model these test cases. In interoperability testing, an analyzer is usually used to collect data between the two devices being tested. The data collected is then decoded as packets. Hence, it is natural to represent the CSP in term of packets. Each packet contains many fields which should be checked against other packets' fields to test for interoperability. Since the constraints exist between the packets' fields, we represent each field as a variable in the CSP. The constraints represent restrictions on these variables.

However, It is a tedious work to state each one of these variables separately because a packet may contain a large number of fields and a tester may not remember all of these for each type of packet. The idea is then to represent a packet definition as a metavariable in the CSP representation and each observed packet as a metavalue. A metavariable or a metavalue is respectively an object or instantiation of an object representing a packet.

For each packet type, a class of objects is defined. Each packet is an object of one of these classes which corresponds to its type. Each class of objects include parameters some of which are the packets' fields and methods needed by these objects to manipulate the packets' data.

Definition 1 (Metavariable) : *A metavariable in the CSP model refers to the representation of a packet that encompasses many variables. Some of these variables are the packet' fields describing the content of the packet. Four other variables are taken from the captured data and added to the metavariable structure are: time, source, protocol, and status. A variable of this metavariable can be itself a metavariable encompassing many other variables. This can be expanded down hierarchically.*

Definition 2 (Metavalue) : *A metavalue in the CSP model refers to the data captured of a packet. This data is used to instantiate a metavariable.*

Definition 3 (Metaconstraint) : *A metaconstraint is a set of constraints relating variables belonging to one or more metavariables. Constraints are defined using variables as their arguments.*

In this paper, we only use unary and binary constraints. A unary metaconstraint is a set of unary constraints belonging to the same metavariable. A binary metaconstraint is a set of binary constraints relating variables belonging to two metavariables. The concept of metaconstraint is an abstract one for representation and design purposes only.

There has been some work combining OO and Constraint Satisfaction (Roy & Pachet 1997) (Paltrinieri 1994a) (Paltrinieri 1994b) (Stone 1995). To our knowledge, no one has used this integration in the same way we present it in this paper. The closest work to ours is what has been done in (Paltrinieri 1994a) (Paltrinieri 1994b). More details on this can be found in the related work section of this paper.

Another advantage of this CSP representation besides its declarative nature is that one can state an object in the model without having to know all the fields of that object. This allows for a very concise CSP model statement. From this CSP model statement, the ADIOP system generates an object corresponding to this CSP model with CSP metavariables as its parameters and constraints as its methods. This model is then integrated to the system and used for testing.

The CSP model is stated in a declarative way. The user needs to specify the packets that are expected to be observed for the test to pass. These packets are represented as objects. An example of a CSP model is stated in (Figure 2) where **1WayIn(A)** and **1WayIn(B)** are the metavariables and **Type**, **Time**, etc are the variables. The variables presented in this figure are only a subset of all the variables.

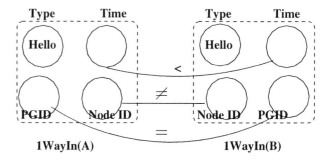

Figure 2: A Modeling Example

A $PACKET statement is used to declare metavariables (packets). More details of the modeling language are provided in a later section of this paper. After defining packets using the $PACKET statement, there is no need to state each variable (packet's field) separately. When a packet is defined, the ADIOP application provides a list generated dynamically from the packet's fields and showing all the variables belonging to this packet (Figure 3). This list can be used for stating constraints between these different variables.

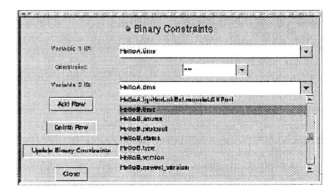

Figure 3: Packet's Parameters List

Modeling with Objects
Modeling of Packets
Interoperability testing of equipment uses packets captured for a specific protocol to determine if a test case passes or fails. These packets contain a number of fields. The values of these fields are checked against some constants or against fields' values from other packets to determine if the test case passes. It is natural to represent this problem using the Object-Oriented approach (OO), where a packet is represented as an object.

Since fields are used to state constraints, it is natural to represent these as variables. This way, an object defines a set of variables. The object also implements methods for decoding the packet it represents.

The use of OO gives us many advantages:

- Each object is a separate entity with its own functionality

- Information hiding of the objects definition as the users do not need to know the details but only the functionality of these objects.

- Inheritance between object allows for a hierarchical definition of packets which matches the way protocols are specified

- The CSP model obtained using objects is concise and expressive

The implementation of these objects as classes uses packages. adiopx is the main package in the ADIOP application, and thus it is the name of the root of the whole ADIOP directory structure. Under this directory there is one subdirectory called *packet* that includes all the classes needed for representing packets. One of these is the class **Packet** which is the parent of all other classes under the **packet**'s directory. This class implements the common parameters and methods for all types of packets. Figure 4 shows a representation of the directory structure of the *packet* package.

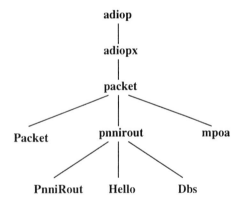

Figure 4: Directory Structure of the *packet* Package

One advantage of this representation is that each class is used for decoding and CSP modeling which saves us resources and provides a clean implementation (no redundancy of functionality).

Class Hierarchy and Inheritance

The classes are stored under the packages as described earlier. These classes are defined in a hierarchical manner to allow for more flexibility of extension and scalability of protocols and packet types being used by the application. The class **Packet** defines the common parameters and methods of all types of packets. As shown in figure (Figure 5), the class **Packet** is the parent of all the classes included in the package *packet*.

In the next level of hierarchy, classes represent a particular protocol type, e.g., PnniRout which stands for PNNI

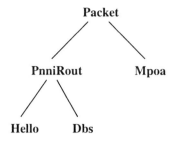

Figure 5: Class Hierarchy of the **Packet** Class

Routing protocol. The class **PnniRout** defines the common parameters and methods of packets of type PNNI Routing. The class **PnniRout** is a subclass of the class **Packet**. This level inherits from the class **Packet** parameters and methods used by ADIOP.

The classes that are children of this protocol type class are the leaves of the class hierarchy and represent the packet types within this protocol (e.g., Hello, Dbs). They inherit parameters and methods that are common to all this protocol packets from their parent **PnniRout**. Each one of these classes implements specific parameters and methods for its own type. The parameters can be of a more complex definition if they are themselves classes. Examples of such parameters are *OneWayInA.aggregToken.length* and *OneWayInA.aggregToken.status*. This is an example of a metavariable (aggregToken) within another metavariable (OneWayInA).

This hierarchy makes it easy to add/remove classes. We can add more protocols and more packet types within protocols. We only need to add the decoder for each one of these packet types to have them available for use by the decoder and the CSP modeling component. When all the hierarchy of packets is defined including parameters and methods, the user can declare an expected observation in a test case model to be one of these types and does not need to know or specify all the details of these packets.

The Decoder also uses the same hierarchy of classes defined in the last subsection. Adding the decoding functionality of a new packet type to ADIOP is a matter of adding one class to the hierarchy. This decoder is used with the monitored observations between two devices to generate the decoded observations which is a set of packets. Each packet is an instantiation of one of the classes in the bottom of hierarchy (leaves). The same classes are used to state the CSP models. A packet is defined in the CSP model by its type which is a leaf in the class hierarchy. Each decoding class contains parameters that represent the specific fields of one type of packets. It also inherits fields from parent decoding classes. This class also contains methods that perform different decoding functions. The advantage of this representation is that the classes used for decoding are also used for modeling, and it provides a concise representation of CSP via objects.

Modeling Interface

The modeling interface is a Graphical User Interface (GUI). A user-friendly interface is important for the ADIOP application so the tester can find it easy to use. The Test Suite Builder (TSB) component of ADIOP provides the functionality for modeling a test case as CSP. The Graphical User Interface (GUI) used for modeling allows the user to declare metavariables, domains, and constraints in a very efficient manner. The user does not have to know the details of the object being manipulated.

From the main menu of the TSB window, the user can choose which protocol they want to use. The list of protocols as shown in figure 6 is constructed from the structure of ADIOP directories. If a new protocol is added to this directory, it will be dynamically loaded and shown in this menu.

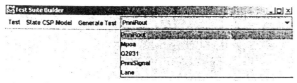

Figure 6: Protocols List in the Test Suite Builder Window

Each test case is built as a file with the *.iop* extension. This file may contain a description of the test case taken usually from the IOP specification document. This file's main section is the CSP model defining the variables and constraints for this test case. The CSP model is defined between two ADIOP keywords, i.e., **$CSP** and **$ENDCSP**.

Variables are not declared individually, but rather when a packet is declared using the **$PACKET** statement, a metavariable representing this packet is created and with it all the corresponding variables. Hence, the declaration of a metavariable is sufficient for defining all the variables within. ADIOP provides a functionality to automatically update the *.iop* file with the variable declaration using the appropriate format.

The packet types shown in figure 7 are also dynamically loaded from the protocol directory structure. For example, if we choose **PnniRout** as the protocol to be used, the packet types list will show: **Dbs, Hello**, etc. But, if we choose **Mpoa** instead to be the protocol, then the packet types list will show: **Cache_Imp_Req, Cache_Imp_Rpl**, etc.

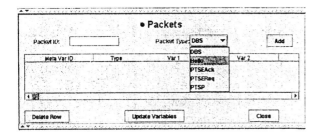

Figure 7: Packet Types List in the Test Suite Builder Window

The domains can be declared as a set of discrete values. These are used to declare unary constraints. A window is provided to add constraints by choosing from existing lists of variables and constraint operations. Constraints can be declared as unary or binary. ADIOP provides a list with all the variables that can be used for this purpose (Figure 3). These variables are dynamically loaded using the structure of the metavariable (packet) they are part of. ADIOP provides also a flexible way to declare general constraints. These are unary or binary constraints that can be of a more complex definition than what is provided in the GUI through the list of available constraint operations. The constraint in this case can be any Java function using one or two variables as its arguments. The constraints can be added to the CSP model definition using the **update** function.

In addition, this GUI is used to decode packets from binary format to readable text format. It also provides the tools for running interoperability tests that have been built and generating reports of testing results. This is not the subject of what we present in this paper.

Test Cases as Objects

When the model definition is completed and the *.iop* file is stored, the user can generate an object from this file. The parameters of this object are the CSP metavariables and the methods are the constraints. This object represents the CSP model of the test case declared, and it will be dynamically added to the Decoder/Diagnoser window menu. By choosing this item from the menu, the user is able to execute this test case on any decoded observations shown on the main Decoder/Diagnoser window.

The set of objects representing test cases are stored under the *testsuite* directory under the appropriate protocol name using a test suite hierarchy (See figure 8).

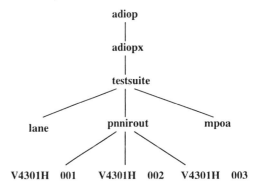

Figure 8: The *testsuite* Directory Hierarchy

ADIOP constructs a menu in the Decoder/Diagnoser window from the structure of the directories under the *testsuite* directory. If a new protocol is added or more test cases are generated, the menu will get updated. Figure 9 shows the menu generated in the Decoder/Diagnoser window.

Modeling Language

The model is stated in a very simple language. The following syntax including keywords and their meaning is used:

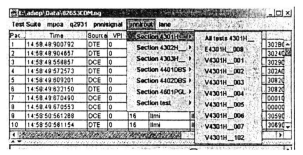

Figure 9: Test Suite Menu

- **$CSP**: This states that the CSP model declaration starts at this point. This statement is added automatically when a test case is created.

- **$ENDCSP**: An optional statement that means that the CSP model declaration ends at this point. If not used, the EOF is used to detect the end of the model declaration. This statement is added automatically when a test case is created.

- **$PROTOCOL protocolTested**: states that this CSP model implements a test case of the 'protocolTested' protocol. This statement is added automatically when a test case is created.

- **$PACKET packet_name packet_type**: This statement states that this test case being modeled contains a packet of type **packet_type** which was given the name **packet_name**. The **packet_type** has to be a leaf of the class hierarchy. (e.g., *Hello*, *DBS*). This statement generates an object of type packet_type and name packet_name.

  From the way objects are implemented, there is no need to know details about packet types when they are being used in the CSP model. The declaration of one packet in the CSP model using **$PACKET packet_name packet_type** is sufficient for defining all the parameters and methods needed for this packet including its fields (CSP variables) that can be used for stating constraints.

- **$DOMAIN domain_name value_1 value_2 ... value_n**: This states that a domain is declared with name **domain_name** and contains values: value_1, ... value_n. All these values are declared as strings.

- **$UNARY_CONSTRAINT variable_name operation domain_name #print_statement#**: This states that the value that can be assigned to variable_name must satisfy the **operation** constraint on the domain_name. For example if the operation is ==, then the value assigned to this variable must be in the domain_name set. variable_name must be one of the parameters in one of the objects declared by **$PACKET**. domain_name must have been declared in **$DOMAIN** or one of the predefined domains in ADIOP. The predefined domains are domains that are always included in all the models and cannot be modified (e.g., *D_Optional* and *D_Mandatory* to state that the existence of a packet in the captured data is optional or mandatory). Alternatively, the user can use a single value instead of a domain_name. **operation** can be one of the

following operations: $==, != , <=, >=, <$ or $>$ if a single value is used, and only $==$ or $! =$ if a domain_name is used. **print_statement** is a statement which will be printed as part of the diagnosis report if this constraint is violated when this test case is used.

- **$BINARY_CONSTRAINT variable1_name operation variable2_name #print_statement#**: variable1_name and variable2_name must be different and have both to be parameters in one or two of the objects declared with **$PACKET**. **operation** can be one of the following operations: $==, != , <=, >=, <, or >$.

- **$CONSTRAINT variable1_name variable2_name f(variable1_name,variable2_name) #print_statement#**: f(v1,v2) is a Java statement that returns a boolean and it is a function with two arguments: v1 and v2, where v1 may be the same as v2. This means that this can be a unary or binary constraint. The idea behind this kind of declaration is to allow for a broader constraint statements. The function used here can be made reusable by storing it under the textit"util" directory of ADIOP. This also allows for the use of a more complex functions.

- Comments can be included using the "// comments"

Example of CSP Modeling for One Test Case

The following is an example of a test case (Test Case ID: V4301H__001) from the PNNI (Private Network-Network Interface) InterOperability Test Suite document (PNNI-IOP 1999):

```
Test Case ID:    V4301H__001
Update Version: 0
Test Description:
Test Case ID: V4301H__001
Test Purpose: Verify that the Hello Protocol is
             running on an operational physical
             link.
Reference: 5.6
Pre-requisite: Both SUTs are SS_M and in the same
             lowest level peer group.
Test Configuration: #1
Test Set-up:
          1. Connect the two SUTs with one physical
             link.
Test Procedure:
          1. Monitor the PNNI (VPI/VCI=0/18) between
             SUT A and SUT B.
Verdict Criteria: Hello packets shall be observed
             in both directions on the PNNI.
Consequence of Failure: The PNNI protocol can not
             operate.
```

The following is a CSP representation of this test using the language presented in the previous section and created using the TSB window from the GUI presented earlier:

```
$CSP
$PROTOCOL  PnniRout

$PACKET    HelloA  Hello
$PACKET    HelloB  Hello

$BINARY_CONSTRAINT   HelloA.source != HelloB.source
$BINARY_CONSTRAINT   HelloA.time <= HelloB.time
$BINARY_CONSTRAINT   HelloA.peer_group_id == HelloB.peer_group_id

$ENDCSP
```

ADIOP generates an object representing this test case with HelloA and HelloB metavariables as its parameters and the three binary constraints as its methods. A menu item with the name of this test case is added to the Decoder/Diagnoser window. This menu item is used to execute this test case by calling its corresponding object.

Application of CSP Modeling

The CSP models are used to diagnose and solve interoperability problems (figure 1). All the test cases built using the ADIOP's modeling component are accessible through the menu in the Decoder/Diagnoser window of ADIOP (figure 9).

The diagnosis component takes the decoded observations from the decoding component and checks if they match the CSP model of the test case being used. In terms of CSP, this means that the decoded observations are metavalues that metavariables can be assigned. The model provides the metavariables that are defined in the test case as well as the constraints that need to be satisfied.

Our motivation for automating the diagnosis of interoperability testing is to save time, reduce repetitive testing, store and reuse knowledge, automate reports generation, and in general to make testing easier and more efficient. Our focus is on how to get a "good" explanation to the problem we are solving.

The advantage of CSP is that it is a reasoning mode that provides both modeling and problem solving within the same framework. The use of CSP for modeling allows us to take advantage of methods and algorithms that already exist for solving CSPs including search and inference. These algorithms are adapted to take advantage of the specialized problem domain structure. This provides a better diagnosis of the interoperability problems including an accurate and concise human-like explanation of the testing performed.

ADIOP uses search supplied by consistency inference methods in a CSP context to support explanations of the problem solving behavior that are considerably more meaningful than a trace of a search process would be. Constraint satisfaction problems are typically solved using search, augmented by general purpose consistency inference methods.

We did an evaluation of ADIOP's debugging component and the summary shows that 50 test cases out of 69 built produced a meaningful explanation, which makes about 73% of test cases.

Related Work

There has been some related work on using the Object-Oriented approach with CSP.

(Stone 1995) presents an Object-Oriented Constraint Satisfaction Planning for whole farm management. A whole-farm planning system (CROPS: Crop ROtation Planning System) has been developed and tested on Virginia farms. The implementation is object-oriented and employs partial arc-consistency algorithms, variable ordering, and constraint relaxation. The paper describes the constraint-based scheduler (CBS), its representation, and how it handles constraint relaxation. The difference between this and our work is that variables are represented as objects in the former and as object's parameters in ours. Constraints also are represented as objects while in our work they are methods of the objects.

(Puget & Leconte 1995) propose to give access to the constraints as first class citizen of the CLP language. They implemented their approach into an OO language, where constraints are explicitly represented by objects. Their implementation, ILOG Solver, used an abstract machine which is implemented in an object oriented programming language, namely C++. Each finite domain variable, each constraint, and even each non deterministic goal is represented by a C++ object. Again this work represents variables and constraints as objects while in ours variables and constraints are respectively represented as the parameters and methods of the objects.

(Roy & Pachet 1997) discuss the problem of the representation of constraints in an object-oriented programming language. They present a class library that integrates constraints within an object-oriented language. The library is based on the systematic reification of variables, constraints, problems and algorithms. The library is implemented in Smalltalk, and is used to state and solve efficiently complex constraint satisfaction involving Smalltalk structures. The same as what we stated in the previous references can be said about the difference between this work and ours.

(Paltrinieri 1994b) has abstracted both variables and constraints as defined in the classical CSP to a new, more compact model, called object-oriented constraint satisfaction problem (OOCSP) by introducing several notions, such as attribute, object, class, inheritance and association. A visual environment for constraint programming based on the OOCSP model has been developed. The OOCSP is converted into an equivalent CSP, which is then solved through a traditional constraint-programming language. The definition of CSP is enhanced through concepts deriving from the object-oriented paradigm. The main difference is that here objects do not have methods (but just data members) since their state is updated by the constraints. (Paltrinieri 1994a) This work is the closest to ours as it models a set of variables as an object. However, objects do not include methods while in our work, there are objects that are used for decoding and stating models and these include decoding methods. We also present objects that represent test cases and have constraints as their methods. Another difference is that this work converts an OOCSP into an equivalent CSP, while we use OOP for defining CSP models and for generating them.

Summary

In this paper we discussed CSP modeling of interoperability testing using Object-Oriented Programming. CSP modeling was introduced in Section 1. The different modeling architectures were presented in Section 2 and why we opted for a many-models architecture. The CSP modeling process using OOP was outlined in Section 4. A more detailed description of how objects are used in modeling is provided in Section 5. In Section 5.2, the class hierarchy and inheritance that we used in CSP modeling are presented. The modeling GUI is covered in Section 6. Section 7 described how the test cases that are modeled as CSPs are converted into usable objects with metavariables and constraints respectively representing their parameters and methods. The more detailed language specification is the subject of Section 8. A full example of

CSP modeling of an interoperability test case is shown in Section 9. We finally present related work in Section 10 on the integration of CSP and OO.

Acknowledgments

This material is based in part on work supported by the National Science Foundation under Grant No. IRI-9504316. Special thanks to the staff and students from the ATM consortium of the InterOperability Lab (IOL) at the University of New Hampshire for their support and feedback. This work has benefited from the reviewers' comments.

References

Campione, M., and Walrath, K. 1998. *The Java Tutorial, Second Edition: Object-Oriented Programming for the Internet (Java Series)*. Addison-Wesley Pub Co.

Paltrinieri, M. 1994a. On the Design of Constraint Satisfaction Problems. In *Principles and Practice of Constraint Programming, Second International Workshop (PPCP94) - Lecture Notes in Computer Science Vol. 874: Alan Borning (Ed.)*, 299–311. Rosario, Orcas Island, Washington, USA: Springer.

Paltrinieri, M. 1994b. Visual Environment for Constraint Programming. In *11th International Symposium on Visual Languages*, 118–119.

PNNI-IOP. 1999. *Interoperability Test for PNNI Version 1.0*. The ATM Forum, Technical Committee. AF-TEST-CSRA-0111.000.

Puget, J.-F., and Leconte, M. 1995. Beyond the Glass Box: Constraints as Objects. In *Logic Programming, Proceedings of the 1995 International Symposium (ILPS): John W. Lloyd (Ed.)*, 513–527. Portland, Oregon: MIT Press.

Riese, M. 1993a. Diagnosis of Communicating Systems: Dealing with Incompleteness and Uncertainty. In *Proceedings IJCAI-93*, 1480–1485.

Riese, M. 1993b. Diagnosis of Extended Finite Automata as a Constraint Satisfaction Problem. In *Proceedings of the Fourth International Workshop on Principles of Diagnosis (DX-93)*, 60–73.

Roy, P., and Pachet, F. 1997. Reifying Constraint Satisfaction in Smalltalk. *Journal of Object-Oriented Programming* 10(4):51–63.

Sqalli, M., and Freuder, E. 1996. A Constraint Satisfaction Model for Testing Emulated LANs in ATM Networks. In *Proceedings of the 7th International Workshop on Principles of Diagnosis (DX-96)*, 206–213.

Stone, N. D. 1995. Object-Oriented Constraint Satisfaction Planning for Whole Farm Management. *AI Applications* 9(1).

Wallace, M. 1996. Practical Applications of Constraint Programming. *Constraints - An International Journal* 1(1-2):139–168.

Index